Understanding Girls' Problem Behavior

HOT TOPICS IN DEVELOPMENTAL RESEARCH

Published

Friends, Lovers and Groups: Key Relationships in Adolescence
Edited by Rutger C. M. E. Engels, Margaret Kerr and Håkan Stattin

What Can Parents Do?: New Insights into the Role of Parents in Adolescent Problem Behavior
Edited by Margaret Kerr, Håkan Stattin and Rutger C. M. E. Engels

Understanding Girls' Problem Behavior

How Girls' Delinquency Develops in the Context of Maturity and Health, Co-occurring Problems, and Relationships

Edited by

Margaret Kerr
Center for Developmental Research, Örebro University, Sweden

Håkan Stattin
Center for Developmental Research, Örebro University, Sweden

Rutger C. M. E. Engels
Behavioural Science Institute, Radboud University, The Netherlands

Geertjan Overbeek
Department of Developmental Psychology, Utrecht University, The Netherlands

Anna-Karin Andershed
School of Law, Psychology and Social Work, Örebro University, Sweden

WILEY-BLACKWELL

A John Wiley & Sons, Ltd., Publication

Wiley-Blackwell is an imprint of John Wiley & Sons, formed by the merger of Wiley's global
Scientific, Technical, and Medical business with Blackwell Publishing.

Registered Office
John Wiley & Sons Ltd, The Atrium, Southern Gate, Chichester, West Sussex, PO19 8SQ, UK

Editorial Offices
The Atrium, Southern Gate, Chichester, West Sussex, PO19 8SQ, UK
9600 Garsington Road, Oxford, OX4 2DQ, UK
350 Main Street, Malden, MA 02148-5020, USA

For details of our global editorial offices, for customer services, and for information about
how to apply for permission to reuse the copyright material in this book please see our website
at www.wiley.com/wiley-blackwell.

The right of Margaret Kerr, Håkan Stattin, Rutger C. M. E. Engels, Geertjan Overbeek and
Anna-Karin Andershed to be identified as the authors of the editorial material in this work
has been asserted in accordance with the UK Copyright, Designs and Patents Act 1988.

Library of Congress Cataloging-in-Publication Data

Understanding girls' problem behavior : how girls' delinquency develops in the
context of maturity and health, co-occurring problems, and relationships /
edited by Margaret Kerr ... [et al.].
    p. ; cm.
  Includes bibliographical references and index.
  ISBN 978-0-470-66632-6 (cloth)
  1. Behavior disorders in children.   2. Behavior disorders in adolescence.
3. Problem children–Mental health.   4. Problem youth–Mental health.   5. Girls–Mental
health.   6. Teenage girls–Mental health.   7. Juvenile delinquency–Etiology.
I. Kerr, Margaret, 1953–
  [DNLM: 1. Juvenile Delinquency.   2. Adolescent Behavior.   3. Adolescent
Development.   4. Aggression.   5. Conduct Disorder. WS 463]
  RJ506.B44U55 2011
  618.92'89075–dc22
                                                          2010035927

A catalogue record for this book is available from the British Library.

Set in 10/12pt Palatino by SPi Publisher Services, Pondicherry, India
Printed and bound in Singapore by Ho Printing Singapore Pte Ltd
1   2011

We dedicate this book to the memory of Xiaojia Ge, a devoted scholar in the area of girls' problem behavior and a valued colleague and mentor

Contents

About the Editors

Anna-Karin Andershed is Assistant Professor of Psychology at Örebro University, Sweden. She earned her PhD at Örebro University. Her research focuses on the development and life-span consequences of antisocial behavior, especially among girls and women. She is currently involved in the development of an assessment instrument for youth with or at risk for antisocial behavior, and a universal/indicated intervention for preschool children.

Rutger C. M. E. Engels is Professor in Developmental Psychopathology at the Radboud University Nijmegen. He is director of the dept. of Developmental Psychopathology, and director of the KNAW-acknowledged (in 2006) Behavioural Science Institute. He received his MA in Social Psychology in 1993 at the University of Groningen and his PhD in 1998 at the Faculty of Medicine, University of Maastricht. In 1998 he became post-doc at the Dept. of Child and Adolescent Studies at Utrecht University, and in 2000 he was appointed as assistant professor. In 2001, he was appointed as full professor at the Radboud University Nijmegen. His research focuses on the interplay between individual characteristics (e.g., personality, outcome expectancies, genes), environmental cues and actual social interactions on the initiation, maintenance and determination of addictive behaviors, such as smoking, alcohol use, overeating, and drug use. His work is characterized by a multi-disciplinary approach with research designs are employed to test our theoretical models ranging from epidemiological survey studies, lab experiments, systematic observational studies in naturalistic settings to genetic research.

Margaret Kerr is Professor of Psychology at Örebro University, Sweden, and Co-director of the Center for Developmental Research. She earned her PhD at Cornell University, USA, and then completed a post-doctoral research fellowship with Richard Tremblay at the University of Montreal, Canada. She has been an associate editor of the *Journal of Research on Adolescence*. Her research focuses on internal and external adjustment in adolescence and their roles in the life course. Her current research interests include adolescents' choices of developmental contexts, parent-child relationships, and peer networks and their roles in the development of internalizing and externalizing problems.

Geertjan Overbeek is Associate Professor of Developmental Psychopathology at Utrecht University, The Netherlands. He earned his PhD at Utrecht University (2003), after which he worked as post-doc and Assistant Professor at the Behavioural Science Institute of the Radboud University Nijmegen for five years. His research focuses on the development of parent-child interactions and adolescents' social-emotional development, with a special interest in the development of internalizing and externalizing forms of problem behavior.

Håkan Stattin is Professor of Psychology at Uppsala and Örebro Universities, Sweden. He earned his PhD at Stockholm University. He co-directs the Center for Developmental Research at Örebro University and has served as President of the European Association for Research on Adolescence and associate editor for the *British Journal of Developmental Psychology*. He is probably best known for his research in three areas: delinquency development, pubertal maturation in adolescent girls, and parental monitoring. His works include an authored book (with David Magnusson in 1990), *Pubertal Maturation in Female Development*. In addition to his continued basic research in these areas, he is conducting prevention trials to reduce alcohol drinking and delinquency among adolescents.

List of Contributors

Anna-Karin Andershed, School of Law, Psychology and Social Work, Örebro University, Örebro, Sweden

Dara Babinski, Center for Children and Families, University of Buffalo, Buffalo, NY, USA

Joanne Belknap, Sociology Department, University of Colorado, Boulder, CO, USA

Michael C. Biehl, Department of Psychology, University of California, Davis, CA, USA

Bonnie Cady, Central Region, Colorado Division of Youth Corrections, Denver, CO, USA,

Jennifer Connolly, LaMarsh Centre for Research on Violence and Conflict Resolution, York University, Toronto, Ontario, Canada

Wendy Craig, Department of Psychology, Queen's University, Kingston, Ontario, Canada

Rutger C. M. E. Engels, Behavioural Science Institute, Radboud University Nijmegen, The Netherlands

Xin Feng, College of Education and Human Ecology, The Ohio State University, Columbus, OH, USA

Nancy L. Galambos, Department of Psychology, University of Alberta Edmonton, Alberta, Canada

Emily Gaarder, Department of Sociology/Anthropology, University of Minnesota-Duluth, Duluth, MN, USA

Xiaojia Ge, Institute of Child Development, University of Minnesota-Twin Cities, Minneapolis, MN, USA

Annika K.E. de Haan, Langeveld Institute, Centre for Cognitive and Motor Disabilities Utrecht University, Utrecht, The Netherlands

Amanda Hinze, Department of Psychiatry, University of Pittsburgh, Pittsburgh, PA, USA

Alison Hipwell, Department of Psychiatry, University of Pittsburgh, Pittsburgh, PA, USA

Kristi Holsinger, Sociology/Criminal Justice-Criminology, University of Missouri-Kansas City, MO, USA

Michele Hubert, Centre for Research in Human Development, Department of Psychology, Concordia University, Montreal, Quebec, Canada

Depeng Jiang, Department of Community Health Science, Faculty of Medicine, University of Manitoba, Canada

Run Jin, Department of Psychology and Child Development, California State University, Stanislaus, CA, USA

Fumiko Kakihara, Center for Developmental Research, Örebro University, Örebro, Sweden

Kate Keenan, Department of Psychiatry Behavioral Neuroscience, University of Chicago, IL, USA

Jane Ledingham, School of Psychology, University of Ottawa, Ottawa, Ontario, Canada

Lisa Leininger, The Ohio State University College of Medicine, Department of Pediatrics, Research Institute at Nationwide Children's Hospital, Columbus, OH, USA

Rolf Loeber, Department of Psychiatry, University of Pittsburgh, Pittsburgh, PA, USA

Andrea Lourie, Research Institute at Nationwide Children's Hospital, Columbus, OH, USA

Sheila K. Marshall, Jack Bell Bldg. School of Social Work, University of British Columbia, Vancouver, British Columbia, Canada

Marlene M. Moretti, Department of Psychology, Simon Fraser University, Burnaby, British Columbia, Canada

Misaki N. Natsuaki, Department of Psychology, University of California, Riverside, CA, USA

Karin S. Nijhof, Behavioural Science Institute, Radboud University Nijmegen, The Netherlands

Ingrid Obsuth, Department of Psychology, Simon Fraser University, Burnaby, British Columbia, Canada

Geertjan Overbeek, Department of Developmental Psychology, Utrecht University, Utrecht, The Netherlands

Kathleen Pajer, The Ohio State University College of Medicine, Department of Pediatrics, Research Institute at Nationwide Children's Hospital, Columbus, OH, USA

Debra Pepler, LaMarsh Centre for Research on Violence and Conflict Resolution, York University, Toronto, Ontario, Canada

Alex E. Schwartzman, Centre for Research in Human Development, Department of Psychology, Concordia University, Montreal, Quebec, Canada

Lisa A. Serbin, Centre for Research in Human Development, Department of Psychology, Concordia University, Montreal, Quebec, Canada

Dale M. Stack, Centre for Research in Human Development, Department of Psychology, Concordia University, Montreal, Quebec, Canada

Magda Stouthamer-Loeber, Department of Psychiatry, University of Pittsburgh, Pittsburgh, PA, USA

Lauree C. Tilton-Weaver, Center for Developmental Research, Örebro University, Örebro, Sweden

Cathy McDaniels Wilson, Department of Psychology, Xavier University-Cincinnati, OH, USA

Acknowledgements

We are grateful to The Swedish Foundation for International Cooperation in Research and Higher Education for supporting the collaborative project between the editors that resulted in the Hot Topics book series.

Introduction
Girls' Problem Behavior: From the What to the Why

Geertjan Overbeek
Utrecht University, The Netherlands

Anna-Karin Andershed
Örebro University, Sweden

Girls' problem behavior, or at least their delinquency, is less rare than commonly thought. Even though girls' issues and girls' problems are of great concern for societies as well as researchers, and despite a growing interest in unravelling the processes and mechanisms behind girls' problem behavior, the knowledge base in this area is still meager. There are exceptions, of course, and what these exceptions indicate is that the causes, expressions, development, and trajectories for many of the problems experienced by young people may differ as a function of gender (Bell, Foster, and Mash, 2005). To date, though, there are only a few longitudinal studies that have provided insight into the potentially different adjustment processes experienced by boys and girls. In addition, studies with a focused female perspective are few, in contrast to the bulk of research and literature directed toward understanding the development of boys. The overarching purpose of this volume is to yield an improved understanding of some of the key aspects of girls' problem behaviors. Drawing on studies of the maturing girl and following her through adolescence, into adulthood, and up to the point where she, herself, becomes a parent, we want to illustrate the process of initiating, establishing, and potentially overcoming problem behavior, and the processes that contribute to this development.

Understanding Girls' Problem Behavior: How Girls' Delinquency Develops in the Context of Maturity and Health, Co-occurring Problems, and Relationships, Edited by Margaret Kerr, Håkan Stattin, Rutger C. M. E. Engels, Geertjan Overbeek and Anna-Karin Andershed © 2011 John Wiley & Sons, Ltd.

GOING FROM THE WHAT TO THE WHY

Despite the increasing prevalence and severity of girls' problem behavior over the past decades, a review of female juvenile delinquency (Hoyt and Scherer, 1998) concluded that delinquent girls are "misunderstood by the juvenile justice system" and "neglected by social science" (p. 81). Specifically, research on the development of girls' problem behavior was virtually non-existent until the 1970s and 1980s, and some argue that the few studies that did focus on girls were characterized by trying to 'fit' girls and women into theoretical models originally designed to explain the development of male problem behavior (i.e., the "add women and stir" approach, Daly and Chesney-Lind, 1988). This is perhaps not so strange, given that the gender gap in serious antisocial behavior is well documented. Boys do suffer more often than girls from this type of psychopathology, and the problem behaviors boys engage in are often more physically harmful to themselves and others than problem behaviors expressed by girls (see Crick and Zahn-Waxler, 2003). Further, childhood risk factors are much poorer predictors of adult criminality for girls than they are for boys, and concurrent associations between risk and protective factors and delinquency are generally weaker for girls than for boys (e.g., Fagan *et al.*, 2007). Hence, boys' and men's adjustment problems are more visible to us – both as researchers and as members of society – and with the theoretical models at hand they are easier to understand and explain. And if these models have worked so well for boys, why not try them out on girls as well?

Clearly, there are findings that support the notion that the mechanisms and processes behind problem behaviors are the same for boys and girls. For example, the same risk and causal factors seem to predict similar trajectories of problem behavior regardless of gender (Moffitt *et al.*, 2001; Lahey *et al.*, 2006; Van Hulle *et al.*, 2007). However, there may be specific gender differences in risk factors that are understudied, and therefore remain to be uncovered. Thus, instead of focusing on differences in the specific types of problem behavior across the sexes –which has been the major research focus until now (Moffitt *et al.*, 2001; Fagan *et al.*, 2007; Van Hulle *et al.*, 2007) – the main topic on our research agenda should be the examination of different *etiologies* of problem behavior for the sexes, which may come about as a result of differences in magnitude of and exposure to actual and perceived risks.

Even though females' problem behavior may be less common and serious than males', this does not mean that they are insignificant for the girls themselves or for society. This volume presents data showing that conduct disorder, which is strongly linked to delinquency, is the second most common psychiatric disorder among girls in the USA, UK, and New Zealand. In addition, girls accounted for a sizeable 24% of arrests for aggravated assault, 35% of forgery arrests, and 40% of embezzlement charges for American delinquents in 2003 (Pajer, Lourie, and Leininger, Chapter 4, this volume). Important to note, also, is that over the past decades girls seem to have 'moved on' from relatively minor misconducts such as shoplifting, social forms of aggression (i.e., actively isolating and gossiping about others), and vandalism to more serious crimes such as assault and robbery. Between 1980 and 2003, arrest rates for assaults by girls in the US increased explosively, by more than 250% (Pajer, Lourie, and Leininger, Chapter 4, this volume). Over the past 23 years in the United States, arrest rates for female juveniles for simple and aggravated assaults have increased, while these same rates for juvenile males decreased. In Canada a similar trend is apparent; between 1996 and 2002 a slight decrease occurred in the rate of violent crime committed by boys but a modest increase surfaced for girls, reflecting more frequent engagement in common assault (Moretti and Osbuth, Chapter 9, this volume). Hence, the fact that girls and women are not engaged in serious antisocial behavior to the same extent as boys and men does not mean that their antisocial behavior should be disregarded. Rather, it seems as if we have to revise some of our preconceptions about female maladjustment.

In addition to these increasing prevalence rates, it is important to note that more than for boys, for girls the development of externalizing behavior seems to be characterized by relatively high levels of functional impairment and comorbidity with other – mostly internalizing – psychopathologies. This is important, because adolescents who suffer from comorbid conditions (e.g., being diagnosed with clinical-level depression and conduct disorder) are at increased risk for a diversity of poor outcomes on domains such as work, friendships and romantic relationships, etc. The increased risk for poor outcomes may be particularly true for girls, as previous studies on suicidal ideation and behavior showed that this behavior was significantly more prevalent in conduct disordered adolescent girls than boys (Keenan, Chapter 6, this volume). For instance, one study showed that highly aggressive girls age 14–15 years have three times the observed rate of attempted suicide that boys have (Cairns, Petersen, and Neckerman, 1988). This means that even though the consequences and correlates of girls' antisocial behavior probably are somewhat different than those of boys', they can be equally detrimental for the individuals themselves and the people around them.

In the 10 years since Hoyt and Scherer drew their conclusion that female delinquency was understudied, there has been a growing consensus that in order to develop a complete understanding of girls' problem behavior, it is necessary to uncover the processes and mechanisms that are unique for the development of misconduct in girls. In more empirical terms, one could say that we need to start treating gender as more than a control variable (Fagan *et al.*, 2007). Knowledge in this area is advancing rapidly now, and because research is presently being conducted from many different theoretical and disciplinary angles, we consider it a 'hot topic' in developmental research. The time is ripe to summarize these advancements. In this volume, we do so by presenting a variety of intriguing studies that go from the what to the why, examining in detail the antecedents, correlates, and consequences of female misconduct.

This volume, we hope, reflects the fact that recent advancements in under-standing girls' problem behavior have come about because of three interrelated features of research that has been conducted. First, most studies presented in this volume are aimed at understanding girls' problem behaviors *in their own right*, without necessarily or exclusively applying theoretical models created for understanding boys' problems. Nevertheless, some other studies presented in this volume increase our knowledge primarily by broadening our empirical scope. They provide first-ever data on (the explanatory mechanisms underly-ing) problem behavior in samples of girls. Second, a crucial feature is that the studies in this volume come from different scientific disciplines and sub-disciplines, from medicine, criminology, and clinical psychology to develop-mental psychology. This allows for an integration of data on physiological processes with perspectives on comorbidity, social contexts (i.e., relationships with parents and peers), and interpersonal reinforcement processes.

These latter issues, of social contexts and interpersonal processes, refer to a third feature of many of the studies presented in this volume – their attention to *contexts* of problem behavior development in girls. The term "contexts", here, is used in the broadest possible sense. It refers to macro-level societal and neighborhood influences as well as the micro-level, moment-to-moment inter-actions within family and peer environments. Why the strong emphasis on social contexts in the development of girls' problem behavior? A growing number of studies suggest that girls' problem behaviors, more than boys', are connected with negative and sometimes even traumatic social experiences and relationship dynamics in childhood and adolescence. Relationships can act both as a precipitating factor, and as a 'maintaining arena' in which problem behaviors find an outlet. This is evident, for instance, in research on conduct problems. Girls' delinquency is mostly adolescent-onset and social in origin (Lahey, Moffitt, and Caspi, 2003), and girls often use their relationships to express aggression and as a means to aggress against others (e.g., Pepler and Craig, 2005; Xie, Cairns, and Cairns, 2005). Hence, we consider the context as crucial to achieving a full understanding of processes and mechanisms behind girls' and women's negative adjustment.

THIS VOLUME

In this volume, we highlight new views in research on girls' problem behavior. The book is divided into three parts. Part 1 focuses on maturity and health, comprising three chapters that deal with female pubertal timing, subjective rep-resentations of maturity and HPA axis functioning in relation to problem behav-ior. Chapter 2 by Ge *et al.* examines a 'contextual amplification hypothesis', which holds that an early onset of puberty in girls increases the risk for develop-ing problem behavior, and that this risk is higher for girls who live in adverse psychosocial contexts (or, in contrast, relatively low for girls who experience a supportive and enriching environment). Chapter 3, by Tilton-Weaver *et al.*, focuses on girls' subjective representations of maturity, more specifically, examining the extent to which discrepancies in adolescents' subjective and desired age (i.e., experiencing a maturity gap or "overfit") links to antisocial behavior, deviant peer associations, and problems in the parent–child relationship. Finally, Chapter 4, by Pajer *et al.*, addresses the understudied question whether (subclinical) conduct disorder in girls is associated with physical discomfort and problems and health risk behaviors in a sample of 278 girls aged 15–16 years.

Part 2 focuses on the etiology leading up to girls' problem behavior and the co-occurrence of girls' problem behavior with internalizing and other psychopathologies. Chapter 5, by Belknap *et al.*, takes a qualitative "pathways" approach to studying the etiology of externalizing behavior in incarcerated adolescent and young adult females. Based on data from focus groups and individual interviews across four studies, the authors emphasize the importance of physically or sexually abusive situations in childhood that lead up to help-seeking behaviors that are themselves criminalized (e.g., running away, self-medication by use of illicit drugs, prostitution, etc.) which, in turn, increase the risk of arrest and incarceration. Next, Chapter 6, by Keenan *et al.*, focuses on the extent to which girls' problem behavior co-occurs with depressive mood or places females at risk (i.e., makes them vulnerable) for the development of depression, based on data from a high risk sample of 232 9-year-old girls and their mothers, who participated in the Pittsburgh Youth Study. Also, this chapter deals with the important question whether this comorbid condition is associated with extra functional impairment in girls.

Part 3 focuses on the relational characteristics and developments associated with girls' problem behavior. It highlights explanatory mechanisms over very short (e.g., development of misconduct or deviant talk in 5-minute time intervals, on a micro-level) or short time intervals (i.e., development of bullying over half-year or one-year), as well as over decades of personal and even intergenerational development. This section contains four chapters. Chapter 7, by De Haan *et al.*, examines whether deviancy training – a reinforcement mechanism in interpersonal contact that has been previously established in boys – stimulates the development of talk about rule-breaking in dyads of incarcerated and non-incarcerated females. Chapter 8, by Pepler *et al.*, examines the development of bullying in adolescent females in relation to the development of parent–daughter conflicts and to the development of physical and emotional health problems. Chapter 9, by Moretti and Obsuth, examines the effectiveness of a parent-training program that teaches relationship principles. Based on a pre-post design with a control group, they present findings on the effectiveness of "Connect", an attachment-based intervention for parents and caregivers with teens who engage in aggressive, antisocial, and delinquent behavior. Finally, Chapter 10, by Serbin *et al.*, focuses on the pathways linking women's histories of childhood behavior problems with their own children's subsequent health and development. This intergenerational transmission mechanism is explored based on data from more than 4000 children from lower

SES urban neighborhoods, who were followed up since 1976, over a 30-year time period. The study focuses on parents' mental and physical health, patterns of spousal and child-directed violence, and socio-economic and environmental risk indicators.

GIRLS' PROBLEM BEHAVIOR: A HOT TOPIC

To conclude this introductory chapter, this volume is the third in a book series on Hot Topics in Developmental Research. The first hot topic was peer relations in adolescence – dealing with issues such as behavioral genetic research on peer relationships, mechanisms of peer influence, romantic relationships, and peers in different contexts. The second hot topic focused on the question "What can parents do?" – integrating new insights into the role of parents in adolescent problem behavior. This third volume now summarizes and integrates the most recent empirical and theoretical advances in research on girls' problem behavior. We have gathered the leading scholars in this field – scholars who are pushing the boundaries of knowledge of girls' problem behavior forward. We believe that the chapters presented here tell a compelling story, because they showcase a variety of different assumptions and hypotheses about the nature of and explanatory mechanisms underlying girls' problem behavior using a variety of sophisticated research strategies. We hope that these differences, and the different types of results and outcomes to which they lead, are 'hot' enough to provoke a scholarly discussion – and in such a way, form the basis for future, enlightening studies on girls' problem behavior.

REFERENCES

Bell, D. J., Foster, S. L., and Mash, E. J. (2005). *Handbook of Behavioral and Emotional Problems in Girls.* New York: Kluwer Academic/Plenum Publishers.

Cairns, R. B., Peterson, G., and Neckerman, H. J. (1988). Suicidal behavior in aggressive adolescents. *Journal of Clinical Child and Adolescent Psychology, 17,* 298–309.

Crick, N. R., and Zahn-Waxler, C. (2003). The development of psychopathology in females and males: Current progress and future challenges. *Development and Psychopathology, 15,* 719–742.

Daly, K. and Chesney-Lind, M. (1988). Feminism and criminology. *Justice Quarterly, 5,* 497–538.

Fagan, A. A., Van Horn, M. L., Hawkins, J. D., *et al.* (2007). Gender similarities and differences in the association between risk and protective factors and self-reported serious delinquency. *Prevention Science, 8,* 115–124.

Hoyt, S. and Scherer, D.G. (1998). Female juvenile delinquency: Misunderstood by the juvenile justice system, neglected by social science. *Law and Human Behaviour, 22,* 81–107.

Lahey, B. B., Moffitt, T. E., and Caspi, A. (2003). *Causes of Conduct Disorder and Juvenile Delinquency.* New York: Guilford Press.

Lahey, B. B., Van Hulle, C. A., Waldman, I. D., *et al.* (2006). Testing descriptive hypotheses regarding sex differences in the development of conduct problems and delinquency. *Journal of Abnormal Child Psychology, 34,* 737–755.

Magnusson, D. and Cairns, R. B. (1996). Developmental Science: Toward a unified framework. In R. B. Cairns, G. H. Elder, and E. J. Costello (eds) *Developmental Science* (pp. 7–30). Cambridge: Cambridge University Press.

Moffitt, T. E., Caspi, A., Rutter, M., *et al.* (2001). *Sex Differences in Antisocial Behavior.* Cambridge: Cambridge University Press.

Pepler, D. J., and Craig, W. M. (2005). Aggressive girls on troubled trajectories: A developmental perspective. In D. J. Pepler, K. C. Madsen, C. Webster, *et al.* (eds) *The Development and Treatment of Girlhood Aggression* (pp. 3–28). Mahwah, NJ: Lawrence Erlbaum Associates, Inc.

Van Hulle, C. A., Rodgers, J. L., D'Onofrio, B. M., *et al.* (2007). Sex differences in the causes of self-reported adolescent delinquency. *Journal of Abnormal Psychology, 116,* 236–248.

Xie, H., Cairns, B. D., and Cairns, R. B. (2005). The development of aggressive behaviors among girls: Measurement issues, social functions, and differential trajectories. In D. J. Pepler, K. C. Madsen, C. Webster, *et al.* (eds) *The Development and Treatment of Girlhood Aggression* (pp. 105–136). Mahwah, NJ: Lawrence Erlbaum Associates, Inc.

PART I

Maturity and Health

CHAPTER 1

A Contextual Amplification Hypothesis: Pubertal Timing and Girls' Emotional and Behavioral Problems

Xiaojia Ge
University of Minnesota-Twin Cities, USA

Misaki N. Natsuaki
University of California, Riverside, USA

Run Jin
California State University, Stanislaus, USA

Michael C. Biehl
University of California, Davis, USA

Preparation of this manuscript was in part supported by the National Institute of Mental Health through funding for the Institute for Social and Behavioral Research (MH48165). Additional funding for the research center and for this project was provided by the National Institute on Drug Abuse, the National Institute on Alcohol Abuse and Alcoholism, and the College of Education and Human Development at University of Minnesota, Twin Cities and the College of Agriculture and Environmental Sciences at UC Davis (CA-D*-HCD-6092-H). Correspondence concerning this chapter should be addressed to Misaki N. Natsuaki, Department of Psychology, University of California, Riverside, California, CA.

It is now common knowledge that a rise in problem behaviors occurs in early adolescence (Moffitt, 1993; Ge *et al.*, 1994; Hankin *et al.*, 1998; Wichstrom, 2001; Ge, Natsuaki, and Conger, 2006c). Trajectories of maladaptive behaviors take an upward swing during the period of pubertal transition. Despite a once-dominant view of externalizing or antisocial behaviors as boys' problems, the

Understanding Girls' Problem Behavior: How Girls' Delinquency Develops in the Context of Maturity and Health, Co-occurring Problems, and Relationships, Edited by Margaret Kerr, Håkan Stattin, Rutger C. M. E. Engels, Geertjan Overbeek and Anna-Karin Andershed © 2011 John Wiley & Sons, Ltd.

increase in maladaptive behaviors can also be seen among girls (Moffitt, 1993). Moreover, girls manifest a greater increase in internalizing symptoms than do boys in early adolescence (Ge *et al.*, 1994; Hankin *et al.*, 1998; Wichstrom, 2001; Ge, Natsuaki, and Conger, 2006c).

The synchrony of the rise of problem behaviors and emotions and the onset of puberty does not seem to be a mere coincidence. Early adolescence, after all, is especially stressful and tumultuous, as it is characterized by rapid physical maturation and a widening array of psychosocial stressors (Cicchetti and Rogosch, 2002). Differential timing of pubertal maturation across adolescents has been noticed for its influence on adolescents' behavioral and emotional development. A rapidly accumulating body of literature has shown that *early* pubertal maturation constitutes a significant risk factor for a variety of girls' emotional and behavioral problems (e.g., Brooks-Gunn and Warren, 1989; Stattin and Magnusson, 1990; Caspi and Moffitt, 1991; Caspi *et al.*, 1993; Ge *et al.*, 1994, 2001c, 2003, 2006a; Ge, Conger, and Elder, 1996, 2001a, 2001b; Graber *et al.*, 1997, 2004; Wichstrom, 2001; Cota-Robles, Neiss, and Rowe, 2002).

Although the findings have been more robust for girls than for boys (Huddleston and Ge, 2003), not every study has found a significant association between early puberty and girls' behavioral and emotional problems. When such an association is observed, the magnitude of the main effect of pubertal timing is, nonetheless, rather modest. These observed inconsistencies in the effects of pubertal timing, we believe, could be systematically sorted out by carefully examining the psychosocial contexts in which pubertal maturation occurs. In this chapter, we propose that the effect of pubertal timing is significantly contingent upon psychosocial contexts. We expect the effects of pubertal timing to be conditional on psychosocial contexts because the meanings and implications of puberty are defined accordingly to these contexts.

Our view of the interactive nature in puberty-context links has its theoretical origin in person-environment interaction perspectives that regard the development of behavior as a result of continuous transactions between biological processes and individuals' social and psychological contexts (Magnusson and Cairns, 1996; Magnusson and Stattin, 1998). According to these perspectives, biological changes should not be examined in isolation; but rather, they should be viewed conjointly with psychosocial contexts within which the developing individual is embedded (Magnusson, 1999; Bergman, Magnusson, and El-Khouri, 2003). Such person-environment interaction models are increasingly adopted for understanding the role that these multifaceted and complex biopsychosocial processes play in behavioral development.

In keeping with this interaction perspective (Susman and Rogol, 2003), we propose that, first, timing of physical maturation has significant implications for multiple dimensions of girls' adjustment during adolescence and beyond. Second, the ontogeny of girls' problem behaviors and emotions is a result of complex interactions between biological changes and psychosocial contexts within which the biological changes take place. It is with this backdrop that we maintain that biological change such as pubertal transition should interact with psychosocial contexts, including familial, peer, school, and neighborhood contexts, so as to place early-maturing girls at risk for elevated emotional and behavioral problems.

A few reminders for the readers are in place. First, the focus of this report is the effect of *pubertal timing* (i.e., early, on-time, or late timing at which an individual undergoes puberty), rather than pubertal maturation (i.e., the degree of physical maturation during puberty) per se. Second, although puberty is a transitional event that occurs for girls as well as boys, this chapter focuses on girls. The link between pubertal maturation and problem behaviors has been demonstrated more robustly for girls than for boys. The association between boys' pubertal timing and their problem behaviors has received mixed results, possibly due to the difficulty in measuring their pubertal maturation as boys do not have any benchmark of puberty as clear as girls' menarche. For more detailed discussion about boys at puberty, we refer readers to the chapter by Huddleston and Ge (2003). Third, it is also important to note that the definition of psychosocial contexts can be sometimes vague. In this chapter, we specifically refer to the contexts with which developing adolescents are directly and routinely in contact with, such as family environment, schools, neighborhoods, same/different sex peers, and stressful life experiences.

PUBERTAL TIMING AND PSYCHOSOCIAL CONTEXTS: THREE USEFUL HYPOTHESES

To help consolidate the existing findings, we propose a conceptual model to capture three substantive hypotheses relevant to the investigation of the interplay of puberty and psychosocial contexts in the development of girls' problem behavior. Figure 1.1 presents an integrative model that summarizes three

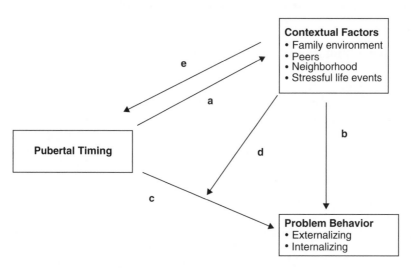

Figure 1.1 The integrative model linking pubertal timing, contexts, and developmental outcomes.

hypotheses delineating the links among pubertal timing, psychosocial contexts, and problem behavior among girls.

The *puberty-initiated mediation hypothesis* (Paths a and b) suggests that girls' early maturation influences their social environments, which in turn, compromises their healthy development. The *contextual amplification hypothesis* (Paths c and d) – the emphasis of our research group and this chapter asserts that there is an interaction between pubertal maturation and psychosocial context, such that early maturation exerts the strongest effect when girls live in adverse contexts. That is, psychosocial contexts are expected to trigger, activate, accentuate, and/or magnify the adverse effect of girls' early maturation. Therefore, according to this hypothesis, adaptation is particularly difficult for children who negotiate an early pubertal transition in a stressful social environment because new challenges at the entry to puberty and a widening array of social stressors may overtax their relatively undeveloped coping resources. This proposition can be worded differently to take into account the other end of continuum: The adverse impact of early physical maturation can be attenuated, compensated, and/or suppressed when early-maturing girls are protected by a nurturing and supportive environment. Finally, although it is not an emphasis of the present chapter, the *evolutionary hypothesis* (Path e) addresses reciprocal causal directions, acknowledging the importance of environmental influence on pubertal timing. Interested readers are referred to the following articles for more details (Belsky, Steinberg, and Draper, 1991; Ellis *et al.*, 1999; Ellis and Garber, 2000; Ellis, 2005). We acknowledge that no single model entirely captures the complexity of the association between puberty and child functioning, and that every piece of the presented model is equally important. However, this chapter mainly focuses on the contextual amplification hypothesis – one of the areas of investigation our research group has been exploring closely.

The Puberty-Initiated Mediation Hypothesis

Because biological changes, particularly development of secondary sex characteristics, have "social stimulus value" (Petersen and Taylor, 1980, p. 137) and psychological meaning, their emergence likely influences girls' social contexts. The puberty-initiated mediation hypothesis proposes that social contexts mediate the association between pubertal maturation and girls' behavioral and emotional problems. Specifically, it is expected that girls' early physical maturation could evoke certain – often challenging – reactions from the surrounding environment, which in turn, leads to their difficulties in emotional and behavioral adjustment.

Though limited, existing evidence has shown that girls' pubertal maturation indeed elicits certain environmental reactions that can be challenging for girls. For instance, daughters' sexual maturation often elicits confusion, discomfort, and awkwardness in parents (Paikoff and Brooks-Gunn, 1991).

A study by Brooks-Gunn and her colleagues (Brooks-Gunn *et al.*, 1994) pro-vides an illustrative example of how girls' breast development demands adjustment in her parents, particularly in fathers. The authors examined adolescent girls' perceptions of parents' reaction after viewing a picture of a family in which a mother was pulling out a bra from a shopping bag in front of a daughter and a father. When asked to illustrate feelings of three pro-tagonists in the picture, the participating girls described the father's reac-tion as either negative (53%) or ambivalent (29%). For instance, a participant in the study described the father's feeling: "He's really kind of embarrassed and he can't stand that his daughter has gotten really big… It's hard for him to understand, because he's a man and his daughter's a girl" (p. 556). Such awkward feelings about daughters' sexual maturation are particularly evi-dent among fathers (Brooks-Gunn *et al.*, 1994).

More direct evidence for the mediating role of psychosocial contexts comes from the classic study by Stattin and Magnusson (1990). The authors suggested that the higher prevalence of problem behaviors among early-maturing girls could result from their tendency to associate with older peers. Their adult-like physical appearance opens a door to social groups of older peers, which in turn may increase early-maturing girls' engagement in adult-like behavior that may be risky for young adolescent girls (Magnusson, Stattin, and Allen, 1985). Conformity to older peers' behavioral norms, thus, places earlier-maturing girls in deviant categories compared to their own age mates.

Based on the afore-mentioned studies, it appears that puberty –an event that occurs within an individual's biological system – elicits social reactions, which in turn affects the person's developmental outcome. This is an important mech-anism to note because it potentially provides implications to prevention and intervention; if attitudes toward girls' precocious puberty and sexual matura-tion in the social environment are somehow changed, the adverse outcome associated with early pubertal maturation may be prevented.

The Contextual Amplification Hypothesis

The contextual amplification hypothesis proposes that contextual processes play a crucial role in amplifying or ameliorating the effects of pubertal transi-tion on the development of girls' emotional and behavioral problems. Unlike the puberty-initiated mediation hypothesis, it is the interaction between puber-tal timing and psychosocial contexts that is emphasized in this hypothesis. Specifically, it is expected that early pubertal maturation exerts the strongest adverse effect when girls live in adverse social contexts. However, an adverse impact of early physical maturation can be mitigated when a supportive and enriched environment protects early-maturing girls. Contextual circumstances can either facilitate or impede early puberty effects through the opportunities, norms, and expectations, as well as through the implicit reward and punish-ment structures that the contexts provide.

This hypothesis, in its broadest sense, acknowledges that human behaviors are usually not randomly distributed. Rather, behaviors are systematically patterned according to characteristics of psychosocial contexts such as history, place, gender, socioeconomic status (SES), race/ethnicity, and past and present life experiences. In fact, the definition of pubertal timing is inherently interactive with context. Unlike pubertal status, which refers to the degree of physical maturation during puberty, pubertal timing is a relative term involving whether the individual's physical development is earlier, at the same time, or later than his/her same-sex, same-age peers (Graber, Petersen, and Brooks-Gunn, 1996). Thus, the age at which a particular level of physical maturation is reached in a particular context is an essential consideration for measuring pubertal timing. Therefore, a girl whose first period occurred at age 12, who may have been labeled as an earlier maturer 100 years ago, is no longer considered an earlier maturer in a contemporary society where the average age at menarche in Western countries is roughly around 12 and 13 years (Parent *et al.*, 2003). The very fact that physical maturation – an event appearing to be universally experienced – affects individuals differently depending on the timing at which it occurs suggests an interaction between puberty and psychosocial context. Moreover, the fact that girls are consistently found to be more negatively affected by early maturation than boys suggests that the pubertal transitional effects are gender-dependent.

The contextual amplification hypothesis is guided by several well-established theories, including the cumulative risk model (Rutter, 1990; Seifer *et al.*, 1992) and diathesis-stress model (Richters and Weintraub, 1990; Caspi and Moffitt, 1991). The cumulative risk model suggests that adverse effects of risks can be cumulative and individuals' behavior and well-being are compounded when experiencing multiple risks, rather than a single risk. From this perspective, girls who undergo early pubertal maturation and experience adverse environmental conditions simultaneously are in more peril of developing behavioral and emotional problems than on-time or later-maturing girls or early-maturing girls who are protected by supportive environments.

Our contextual amplification formulation is also conceptually consistent with the diathesis-stress model. Here, diathesis refers to salient vulnerabilities an individual possesses. Early physical maturation can be viewed as a diathesis because it has been shown to increase girls' risk for problem behaviors and emotions. Stress involves precipitating factors, such as adverse circumstances and stressful life experiences, which operate to exacerbate the harmful impact of the diathesis. According to this model, liability carried by a diathesis reaches its threshold potential when it is coupled with psychosocial stressors. In this instance, problem behaviors and emotional difficulties are triggered or activated when early maturation is combined with certain harmful contextual features.

The contextual amplification hypothesis also incorporates theories of social support: Early-maturing girls may not necessarily suffer from negative consequence in supportive environments. In this sense, this formulation incorporates the well-documented buffering model whereby beneficial effects of a supportive and resourceful environment provided by friends, family, and/or significant others are expected to reduce or neutralize the negative impact of maturing earlier than peers (Cohen and Wills, 1985). Protective circumstances, we believe, should serve to compensate the detrimental effect of a diathesis. For example, early-maturing girls in the Dunedin study did not manifest problem behaviors when they were in girls-only schools, as opposed to mixed-sex schools (Caspi et al., 1993). Incorporating the ameliorating function of protective environmental context, therefore, makes it easier for the model to explain why in some studies early maturation does not always lead to adverse outcomes.

Research has begun to document the evidence for a crucial role of psychosocial contexts in moderating the effects of early pubertal maturation on adolescent developmental outcomes (e.g., Brooks-Gunn and Warren, 1989; Caspi et al., 1993; Ge et al., 1996; Ge et al., 2002; Obeidallah et al., 2004). Recent studies have documented interactions of girls' pubertal timing with various psychosocial contexts, including race and ethnicity (Cavanagh, 2004), stressful life events (Ge, Conger, and Elder, 2001a), peers (Ge, Conger, and Elder, 1996; Ge et al., 2002; Haynie, 2003; Nadeem and Graham, 2005; Compian, Gowen, and Hayward, 2004; Conley and Rudolph, 2009), family (Dick et al., 2001; Ge et al., 2002; Haynie, 2003), school structures and school sex composition (Blyth, Simmons, and Zakin, 1985; Caspi et al., 1993), and neighborhood (Dick et al., 2000; Ge et al., 2002; Obeidallah et al., 2004). In the sections that follow, we will provide a brief overview of each salient context.

Family matters   The evidence for an interaction between pubertal timing and familial contexts largely came from the studies conducted in our lab. One of our earlier studies (Ge et al., 1995) found that the negative influence of fathers' psychological distress was significantly more pronounced among daughters who had experienced pubertal transition. A further investigation revealed that adverse effects of fathers' hostile feelings on girls' psychological distress are more pronounced for early-maturing girls than their on-time and later-maturing peers (Ge, Conger, and Elder, 1996). Extending this finding to African American families, Ge et al. (2002) discovered that, indeed, pubertal transition varied in its behavioral impact depending on the family context where a growing girl lived. African American children who were early maturers showed more problem behaviors when living with parents who were more irritable, harsher, and hostile in their disciplinary practices. It appears that early maturation may increase children's vulnerability to even normally occurring variations in parents' moods and behaviors, although why this should be the case remains still under-explored.

School matters   Three studies are prominent in documenting the moderating influence of school contexts in the link between puberty and behaviors. As early as two decades ago, Simmons and Blyth (1987) showed the dampening effects of overlapping school and pubertal transitions on girls' emotional well-being. At about the same time, Brooks-Gunn and colleagues (Gargiulo *et al.*, 1987) reported a puberty–school interaction effect on female adolescents' behaviors. These authors found that physical maturation was related to girls' dating behavior and body image only in a ballet school context. No such effect was observed in non-ballet schools. Search for a puberty X school context interaction has burgeoned since then. An early effort to test sex composition in school context as a moderator of the puberty-behavior link came from Caspi *et al.* (1993). Based on the Dunedin sample, these authors reported that early-maturing girls in mixed-sex schools were more likely to engage in problem behaviors than were their peers. In contrast, earlier-maturing girls in single-sex schools did not manifest such problems. Despite the fact that Simmons and Blyth focused on multiple transitions, that Brooks-Gunn and colleagues emphasized the nature of the school (ballet or non-ballet schools), and that Caspi and colleagues placed their reasoning on the different behavioral norms in the same-sex and mixed-sex school settings, the interaction effects demonstrated by these studies had important theoretical implications for how to look at biological changes in school contexts.

Why does school context matter? It matters because school has become an increasingly important social arena where children find themselves upon entering into adolescence. Coinciding with the time of pubertal timing, behavioral norms at school become particularly influential in middle school and youths find themselves feeling pressure to "fit in" to the norm. For instance, heightened desires for a pre-puberty physique among girls attending ballet school was an explanation why females in a ballet school were particularly affected by earlier maturation (Gargiulo *et al.*, 1987). School matters also because the transition to middle school is stressful, which adds an extra load of stressors to early-maturing youths who are undergoing stressful physical maturation at the same time (Simmons and Blyth, 1987).

Place matters   It seems that place of residence does matter when examining the pubertal timing effect. In an innovative study based on a sample of Finnish twins, R. J. Rose *et al.* (2001) reported that the effect of pubertal timing on drinking behaviors among girls was contingent upon whether the girls lived in a rural or an urban setting. Following this line of reasoning, Ge *et al.* (2002) showed that disadvantaged neighborhoods operated to exacerbate the adverse impact of pubertal timing on a sample of African American children's behaviors. This same effect was further demonstrated by Obeidallah *et al.* (2004) in the Chicago neighborhood project: early-maturing girls residing in highly disadvantaged neighborhoods were more likely to engage in violent behaviors.

These findings make a great deal of theoretical sense when we consider two potential explanatory factors: availability and life experiences. It is well known that deviant activities and antisocial peers are disproportionately distributed across places or neighborhoods. For instance, drinking friends or peers would be more readily available in urban rather than rural settings (R. J. Rose *et al.*, 2001), and deviant peers are readily accessible in disadvantaged neighborhoods. Residents living in disadvantaged neighborhoods tend to have limited access to social and economic resources (Leventhal and Brooks-Gunn, 2000), experience declining collective efficacy and eroding informal social ties (Sampson, Raudenbush, and Earls, 1997). Furthermore, their life experiences tend to be more stressful and disruptive. Adaptation may be particularly difficult for girls who negotiate an early pubertal transition in such a high-stress environment because new challenges at the entry to puberty and a widening array of social stressors may overtax their relatively undeveloped coping resources. In fact, evidence shows that early maturation interacted with greater exposure to life stressors to increase girls' depressive symptoms (Ge, Conger, and Elder, 2001a). It is important to note, however, that neighborhoods are intimately related to school and family socioeconomic background, at least in the United States. Separating the neighborhood effect from that of other contextual factors remains to be a methodological challenge as these are intricately confounded.

Peers matter   Early-maturing girls appear to be sensitive to peer influence, particularly from older ones and boys (Stattin and Magnusson, 1990; Caspi *et al.*, 1993; Ge, Conger, and Elder, 1996; Conley and Rudolph, 2009). Stattin and Magnusson's (1990) influential book was among the first to direct our attention to the importance of peers and age of peers. Speculation about the importance of sex of peers is also acknowledged by Simmons and colleagues (1987) who showed the sexual pressure by older, male peers dampened early-maturing girls' self perception. Caspi *et al.* (1993) further reasoned that earlier-maturing girls' conformation to the behavior norms of older peers could automatically put them into deviant categories. Building upon these findings, Ge, Conger, and Elder (1996) demonstrated that early-maturing girls with mixed-sex friends manifested higher levels of psychological distress.

The heightened importance of peer relationships in adolescence provides theoretical meanings to a prediction of puberty X peer context interaction. Upon entering adolescence, children are faced with an increasingly complex and expanding social network of friends. At the same time, the widening peer networks often are accompanied by increased disturbances, tensions, turmoil, and strains in peer domains (Brown, 1990). Coupled with their stronger interpersonal orientations and greater emphasis on success in relational arena, girls are more likely than boys to be affected by what happened in interpersonal domains (A. J. Rose and Rudolph, 2006).

An interesting pattern that we see in the literature is that the presence of males in the peer circle brings a new meaning to pubertal maturation for girls, particularly if girls are maturing early. As we have seen previously, early-maturing girls tend to exhibit heightened levels of emotional and behavioral problems when their social network includes boys (Caspi *et al.*, 1993; Ge, Conger, and Elder, 1996). More detailed investigation is needed to examine what it is about the affiliation with boys that accentuates the adverse effect of girls' early maturation. Perhaps, close contact with boys may magnify the puberty-related risk factors such as sexual pressure (Simmons and Blyth, 1987) and post-puberty body image that are perceived to be different from the ideal for successful romantic relationships (Paxton *et al.*, 1999). In general, it seems that the presence of boys in girls' peer circles exposes them to behavioral norms that are different from those in girl-only contexts.

In sum, the series of studies reviewed here speaks for the importance of studying puberty in its context. Although puberty itself is a biological event that occurs within each person, its effect on developmental outcomes is better understood if it is examined in context.

RESEARCH FROM OUR LABORATORY: TESTING THE CONTEXTUAL AMPLIFICATION HYPOTHESIS

During the past decade, our research program has accumulated some important knowledge on the effects of pubertal timing in context. The following section summarizes a series of empirical studies from our laboratory that have contributed to the evolution of our conceptualization about the roles of puberty and psychosocial context in adolescent development. In these studies, we have found that early pubertal timing has negative effects both across gender and ethnicity, on different developmental outcomes (internalizing and externalizing problems, depression, and alcohol and substance use) at both the symptom and diagnostic levels, and that these effects often have long-term consequences that go beyond the pubescent years. Most importantly, we have learned that biological maturation occurs within psychosocial contexts both of which contribute, independently and jointly, to adolescents' emotional and behavioral problems.

Evidence for the Contextual Amplification Hypothesis

This intellectual venture started with a study on trajectories of depressive symptoms in adolescence (Ge *et al.*, 1994). The study revealed that the emergence of gender differences occurred around the age of 13: Girls became significantly more depressed than boys at this age and the gender differences persisted into adulthood. This finding naturally led to the next question: what is happening around age 13?

As one of the most salient factors around this age, puberty became a subject of interest. Motivated to explore the effects of the pubertal transition, we conducted a subsequent study on pubertal timing and girls' psychological distress (Ge, Conger, and Elder, 1996). In this study, we observed a significant main effect of pubertal timing: Starting from eighth grade, girls who matured earlier were significantly more distressed than their on-time and later-maturing counterparts. The significant effect of early maturation persisted into 10th grade. What is interesting and relevant to the contextual amplification hypothesis is that the impact of familial and peer factors were significantly larger among earlier-maturing girls than on-time and later-maturing girls. Specifically, compared with both on-time and later-maturing girls, earlier-maturing girls experienced higher levels of psychological distress over time, particularly when they associated with mixed-sex peer groups. They were also more vulnerable to psychological problems, deviant peer pressure, and father's hostile feelings. These findings were our first evidence for the contextual amplification hypothesis: pubertal timing interacts with familial and peer contexts to impinge on girls' emotional health.

Two key findings are particularly noteworthy from these afore-mentioned studies. First, pubertal timing appears to play an important role in girls' troubled emotions and behaviors. Second, gender differences in psychological distress and internalizing problems emerge around the time of pubertal transition. Putting these pieces of information together, we raised this question: does pubertal timing indeed explain the emerging gender differences in psychological distress? We suspected that it might be the depression levels of early-maturing girls that drove the emergence of the observed female preponderance for depression. In order to test this hypothesis, we divided girls into three groups (i.e., early, on-time, and late-maturing) in a subsequent study (Ge,Conger, and Elder, 2001a). As expected, the early-maturing girls manifested disproportionately high rates of depressive symptoms. Interestingly, once the early-maturing group was removed from the analysis, depressive symptoms of the on-time and later-maturing girls were no longer significantly different from those of boys, suggesting that pubertal timing explained, at least in part, the observed emergence of gender differences in depressive symptoms. More relevant to the contextual amplification hypothesis, this study showed that stressful life events not only had a main effect on depressive symptoms, but also interacted with pubertal timing to further increase girls' risk for depressive symptoms.

Early adolescence is the time for drastic changes in various aspects of youths' lives, and all dimensions of changes are intertwined with each other. One area of change, of course, is the biological transformation from child-like physique in childhood to sexually mature body in adolescence. Another, with developing autonomy and physical mobility in adolescence, is an increasing exposure to a widening range of social environments. We suspected that the meaning and value attached to puberty, and psychosocial resources needed to negotiate a smooth pubertal transition would vary depending on the family and social environments adolescents are exposed to. For instance, menarche may be particularly stressful and confusing for a maturing girl if an adult has not discussed and prepared her for the onset of menarche. Menarche can be shocking for maturing girls who live in places where the information is difficult to ask for or acquire. However, if her mother provides her guidance and resources to handle the first period, menarche could be less unexpected and stressful for her. Similarly, in neighborhoods where information about menarche is available and individuals are more open to discussing this information, it may provide a context to make this transition less abrupt and confusing.

Given the importance of family and neighborhood environments in adolescents' lives, we tested whether early pubertal timing differentially affected adolescents who lived in different neighborhoods and familial contexts (Ge et al., 2002). Results indicated that early-maturing children residing in more disadvantaged neighborhoods were more likely to affiliate with deviant peers, and early-maturing children with harsh and inconsistent parents were more likely to show problem behaviors. These interaction effects were not specific to girls. This study is important in the formulation of the contextual amplification hypothesis because it directly demonstrates that the pubertal timing effect may vary by contextual factors on both family and neighborhood levels.

Our previous studies had mainly tested the contextual amplification hypothesis using two child outcomes: depression and delinquency. However, the hypothesis seemed to be applicable to a wide range of child outcomes, including substance use. Indeed, the results of a study based on African American adolescents (Ge et al., 2006b) indicated that the effects of pubertal timing differed by peer context in predicting adolescent substance use. First, we found that there was a substantial increase in the risks for substance use from fifth to seventh grades: in seventh grade, adolescents were more willing and intended to use substances if available, and girls, in particular, were more likely to hold favorable impressions toward peers who used substances. More importantly, pubertal timing interacted with peer substance use such that early-maturing adolescents whose friends were substance users were more likely to develop favorable perceptions about substance use and to be at risk for substance use problems.

Altogether, the evidence has converged to suggest that biological changes and social challenges in adolescence operate jointly to affect various adolescent developmental outcomes, including depression, delinquency, deviant-peer associations, and substance use. Generally, the results from these studies appear to purport the following implications in our current thinking of puberty research: (a) pubertal maturation is directly and indirectly related to adolescents' emotional and behavioral problems, particularly for girls, and (b) the adverse effect of early maturation is exacerbated in challenging psychosocial contexts.

Replication across Racial/Ethnic Groups

Although the effects of pubertal timing in European American teenagers had been well documented, little attention was paid to extend the research to non-Caucasian samples before 2000. Given the fact that timing of pubertal maturation differs across ethnicity (Herman-Giddens et al., 1997), it was important to test whether pubertal timing differed in explaining adolescents' emotional and behavioral problems across racial/ethnic groups. One of our earlier studies was designed to accomplish this task by examining the link between early physical maturation and the development of self-esteem and body image across gender and ethnic groups (Ge *et al.*, 2001c). Based on the analysis of the data from the National Longitudinal Survey of Adolescent Health (Add Health), we found that early maturation was associated with perceptions of being overweight and increased somatic complaints across all ethnicities for girls. The association of perception of being overweight and self-esteem was statistically significant only for Anglo-American and Hispanic girls, but not for African American girls. This study suggests that meanings and implications of early maturation vary by gender and by race/ethnicity. Pubertal maturation is a universal event for all racial/ethnic groups, but it possibly connotes different meanings depending on ethnic cultural contexts that may yield different child outcomes.

The Roles of Pubertal Timing and Contexts Beyond Adolescence

While contemporaneous associations between puberty, social contexts, and girls' developmental outcomes are relatively well documented, little is known how these biological transitions in adolescence influence the later courses of adolescents' lives. Although pubertal transition itself is typically completed in adolescence, when and how individuals undergo pubertal maturation in adolescence could potentially leave an important mark in life trajectories that may affect their later life course. Asking questions of whether the adverse effects of early pubertal timing and psychosocial contexts extend into young adulthood, we have been extending our perspective to the investigation of long-term effects of pubertal timing.

To date we have conducted three studies (Ge, Conger, and Elder, 2001a; Biehl, Natsuaki, and Ge, 2007; Natsuaki, Biehl, and Ge, 2009) that have sought to explore the possibility of long-term effect of pubertal timing. The first of these studies examined whether the effects of pubertal timing persisted on depressive symptoms throughout the years in high school (Ge, Conger, and Elder, 2001a). Using data collected from the Iowa Youth and Families Project in which seventh through 12th graders were followed, Ge and colleagues (2001a) showed that the effects of early pubertal maturation were not limited to the transitional years, but persisted at least to the end of high school years. In order to examine if these effects were evident at even older ages, Biehl, Natsuaki, and Ge (2007) used three waves of data from the Add Health study to examine the effects of pubertal timing on trajectories of alcohol use from ages 12 to 23. Extending our previous findings, results showed that early pubertal timing was associated with increases in alcohol use, and the effect was persistent over time. Furthermore, results supported the contextual amplification hypothesis such that early-maturing individuals who associated with alcohol-drinking friends were likely to develop higher levels of alcohol use over time. The third study (Natsuaki *et al.* 2009a) applied the contextual amplification hypothesis to trajectories of depressive symptoms tracing from ages 13 to 23. Intricate pictures regarding age, context, and timing of puberty emerged: early-maturing girls who dated early exhibited the highest levels of depressive symptoms during adolescence although the difference in the levels of depressive symptoms between these girls and other peers dissipated over time.

These three studies, although preliminary, appear to suggest that timing of pubertal transition may not be a mere predictor of transitory perturbation in behavior and emotion during early adolescence. Rather, it may have the potential to alter later developmental trajectories. If, indeed, pubertal timing exerts long-term effects on individuals' developmental life courses, the elucidation of how puberty – a transitional event that is typically completed in adolescence – shapes later outcomes needs to be one of the research priorities. A few interesting questions arise. Do pubertal timing and social contexts in adolescence exert direct effects on later outcomes? Or, is it likely that early maturation and adverse psychosocial contexts conjointly generate negative adolescent outcomes, which later unfold to undesirable adulthood outcomes?

Uncovering a Pubertal Timing X Context Interaction: Stress Sensitivity as a Possibility

As empirical evidence for the contextual amplification hypothesis has accumulated from inside and outside our laboratory, we begin to ponder a conceptual question: what is the underlying mechanism of the statistical interaction we have seen between pubertal timing and context? A statistical puberty X context interaction means that, as consistent with the contextual amplification hypothesis, the effect of pubertal timing depends on context. However, the mechanisms underlying this statistical interaction remain unclear. Focusing on the role of adolescents' stress sensitivity, we asked the following question: Are early maturing girls more depressed and anxious than their peers because they are more sensitive to the effects of interpersonal stress in adverse contexts? Using cortisol reactivity to interpersonal challenges as a physiological assessment of stress sensitivity, we examined the link between pubertal timing and stress reactivity to explain early-maturing girls' internalizing psychopathology (Natsuaki et al., 2009b). Results indicated that, early maturing girls' higher levels of internalizing problems were at least partially attributed to their heightened sensitivity to interpersonal stress. In other words, stress sensitivity is one of the potential mechanisms that explain the contextual amplification hypothesis: early-maturing girls tend to experience elevated levels of internalizing problems because they react strongly to interpersonal stress. Similar results have been reported recently by Smith and Powers (2009). Readers are reminded, however, that because this area of investigation is still at nascence, further validation is undoubtedly needed.

CONCLUSION

Early adolescence is a period characterized by a myriad of changes in biological, cognitive, and social domains. Perhaps because of the multi-faceted changes in this age period, research on the link between puberty and behaviors demands a great complexity in theoretical formulation and fuller appreciation of interaction effects in this stage of life. The conceptualization of pubertal maturation and girls' emotional and behavioral problems proposed in this chapter responds directly to this theoretical challenge and acknowledges its complexity. Previous theorizing (Simmons and Blyth, 1987; Stattin and Magnusson, 1990; Caspi and Moffitt, 1991; Brooks-Gunn et al. 1994), as well as accumulating empirical evidence, both from our laboratory and others' research programs, have convinced us that studying puberty in psychosocial context represents a fruitful avenue to enhance our understanding of adolescent emotional and behavioral problems.

While the importance of incorporating a puberty-contextual transaction approach in puberty research has been well recognized generally for the last two decades, conceptualization of how these two are intertwined has been less of a focus. In our attempt to sort out possible pathways in which pubertal transition and contexts interactively operate to influence adolescent emotional and behavioral problems, we have proposed an integrative model that embeds three hypotheses: the puberty-initiated mediation hypothesis, the evolutionary psychology hypothesis, and most importantly for this chapter, the contextual amplification hypothesis.

It is our hope that we have made the case through this chapter that investigation of pubertal timing is inherently contextually dependent. Enlargement of breast size, accumulation of puberty-associated fat, appearance of acne, and experience of menarche are biological transformations that themselves do not comprise social reference. However, whether these events happen earlier, on-time, or later are determined by the comparisons to their close reference group, the same-age, same-sex peers. Also, as various studies supporting the contextual amplification hypothesis have suggested, the meaning of pubertal timing and, thus, its effect on developmental outcomes, appear to differ significantly across the psychosocial contexts (i.e., school, neighborhood, family, peers) where physical maturation takes place. In this sense, studies of pubertal timing need to take multiple layers of contexts into consideration.

Our conceptual model of puberty and context has important practical implications. Most importantly, it suggests that making youths' psychosocial contexts more supportive can mitigate risks associated with pubertal maturation. The alleviation of contextual risks and adversities appears to be particularly crucial for early-maturing girls because it is these girls who appear to be most vulnerable to those adversities. It is likely that a successful navigation through the pubertal transitional period is not simply a matter of attending to the physical changes, but rather, it requires well-coordinated social and psychological preventive intervention programs.

Now that the significance of studying interactions between pubertal timing and psychosocial contexts is recognized in the field (at least we hope that we have done so in this chapter), it is also important to acknowledge how much remains to be understood. For example, what are the social and psychological meanings of earlier or later timing of physical maturation, aside from its biological nature? What are the reasons for pubertal timing to interact with psychosocial contexts to affect girls' problem behavior? Our future research will continue to focus on refining and testing the model in more detailed fashion. We believe that such efforts will add to the understanding of the interplay of the biological and social worlds of teenagers and the knowledge of how to prevent the development of girls' problem behaviors.

REFERENCES

Belsky, J., Steinberg, L., and Draper, P. (1991). Childhood experience, interpersonal development, and reproductive strategy: An evolutionary theory of socialization. *Child Development, 62*, 647–670.

Bergman, L. R., Magnusson, D., and El-Khouri, B. M. (2003). Studying individual development: A person-oriented approach. In D. Magnusson (ed.), *Paths through Life* (Vol. 4). Mahwah, NJ: Lawrence Erlbaum Associates, Inc.

Biehl, M. C., Natsuaki, M. N., and Ge, X. (2007). The influence of pubertal timing on alcohol use and heavy drinking trajectories. *Journal of Youth and Adolescence, 36*(2), 153–167.

Blyth, D. A., Simmons, R. G., and Zakin, D. F. (1985). Satisfaction with body image for early adolescent females: The impact of pubertal timing within different school environments. *Journal of Youth and Adolescence, 14*(3), 207–225.

Brooks-Gunn, J., Newman, D. L., Holderness, C., et al. (1994). The experience of breast development and girls stories about the purchase of a bra. *Journal of Youth and Adolescence, 23*(5), 539–565.

Brooks-Gunn, J., and Warren, M. P. (1989). Biological and social contributions to negative affect in young adolescent girls. *Child Development, 60*(1), 40–55.

Brown, B. B. (1990). Peer groups and peer cultures. In S. S. Feldman and G. R. Elliott (eds), *At the Threshold: The Developing Adolescent* (pp. 171–196). Cambridge, MA: Harvard University Press.

Caspi, A., Lynam, D., Moffitt, T. E., et al. (1993). Unraveling girls delinquency: Biological, dispositional, and contextual contributions to adolescent misbehavior. *Developmental Psychology, 29*(1), 19–30.

Caspi, A., and Moffitt, T. E. (1991). Individual differences are accentuated during periods of social change: The sample case of girls at puberty. *Journal of Personality and Social Psychology, 61*(1), 157–168.

Cavanagh, S. E. (2004). The sexual debut of girls in early adolescence: The intersection of race, pubertal timing, and friendship group characteristics. *Journal of Research on Adolescence, 14*(3), 285–312.

Cicchetti, D., and Rogosch, F. A. (2002). A developmental psychopathology perspective on adolescence. *Journal of Consulting and Clinical Psychology, 70*(1), 6–20.

Cohen, S., and Wills, T. A. (1985). Stress, social support, and the buffering hypothesis. *Psychological Bulletin, 98*(2), 310–357.

Compian, L., Gowen, L. K., and Hayward, C. (2004). Peripubertal girls' romantic and platonic involvement with boys: Associations with body image and depression symptoms. *Journal of Research on Adolescence, 14*(1), 23–47.

Conley, C. S., and Rudolph, K. D. (2009). The emerging sex difference in adolescent depression: Interacting contributions of puberty and peer stress. *Development and Psychopathology, 21*, 593–620.

Cota-Robles, S., Neiss, M., and Rowe, D. C. (2002). The role of puberty in violent and nonviolent delinquency among Anglo American, Mexican American, and African American boys. *Journal of Adolescent Research, 17*(4), 364–376.

Dick, D. M., Rose, R. J., Pulkkinen, L., *et al.* (2001). Measuring puberty and understanding its impact: A longitudinal study of adolescent twins. *Journal of Youth and Adolescence, 30*(4), 385–399.

Dick, D. M., Rose, R. J., Viken, R. J., *et al.* (2000). Pubertal timing and substance use: Associations between and within families across late adolescence. *Developmental Psychology, 36*(2), 180–189.

Ellis, B. J. (2005). Timing of pubertal maturation in girls: An integrated life history approach. *Psychological Bulletin, 130*, 920–958.

Ellis, B. J., and Garber, J. (2000). Psychosocial antecedents of variation in girls' pubertal timing: Maternal depression, stepfather presence, and marital and family stress. *Child Development, 71*(2), 485–501.

Ellis, B. J., McFadyen-Ketchum, S., Dodge, K. A., *et al.* (1999). Quality of early family relationships and individual differences in the timing of pubertal maturation in girls: A longitudinal test of an evolutionary model. *Journal of Personality and Social Psychology, 77*(2), 387–401.

Gargiulo, J., Attie, I., Brooks-Gunn, J., *et al.* (1987). Girls' dating behavior as a function of social context and maturation. *Developmental Psychology, 23*(5), 730–737.

Ge, X., Lorenz, F. O., Conger, R. D., *et al.* (1994). Trajectories of stressful life events and depressive symptoms during adolescence. *Developmental Psychology, 30*(4), 467–483.

Ge, X., Conger, R. D., Lorenz, F. O., *et al.* (1995). Mutual influences in parent and adolescent psychological distress. *Developmental Psychology, 31*(3), 406–419.

Ge, X., Conger, R. D., and Elder, G. H. (1996). Coming of age too early: Pubertal influences on girls' vulnerability to psychological distress. *Child Development, 67*(6), 3386–3400.

Ge, X., Conger, R. D., and Elder, G. H. (2001a). Pubertal transition, stressful life events, and the emergence of gender differences in adolescent depressive symptoms. *Developmental Psychology, 37*(3), 404–417.

Ge, X., Conger, R. D., and Elder, G. H. (2001b). The relation between puberty and psychological distress in adolescent boys. *Journal of Research on Adolescence, 11*(1), 49–70.

Ge, X., Elder, G. H., Regnerus, M., *et al.* (2001c). Pubertal transitions, perceptions of being overweight, and adolescents' psychological maladjustment: Gender and ethnic differences. *Social Psychology Quarterly, 64*(4), 363–375.

Ge, X., Brody, G. H., Conger, R. D., *et al.* (2002). Contextual amplification of pubertal transition effects on deviant peer affiliation and externalizing behavior among African American children. *Developmental Psychology, 38*(1), 42–54.

Ge, X., Kim, I. J., and Brody, G. H., *et al.* (2003). It's about timing and change: Pubertal transition effects on symptoms of major depression among African American youths. *Developmental Psychology, 39*(3), 430–439.

Ge, X., Brody, G. H., Conger, R. D., *et al.* (2006a). Pubertal maturation and African American children's internalizing and externalizing symptoms. *Journal of Youth and Adolescence, 35*, 531–540.

Ge, X., Jin, R., Natsuaki, M. N. *et al.* (2006b). Pubertal maturation and early substance use risks among African American children. *Psychcology of Addictive Behaviors, 20*(4), 404–414.

Ge, X., Natsuaki, M. N., and Conger, R. D. (2006c). Trajectories of depressive symptoms and stressful life events among male and female adolescents in divorced and non-divorced families. *Development & Psychopathology, 18*, 1–21.

Graber, J. A., Petersen, A. C., and Brooks-Gunn, J. (1996). Pubertal processes: Methods, measures, and models. In: *Transitions through Adolecence: Interpersonal Domains and Context*. Hillsdale, NJ: Lawrence Erlbaum Associates, Inc.

Graber, J. A., Lewinsohn, P. M., Seeley, J. R., *et al.* (1997). Is psychopathology associated with the timing of pubertal development? *Journal of the American Academy of Child and Adolescent Psychiatry, 36*(12), 1768–1776.

Graber, J. A., Seeley, J. R., Brooks-Gunn, J., *et al.* (2004). Is pubertal timing associated with psychopathology in young adulthood? *Journal of the American Academy of Child and Adolescent Psychiatry, 43*(6), 718–726.

Hankin, B. L., Abramson, L. Y., Moffitt, T. E., *et al.* (1998). Development of depression from preadolescence to young adulthood: Emerging gender differences in a 10-year longitudinal study. *Journal of Abnormal Psychology, 107*(1), 128–140.

Haynie, D. L. (2003). Contexts of risk? Explaining the link between girls' pubertal development and their delinquency involvement. *Social Forces, 82*(1), 355–397.

Herman-Giddens, M. E., Slora, E. J., Wasserman, R. C., *et al.* (1997). Secondary sexual characteristics and menses in young girls seen in office practice: A study from the pediatric research in office settings network. Pediatrics, *99*, 503–512.

Huddleston, J., and Ge, X. (2003). Boys at puberty: Psychosocial implications *Gender differences at puberty* (pp. 113–134). New York, NY: Cambridge University Press.

Leventhal, T. and Brooks-Gunn, J. (2000). The neighborhoods they live in: The effects of neighborhood residence on child and adolescent outcomes. *Psychological Bulletin, 126*(2), 309–337.

Magnusson, D., Stattin, H., and Allen, V. L. (1985). Biological maturation and social development: A longitudinal study of some adjustment processes from mid-adolescence to adulthood. *Journal of Youth and Adolescence, 14*(4), 267–283.

Magnusson, D., and Cairns, R. B. (1996). Developmental Science: Toward a unified framework. In R. B.Cairns, G. H., Elder, and E. J. Costello, (eds), *Developmental Science* (pp. 7–30). Cambridge: Cambridge University Press.

Magnusson, D., and Stattin, H. (1998). Person-context interaction theories. In W. Damon and R. M. Lerner (eds), *Handbook of Child Psychology: Volume 1: Theoretical Models of Human Development* (5th ed.) (pp. 685–759). Hoboken, NJ: John Wiley & Sons, Inc.

Magnusson, D. (1999). On the individual: A person-oriented approach to developmental research. *European Psychologist, 4*, 205–218.

Moffitt, T. E. (1993). Adolescence-limited and life-course-persistent antisocial behavior: A developmental taxonomy. *Psychological Review, 100*(4), 674–701.

Nadeem, E., and Graham, S. (2005). Early puberty, peer victimization, and internalizing symptoms in ethnic minority adolescents. *Journal of Early Adolescence, 25*(2), 197–222.

Natsuaki, M. N., Biehl, M. C., and Ge, X. (2009a). Trajectories of depressed mood from early adolescence to young adulthood: The effects of pubertal timing and adolescent dating. *Journal of Research on Adolescence, 19*, 47–74.

Natsuaki, M. N., Klimes-Dougan, B., Ge, X.*et al.* (2009b). Early pubertal maturation and internalizing problems in adolescence: Sex differences in the role of cortisol reactivity to interpersonal stress. *Journal of Clinical and Child and Adolescent Psychology, 38*, 513–524.

Obeidallah, D., Brennan, R. T., Brooks-Gunn, J., *et al.* (2004). Links between pubertal timing and neighborhood contexts: Implications for girls' violent behavior. *Journal of the American Academy of Child and Adolescent Psychiatry, 43*(12), 1460–1468.

Paikoff, R. L., and Brooks-Gunn, J. (1991). Do parent-child relationships change during puberty? *Psychological Bulletin, 110*(1), 47–66.

Parent, A. S., Teilmann, G., Juul, A., *et al.* (2003). The timing of normal puberty and the age limits of sexual precocity: Variations around the world, secular trends, and changes after migration. *Endocrine Reviews, 24*, 668–693.

Paxton, S. J., Schutz, H. K., Wertheim, E. H., *et al.* (1999). Friendship clique and peer influences on body image concerns, dietary restraint, extreme weight-loss behaviors, and binge eating in adolescent girls. *Journal of Abnormal Psychology, 108*(2), 255–266.

Petersen, A. C., and Taylor, B. (1980). The biological approach to adolescence. In J. Adelson (ed.), *Handbook of Adolescent Psychology* (pp. 117–155). New York: Wiley.

Richters, J. E., and Weintraub, S. (1990). Beyond diathesis: Toward an understanding of high-risk environments. In J. E. Rolf, A. S. Masten, D. Cicchetti, *et al.* (eds), *Risk and Protective Factors in the Development of Psychopathology* (pp. 67–96). New York, NY: Cambridge University Press.

Rose, A. J., and Rudolph, K. D. (2006). A review of sex differences in peer relationship processes: Potential trade-offs for the emotional and behavioral development of girls and boys. *Psychological Bulletin, 132*, 98–131.

Rose, R. J., Dick, D. M., Viken, R. J., *et al.* (2001). Drinking or abstaining at age 14? A genetic epidemiological study. *Alcoholism-Clinical and Experimental Research, 25*(11), 1594–1604.

Rutter, M. (1990). Psychosocial resilience and protective mechanisms. In J. E. Rolf, A. S. Masten, D. Cicchetti, *et al.* (eds), *Risk and Protective Factors in the Development of Psychopathology.* (pp. 181–214). New York, NY: Cambridge University Press.

Sampson, R. J., Raudenbush, S. W., and Earls, F. (1997). Neighborhoods and violent crime: A multilevel study of collective efficacy. *Science, 277*(5328), 918–924.

Seifer, R., Sameroff, A., Baldwin, C. P., *et al.* (1992). Child and family factors that ameliorate risk between 4 and 13 years of age. *Journal of the American Academy of Child & Adolescent Psychiatry, 31*, 893–903.

Simmons, R. G., and Blyth, D. A. (1987). Moving into adolescence: The impact of pubertal change and school context. In: *Moving into Adolescence: The Impact of Pubertal Change and School Context.* Hawthorne, NY: Aldine.

Smith, A. E., and Powers, S. I. (2009). Off-time pubertal timing predicts physiological reactivity to postpuberty interpersonal stress. *Journal of Research on Adolescence, 19*, 441–458.

Stattin, H., and Magnusson, D. (1990). Pubertal maturation in female development. In D. Magnusson (ed.), *Paths through Life* (Vol. 2): Hillsdale, NJ: Lawrence Erlbaum Associates, Inc.

Susman, E. J., and Rogol, A. D. (2003). Puberty and psychological development. In R. M. Lerner (ed.), *Handbook of Developmental Psychology.* Hillsdale, NJ: Lawrence Erlbaum Associates, Inc.

Wichstrom, L. (2001). The impact of pubertal timing on adolescents' alcohol use. *Journal of Research on Adolescence, 11*(2), 131–150.

CHAPTER 2

Fits and Misfits: How Adolescents' Representations of Maturity Relate To Their Adjustment

Lauree C. Tilton-Weaver
Örebro University, Sweden

Fumiko Kakihara
Örebro University, Sweden

Sheila K. Marshall
University of British Columbia, Canada

Nancy L. Galambos
University of Alberta, Canada

> *To be concerned about being grown up, to admire the grown up because it is grown up, to blush at the suspicion of being childish; these things are the marks of childhood and adolescence. And in childhood and adolescence they are, in moderation, healthy symptoms. Young things ought to want to grow.*
>
> –C. S. Lewis

Adolescence has been characterized as a time in which individuals are caught "betwixt and between" – too old to be treated as children, too young to be treated as adults. Adolescents, to varying degrees, appear to be aware of this. Theorists have pointed to this phenomenon as a reason for adolescents' engagement in problem behavior. Moffitt's (1993) notion of a maturity gap – that adolescents engage in misbehavior as a means of laying claim on more mature status – is probably one of the best known. In this chapter, we explore the idea of maturity gap and other configurations of maturity perceptions in order to better understand the relationship of subjective maturity to adolescents'

Understanding Girls' Problem Behavior: How Girls' Delinquency Develops in the Context of Maturity and Health, Co-occurring Problems, and Relationships, Edited by Margaret Kerr, Håkan Stattin, Rutger C. M. E. Engels, Geertjan Overbeek and Anna-Karin Andershed © 2011 John Wiley & Sons, Ltd.

adjustment. We also compare these issues for girls and boys, to determine the extent to which these issues are linked to adjustment primarily for girls.

BACKGROUND

How old an adolescent feels, dubbed subjective age, provides insight into perceptions of maturity, so it is interesting that feeling older than one's chronological age is a common phenomenon in adolescence (Hubley and Hultsch, 1994; Montepare and Lachman, 1989; Galambos *et al.*, 1999). Moreover, feeling older is linked to a greater level of engagement in problem behavior and association with deviant peers in adolescence (Stattin and Magnusson, 1990; Galambos *et al.*, 1999; Arbeau, Galambos, and Jansson, 2007). The linkage may be somewhat bidirectional: adolescents who feel older increase in smoking and those who have sex, drink alcohol, or smoke subsequently feel older (Galambos, Albrecht, and Jansson, 2009). This link between an older subjective age and engagement in problem behaviors supports the existence of adultoid or pseudomature adolescents who have been described in theoretical literature, but until recently, remained unidentified empirically.

PSEUDOMATURITY

Theoretical accounts describe adultoid or pseudomature adolescents as youth who gain the image of social maturity through engagement in behaviors seen as acceptable and desirable in adults (e.g., drinking alcohol). Greenberger and Steinberg (1986) argued that although pseudomature adolescents may be viewed by themselves and others as more mature, they lack the genuine psychosocial maturity (i.e., strong work ethic and identity) necessary for successfully negotiating the transition to adulthood. "'Adultoid' behavior simply mimics adult activity without being accompanied by the underlying perceptions, beliefs, or understanding that a person who is psychologically adult would bring to a similar situation" (p. 174).

Other scholars have also suggested that engagement in problem behaviors may be a venue through which adolescents lay claim to a greater sense of maturity, particularly those who are driven to grow up and enjoy the privileges of adulthood. Jessor (1992) and Moffitt (1993) argued that engagement in problem behavior allows access to more mature status, a valued resource among adolescents. "[D]elinquency must be a social behavior that allows access to some desirable resource. I suggest that the resource is mature status, with its consequent power and privilege" (Moffitt, 1993, p. 686).

In two separate studies, Galambos and colleagues empirically identified pseudomature adolescents, using a pattern-centered approach that allowed pseudomature adolescents to be compared to mature and immature adolescents (Galambos and Tilton-Weaver, 2000; Galambos, Barker, and Tilton-Weaver,

2003). These comparisons showed that pseudomature adolescents felt significantly older and engaged in more problem behaviors, but were less psychosocially mature than both mature and immature adolescents. Moreover, additional analyses and follow-up studies show pseudomature adolescents are more independent, more invested in peers and pop culture, and have more conflicted relationships with their parents. They expect to gain privileges sooner than their peers or their parents want them to, and they avoid taking on responsibilities. In short, they appear to want the status of being more mature, without wanting or understanding the responsibilities that go with it.

It is especially interesting that pseudomature adolescents not only felt older than other adolescents, but they wanted to be older still. This, combined with their involvement with peers and problem behavior, is reminiscent of the youth described by Moffitt (1993) as "adolescence-limited" delinquents, for whom engagement in problem behaviors provides an opportunity to gain more mature status in the eyes of their peers. Thus, there is reason to think that pseudomature adolescents may also be on Moffitt's adolescence-limited trajectory of problem behavior.

OTHER REPRESENTATIONS OF MATURITY

In a study of adolescents' implicit theories of maturity, Tilton-Weaver, Galambos, and Vitunski (2001) asked adolescents to describe peers who seemed more "grown up" than other peers. Adolescents described attributes of adulthood – physical development, power, status, privileges, and responsibilities. They differed in which attributes of adulthood they saw as relevant to the concept of being grown up. Some described individuals with an age-appropriate balance of these attributes. These "grown up" peers closely resembled the "mature" adolescents of Galambos' studies (Galambos and Tilton-Weaver, 2000; Galambos, Barker, and Tilton-Weaver, 2003). Other participants from Tilton-Weaver, Galambos, and Vitunski (2001) described individuals who seemed to be focused on privileges. These descriptions mirrored empirical accounts of pseudomature adolescents. This provided evidence that adolescents differ in how they construe maturity. Such representations may constitute implicit theories, guiding adolescents' understandings of maturity and perhaps acting as guideposts for their own behavior and development.

MOFFITT'S MATURITY GAP

The link between perceived maturity status and adjustment is perhaps most clearly explored in Moffitt's (1993, 2006) theory positing differences between adolescence-limited and life-course persistent antisocial trajectories. Moffitt suggested that the antisocial behavior of life-course persistent delinquents would be seen as desirable during adolescence, leading to higher status among peers. Other adolescents would then mimic the antisocial behavior, as a way of gaining similar status. Adolescents not previously engaged in problem behaviors would be drawn in because of a "maturity gap." According to Moffitt, adolescents entering puberty (who are not life-course delinquents) feel a disjuncture between their biological and their social ages, unable to access the desirable resources of adulthood.

Moffitt's notion of maturity gap, however, seems to apply somewhat uniformly across adolescence. Moffitt suggests that the maturity gap refers to the relatively normless period between biological maturation (puberty) and the assumption of rights and privileges associated with adulthood. Moffitt further suggested there were several conditions under which adolescents would likely not be pulled into delinquent activities: when (a) puberty is delayed, (b) they have access to roles respected by adults, (c) they are in contexts limiting opportunities to learn about delinquency, (d) they have personal characteristics that act to exclude them from delinquent peer groups, or (e) any combination of these conditions. Of these, only delayed puberty and access to respected roles would reduce or nullify the effects of a maturity gap without engagement in delinquency. Those with delayed puberty would not sense a difference between their biological and social ages, and those with access to respected adult roles would have a means of securing a sense of maturity without misbehavior. It could be expected then, that most adolescents would have maturity gaps to some extent.

The diversity in the types of maturity found in previous research (i.e., Galambos and Tilton-Weaver, 2000) and in adolescents' descriptions of maturity (Tilton-Weaver, Galambos, and Vitunski, 2001) suggest that there is more variability in maturity perceptions than is represented by Moffitt's theory. That is, feeling older, but wanting to be even older (as do pseudomature adolescents) is one way of construing a mismatch between subjective and desired maturity. In the studies of pseudomaturity, only part of the adolescents felt this way. We argue that it is important to understand this variability, and to consider the conditions under which some adolescents experience maturity gaps as well as the extent to which feeling a gap portends problems.

MATURITY "OVERFIT"

Moffitt (1993) also did not discuss the possibility that some adolescents may feel older than they want to be. Because youths differ in the degree to which they feel and want to feel older, there may be experiences that lead adolescents to feeling older, but more so than they desire. We dub this a maturity *overfit*. It is understandable that Moffitt did not discuss this type of "gap," as Moffitt's theory is meant to explain delinquency and not other potential adjustment issues. However, an overfit is an intriguing possibility hinted at in research.

There may be several sources for feeling older than one desires or being treated more maturely than one desires. Such youths may feel younger than their peers, like the immature adolescents in the studies of pseudomaturity (Galambos and Tilton-Weaver, 2000; Galambos, Barker, and Tilton-Weaver, 2003), or feel older, but desire to be younger. Sources for a discrepancy like this may come from being thrust into experiences that one does not feel prepared for. These may include adult-like experiences that are not age appropriate.

We speculate that early pubertal development may be a source of such feelings. We suggest that this is particularly true for early maturing girls, because they are most physically different from their age mates (Stattin and Magnusson, 1990). Although early pubertal development has been linked to pseudomaturity, and thus a maturity gap, this does not rule out the possibility that for some, early development leads to feeling that one is more mature, or treated more maturely, than is desired.

Another potential source is treatment by others. Adolescents whose roles with parents have been reversed and are in the position of being caretaker (i.e., parentified adolescents, Earley and Cushway, 2002) may feel this way. For example, Koerner, Kenyon, and Rankin (2006) found that adolescents whose divorced mothers disclosed financial and job concerns felt older than their peers whose divorced mothers did not disclose as much. Sexual abuse is another example. Turner, Runtz, and Galambos (1999) found that girls who self-reported sexual abuse felt significantly older than their peers who had not been abused. In sum, some adolescents may feel older than they desire, or may feel they are being treated older than they desire and this may create discomfort contributing to adjustment difficulties.

FITS AND MISFITS

We can conceptualize, then, three types of maturity fits and misfits: fit, gap, and overfit. Each is characterized by either a match or mismatch between adolescents' perceptions of maturity and their desires for maturity (see Table 2.1). That is, adolescents with maturity fits have a match between their perceived maturity and their desire for maturity. In contrast, adolescents with maturity gaps desire more maturity than they feel, and adolescents with maturity overfits feel more maturity than they desire. We posit that these perceptions arise from different contexts and have differential consequences for adolescents' development.

GENDER

One of the primary purposes of this group of studies was to explore the meaning of maturity representations for girls in particular. Although Moffitt (2006) suggested that maturity gaps may apply to both male and female adolescents, we wondered if some representations or some linkages to adjustment might be specific to girls. For example, if early pubertal maturation is associated with an

Table 2.1 Conceptual guide to types of maturity fits and misfits.

		Operationalization		
Type of fit	Description	Study 1: Categorized	Study 2: Interactions	Study 3: Categorized
Maturity fit	Match between feelings of maturity and desire for maturity	Desired age is roughly equal to subjective age	High or low on both desired treatment and perceived treatment	Treated about as maturely as desired
Maturity gap	Mismatch characterized by desire for more maturity than is felt	Desired age is greater than subjective age	Desires more mature treatment & treated less maturely	Treated less maturely than desired
Maturity overfit	Mismatch characterized by more felt maturity than is desired	Subjective age is greater than desired age	Desires less mature treatment & treated more maturely	Treated more maturely than desired

overfit, this might be particularly true for girls, whose early maturation makes them more likely to stand apart from their peers. For them, the difference between their physical maturity and their experiences may be more salient. Girls may also react differently to a lack of fit, perhaps showing depressive symptoms more than boys. Thus, we examined gender differences in dispersion of fits and misfits and sought to determine if the relationships with other constructs depended on gender.

DEVELOPMENTAL ISSUES

Although there is some suggestion of change over time in adolescents' perceptions of maturity, developmental shifts in maturity perceptions has not been explored. Cross-sectional evidence suggests that there are shifts in subjective age, with a cross-over from most adolescents having older subjective ages to younger subjective ages sometime during the second decade of life (Galambos, Turner, and Tilton-Weaver, 2005). These studies, however, did not directly assess fit.

With respect to maturity gaps, Moffitt's (1993) writings suggest a trajectory. Maturity gap may be most common in early adolescence, when pubertal development is a salient feature of youths' experiences. In early adulthood, gaps should close, as the delinquent behavior that was previously rewarding becomes punishing, because of the consequences misconduct has for the assumption of many adult roles (e.g., criminal records interfere with finding gainful employment). In between these two periods, gaps should lessen, because older adolescents tend to engage in more problem behaviors than younger adolescents and the engagement in problem behaviors could be expected to lend adolescents the feeling of being more mature. Hence, younger adolescents should experience maturity gaps more than older adolescents do.

However, we suggest an alternate possibility. It is possible that engagement in behaviors, while lending a sense of greater maturity, does not wholly satisfy adolescents' desires. If so, the closer they are to adulthood, the more keenly they may feel the gap. In this scenario, either older adolescents would be more likely than younger to have gaps or there would be no significant differences. Where, though, would we find overfits? Although older adolescents are expected to take on more responsibilities than younger adolescents, adolescents in general lag behind their parents in wanting to assume them (Feldman and Rosenthal, 1991). We suspect that this may make some older adolescents feel uncomfortable, creating an overfit. Similarly, older youths are granted more independence than younger adolescents (Feldman and Quatman, 1988). Again, this might make some uncomfortable. In sum, we expect overfits to be found more among older than younger adolescents.

We thought there might also be development differences in the correlates of maturity fit and misfits. We speculated, for example, that early adolescents might feel the circumstances creating gaps and overfits (i.e., restrictive parenting or being exposed to adult-like behaviors) more keenly than older adolescents, because pubertal development is so salient. If so, there should be age differences in the relationships of fit to contextual features such as restrictive parenting or involvement with deviant peers. We also thought that the consequences of gaps and overfits might differ across adolescence. Older adolescents, who are closer to adulthood than younger adolescents, might find a maturity gap particularly disagreeable. If this is the case, the link between fit and adjustment should be stronger for older than for younger adolescents. In short, we looked at whether correlates of maturity fits and misfits depended on age.

THE PRESENT STUDIES

The studies we have reviewed draw attention to individual differences and possibly developmental differences in adolescents' cognitive representations of maturity. In this chapter, we present a series of studies examining these representations in three different ways, in three different samples (see Table 2.1), with the intention of delving into potential antecedents and consequences. Our primary objective was to find a way to measure maturity gap, maturity fit, and overfit. From the finding that adultoid adolescents not only felt older, but wanted to be older than their mature and immature peers (Galambos and Tilton-Weaver, 2000), we deduced that there were differences that could be reliably measured. Assuming reliable measurement, these questions guided the work: (1) Are there individual differences, such as gender and age differences, in perceptions of maturity and maturity fit? (2) Are different types of maturity fit differentially related to adjustment? Although Moffitt's (1993) concept of maturity gap is a mechanism explaining externalizing problems, we speculated that maturity gaps and overfits might be related to internalizing problems as well. We also asked: (3) Are there contextual (peer, family) differences in fits? We expected adolescents with maturity gaps to be more peer-oriented and to have more deviant peers than their fit counterparts. We also expected to find differences in the ways they are parented and in their relationships with parents. We expected that adolescents with gaps might feel more restricted and less accepted by their parents and experience more conflict with them than the others.

In the first study, we use subjective age and desired age to create an index of maturity gap. In the second study, we explore maturity gap by examining the discrepancy between adolescents' perceptions of how maturely they are treated and the importance of being treated maturely. The final study uses this newly created measure of maturity gap in another sample, in order to both validate the measure and to further explore the construct. We looked for age-related differences in the composition of these groups as well as the possibility of age-related differences in correlates. We also examined gender differences, so as to understand which issues are particularly relevant to girls.

STUDY 1

This study was our first attempt to measure and capture maturity fits and misfits. Given the acceptance of subjective age measures among researchers, and the existence of valid measures of desired age, it made sense to first use these two constructs to tap into perceptions of feeling older than one desires and vice versa. We examined individual and contextual variation between these groups, with the expectation that adolescents with maturity fits would be better adjusted and have better peer and family contexts than those with gaps or overfits.

Addressing expectations for those with maturity gaps first, we expected them to look like the adolescence-limited delinquents described by Moffitt or the pseudomature adolescents found by Galambos and colleagues. We expected that boys and physically mature adolescents would be over-represented in the maturity gap group. However, Moffitt (2006) recently applied her theory to both boys and girls, so there may be no gender differences in who experiences a maturity gap. With respect to age, there were multiple possibilities. Gaps could be more prevalent in younger or in older adolescents, or there might be no significant differences at all. So, we made no specific hypothesis. Like pseudomature youths, we expected adolescents with maturity gaps to have more adjustment difficulties, evincing more problem behavior and less psychosocial maturity than the other groups. Also like pseudomature youths, we expected adolescents with maturity gaps to be more peer-oriented (i.e., more time with peers, more deviant, fewer prosocial peers), to be more behaviorally independent, and pop-culture oriented than the other adolescents. We also expected them to be like pseudomature youth in their experiences with their parents – having more conflict and feeling less acceptance from their parents than youths with fits or overfits.

With respect to those with overfits, recall that we speculated the feeling of being more mature than one desired might come from early pubertal maturation, particularly if the early maturing adolescent is a girl. They may also be more independent, but feel less sure of themselves than adolescents with maturity fits. We expected that this might translate into being less self-reliant and having less consolidated identities than adolescents with maturity fits. Based on Eccles' stage-environment fit (Eccles *et al.*, 1993), we speculated that adolescents with overfits might experience more parent-adolescent conflict or less parental acceptance than adolescents with maturity fits. If so, they may also be drawn to peer contexts more than those with maturity fits.

Methods

Sample and procedures

Data for this study come from the Victoria Adolescence Project (VAP), a three-year cohort-sequential study examining psychosocial development. The full sample consisted of 452 students who were initially in grades 6 ($n = 220$; 110 females, 100 males) and 9 ($n = 232$; 113 females, 119 males). Mean ages were 11.96 years ($SD = 0.32$) for the sixth graders and 15.07 years ($SD = 0.42$) for the ninth graders. The participants were primarily European Canadians (85%), with a minority of Asians (10%), First Nations (3%), and other ethnic groups (2%). Most came from two-parent households (76%), including 8% from mother/stepfather homes and 2.4% from father/stepmother homes. Another 22% were living in single-parent households (including those sharing joint custody), with the remaining 2% living with other relatives or non-relatives. The socioeconomic levels were similar to those of families in the region from which the sample was drawn.

The adolescents were recruited from and initially sampled in the classrooms of eight elementary schools (Grades K-7), two junior high schools (Grades 8–10), and one high school (Grades 8–12). Passive consent procedures were used in all but one elementary school ($n = 18$) and one junior high school ($n = 22$), where active consent procedures were required by the principals. Students filled out questionnaires during class time (approximately 1 hour), where teachers were generally not present. Following completion of the questionnaire, the classes were provided $5 for each student who participated. Successive waves of data collection were collected using active consent, mailing packages to the adolescents' homes, where they completed and returned by mail. Adolescents were provided with $5 honorariums for successive waves of participation. In this study, the second wave of data was used, which was collected approximately one year after the initial collection. Longitudinal data were provided by 157 adolescents. Additional sample and procedural information is available in Galambos, Barker, and Tilton-Weaver (2003).

Measures

Subjective and desired age   The mean of seven items (Galambos and Tilton-Weaver, 2000; Montepare et al., 1989) assessed subjective age or how old adolescents feel relative to their chronological age. Using a seven-point scale ranging from 1 (a lot younger than my age) to 7 (a lot older than my age), adolescents responded to items such as "Compared to most girls [boys] my age, most of the time I feel…" "Compared to most girls [boys] my age, most of the time I look…" and "My girl [boy] friends act toward me as if I am…" Higher scores indicated an older subjective age (Time 1: $\alpha = 0.82$, M = 4.37, SD = 0.83; Time 2: $\alpha = 0.86$, M = 4.57, SD = 0.76).

The same set of items, with the wording altered to reflect the adolescents *desired age* were used (e.g., "Compared to my present age, most of the time I would like to look…"), using the same 7-point response scale. Higher scores indicated an older desired age (Time 1: $\alpha = 0.88$, *M* = 4.76, *SD* = 0.88; Time 2: $\alpha = 0.87$, *M* = 4.70, *SD* = 0.73).

To categorize youths according to their maturity fits, we created discrepancy scores by subtracting each desired age item from its respective subjective age item, and calculating the mean of the 7 items. Thus, potential scores would range from −6 (a mean score of 1 for desired age and 7 for subjective age) to 6 (a mean score of 7 for desired age and 1 for subjective age). Positive values indicated maturity gaps, whereas negative values indicated maturity overfits. Cronbach alphas for the derived scores were acceptable: Time 1 = 0.76, Time 2 = 0.78. We then created categorical variables by roughly dividing the sample into three groups. Adolescents with values from −6.00 to −0.15 were categorized as having maturity overfits, from −0.14 to 0.14 were categorized as having maturity fits, and from 0.15 to 6 were categorized as having maturity gaps. Orthogonal codes were then created, with the first orthogonal code contrasting adolescents with overfits (−1) to adolescents with fits (1); the second orthogonal code compared overfit and fit groups (−1) to those with maturity gaps (2).

Problem behavior   Twenty-three items, comprising three scales, were used to assess adolescents' problem behaviors (Brown, Clasen, and Eicher, 1986; Maggs, Almeida, and Galambos, 1995). Adolescents reported the frequency with which they disobeyed parents, used substances, or engaged in antisocial behaviors in the month prior to testing, using a 5-point scale ranging from never to almost every day. Higher mean scores reflect higher levels of problem behaviors (for disobeying parents, Time 1: $\alpha = 0.80$, M = 2.08, SD = 0.82; Time 2: $\alpha = 0.78$, M = 1.91, SD = 0.77; for substance use, Time 1: $\alpha = 0.88$, M = 1.49, SD = 0.82; Time 2: $\alpha = 0.88$, M = 1.52, SD = 0.84; for antisocial behaviors, Time 1: $\alpha = 0.86$, M = 1.22, SD = 0.39; Time 2: $\alpha = 0.56$, M = 1.13, SD = 0.31).

Psychosocial development   Greenberger's individual adequacy (autonomy) subscales from the Psychosocial Maturity Inventory (PMI; Greenberger and Bond, 1984) were used. Assessing self-reliance, identity, and work orientation, each subscale is composed of ten items, responded to on a 4-point Likert scale ranging from 1 (agree strongly) to 4 (disagree strongly). Higher mean scores indicated greater self-reliance (Time 1: α = 0.67, M = 3.05, SD = 0.47; Time 2: α = 0.65, M = 3.23, SD = 0.43), a more consolidated identity (Time 1: α = 0.71, M = 3.15, SD = 0.49; Time 2: α = 0.74, M = 3.27, SD = 0.47), and a stronger work orientation (Time 1: α = 0.60, M = 2.78, SD = 0.49; Time 2: α = 0.70, M = 2.89, SD = 0.50).

Pubertal development   Pubertal development was measured using the Pubertal Development Scale (PDS, Petersen, Crockett, Richards, et al., 1988), a well-established self-report measure that assesses pubertal change with items asking about hair and skin changes, breast development and menstruation (for girls), and vocal changes (for boys). The scales are calculated separately for boys and girls, with higher values indicating more advanced pubertal development (for boys, Time 1: α = 0.83, M = 2.51, SD = 0.83; for girls, Time 1: α = 0.74, M = 2.78, SD = 0.82).

Deviant/prosocial friends   Two scales used 4 items each to assess the deviant and prosocial orientation of the adolescents' friends. Sample items are "Lots of my friends smoke cigarettes" and "Most of my friends would jump in and help a stranger in trouble". Mean scores from items rated on a scale ranging from 1 (agree strongly) to 4 (disagree strongly) indicate adolescents perceived their friends were more deviant (Time 1: α = 0.74, M = 2.16, SD = 0.77; Time 2: α = 0.80, M = 2.13, SD = 0.79) or more prosocial (Time 1: α = 0.63, M = 2.96, SD = 0.60; Time 2: α = 0.69, M = 3.21, SD = 0.57).

Time with peers   The mean monthly frequency of four self-reported behaviors (e.g., spent a day or an evening doing something with friends) was used to assess peer involvement (Brown, Clasen, and Eicher, 1986). Rated on a scale ranging from 1 (never) to 5 (almost every day), higher scores indicated more time spent with peers (Time 1: α = 0.77, M = 2.74, SD = 0.91; Time 2: 0.76, M = 3.03, SD = 0.90).

Behavioral independence   Four items (e.g., went shopping without an adult) previously used by Simmons and Blyth (1987) were used to assess behavioral independence. Mean scores on responses using a scale ranging from 1 (never) to 5 (almost every day) indicated higher levels of independence (Time 1: α = 0.80, M = 2.79, SD = 1.16; Time 2: α = 0.81, M = 3.05, SD = 1.10).

Investment in pop culture   Mean scores from four items created for the project were used to have adolescents indicate the frequency of pop-culture related activities in the month prior to testing (e.g., "Read a magazine for teenagers," "Watched Much Music"). Adolescents responded using a scale ranging from 1 (never) to 5 (almost every day). Higher scores indicated more investment in pop culture. This variable was available for Time 1 only (α = 0.73, M = 2.60, SD = 0.94).

Parent–adolescent conflict   A 15-item revision (Galambos and Almeida, 1992) of the Issues Checklist (IC; see Prinz et al., 1979) was used to assess adolescents' conflict with their mothers and fathers. Adolescents indicate whether they have discussed any of the 15 topics (e.g., cleaning up their bedroom) in the last two weeks. For each topic discussed, the intensity of the discussion is rated on a scale ranging from 1 (very calm) to 5 (very angry). Conflict frequency was calculated as the sum of all topics rated 2 or greater and intensity as the mean level of intensity for all topics. Conflict frequency and intensity were then standardized and averaged, such that higher values indicate higher levels of conflict (for mothers, Time 1: $M = 0.00$, $SD = 0.97$ and Time 2: $M = 0.00$, $SD = 0.97$; for fathers, Time 1: $M = 0.01$, $SD = 0.97$ and Time 2: $M = 0.00$, $SD = 0.97$).

Parental acceptance   The acceptance subscale of the Child's Report of Parental Behavior Inventory (CRPBI; Schaefer, 1965; Burger and Armentrout, 1971) was used to measure the amount of warmth and support provided adolescents by their parents. The mean of 24 items (e.g., "She [he] almost always speaks to me in a warm and friendly voice."), rated on a scale of 1 (very much unlike her [him]) to 5 (very much like her [him]) has adequate psychometric properties (for mothers, Time 1: $\alpha = 0.97$, $M = 3.76$, $SD = 0.87$ and Time 2: $\alpha = 0.98$, $M = 3.76$, $SD = 0.89$; for fathers, Time 1: $\alpha = 0.98$, $M = 3.67$, $SD = 0.93$ and Time 2: $\alpha = 0.97$, $M = 3.63$, $SD = 0.85$).

Plan of analyses

To test for differences in gender and age, we used chi-square tests. All other differences were tested using hierarchical regressions. For each dependent variable (with the exception of pubertal development), five steps of predictors were entered. Gender and grade (effect coded, girls and ninth graders were assigned 1) were entered first, followed by the linear orthogonal codes, with the interaction of gender and age entered third, the two-way interactions between gender and each orthogonal code entered fourth, and with the three-way interactions between grade, gender, and codes entered last. Because the pubertal development scales are assessed separately for boys and girls, the regressions for pubertal development were conducted separately by gender, without gender or gender interactions included.

Results

We first sought to determine if there were gender, grade, or pubertal maturation differences in the prevalence of fits or misfits. No gender differences emerged, $\chi^2(2,443) = 4.18$, $p > 10$. However, significant differences were found for grade, $\chi^2(2,443) = 12.36$, $p < 0.01$. The largest groups were those with maturity gaps ($n = 269$, 60.4% of the sample) with slightly more sixth graders ($n = 139$, 31.2%) than ninth graders ($n = 130$, 29.2%). The smallest groups were those with maturity fits ($n = 63$, 14.2%), with more sixth graders ($n = 38$, 8.5%) than ninth graders ($n = 25$, 5.6%). Differences were most obvious among those with overfits ($n = 113$,

Table 2.2   Summary of significant fit comparisons for study 1.

Construct	Fit versus overfit	Fit/Overfit versus gap	X gender	Increases
Pubertal development	—	—	Girls only: OF more than F	—
Disobeying parents	OF more than F	MG more than F/OF	—	—
Psychosocial maturity				
Self reliance	—	F/OF more than MG	—	—
Identity	F more than OF	F/OF more than MG	—	—
Work orientation	F more than OF	F/OF more than MG	—	—
Peers				
Time spent with peers	—	—	—	OF more than F
Deviant peers	—	MG more than F/OF	—	—
Independence	OF more than F	—	—	—
Parenting				
Conflict with mother	—	—	—	MG more than F/OF
Conflict with father	—	—	Girls only: MG more than F/OF	—
Maternal acceptance	—	—	—	—
Paternal acceptance	—	F/OF more than MG	—	—

Note: F = fit, OF = overfit, MG = maturity gap. Increases denotes residual change from T1 to T2.

25.4%), with more ninth graders ($n = 73$, 16.4%) than sixth graders ($n = 40$, 9.0%). These results were largely consistent with our expectations.

We next examined differences in pubertal maturation (see Table 2.2 for a summary of all comparisons). Recall that we expected early maturing adolescents to be over-represented in groups with gaps and overfits. We expected this to be particularly true for girls. The regressions for boys were not significant – none of the codes or interactions suggested significant differences. On the other hand, girls with maturity overfits were more physically mature than girls with maturity fits, $\beta = -0.25$, $t(198) = -3.29$, $p < 0.01$. This partially supports our expectations.

Testing next for differences in adjustment, we expected adolescents with gaps and overfits to evince more problem behavior and perhaps less psychosocial adjustment. Of the three problem behavior scales, the regressions confirmed this only for disobeying parents. We found that adolescents with overfits disobeyed parents more than adolescents with fits, $\beta = -0.09$, $t(439) = -1.93$, $p < 0.10$, and adolescents with maturity gaps disobeyed parents more than both adolescents with fits and overfits, $\beta = 0.10$, $t(439) = 2.08$, $p < 0.05$. No interactions were significant. We also expected youths with maturity gaps to be less psychosocially immature than their counterparts, but suspected youths with overfits could be either more or less psychosocially mature than those with maturity fits. We found that adolescents with maturity fits had more consolidated identities, $\beta = 0.10$, $t(433) = 1.95$, $p < 0.10$; and greater work orientation, $\beta = 0.09$, $t(433) = 1.92$, $p < 0.10$, than adolescents with overfits. These two groups together were more self-reliant, $\beta = -0.15$, $t(434) = -3.23$, $p < 0.01$; had more consolidated identities, $\beta = -0.23$, $t(433) = -4.70$, $p < 0.01$; and greater work orientation, $\beta = -0.17$, $t(433) = -3.54$, $p < 0.01$ than adolescents with maturity gaps. This supports the argument that adolescents with maturity gaps are less well-adjusted than others, and revealed that adolescents with overfits also have adjustment difficulties, albeit at lower levels than youths with maturity gaps.

We next looked for differences in independence, as well as peer and pop culture orientations. We expected that adolescents with maturity gaps and overfits might be more independent, but found significant differences only between those with overfits and fits. Adolescents with overfits were more behaviorally independent than adolescents with maturity fits, $\beta = -0.12$, $t(437) = -2.94$, $p < 0.01$. We also expected adolescents with gaps and overfits to be more peer-oriented than those with fits. Consistent with research on pseudomaturity, we found that adolescents with gaps have more deviant friends than the other two groups, $\beta = 0.11$, $t(421) = 2.47$, $p < 0.05$. Lastly, we expected adolescents with gaps to be more pop-culture oriented. This was not the case. Our expectations, then, were only partially supported for those with maturity gaps, but not those with overfits.

Finally, we compared the three groups on the parent variables. Because groups with maturity gaps and with misfits are both "mismatches" according to stage-environment fit (Eccles *et al.*, 1993), we expected they would report greater conflict and less acceptance than the adolescents with maturity fits. One marginally significant interaction was found: the comparison of adolescents with fits and overfits to those with maturity gaps depended on adolescents' gender, $R^2\Delta = 0.01$, $F\Delta(2, 410) = 2.53$, $\beta = 0.10$, $t(410) = 1.69$, $p < 0.10$. Probing showed that for boys, there were no differences in conflict with fathers. For girls, however, those with maturity gaps reported experiencing more conflict with their fathers than girls with fits or overfits, $\beta = 0.17$, $t(246) = 2.48$, $p > 0.05$. In sum, our expectations were partially supported with regard to those with a maturity gap, but not those with maturity overfits.

We repeated the regressions, using Time 2 scores as the outcome and Time 1 as a covariate in the first step. Using this ANCOVA approach to change, successive steps examine residualized change in the variable of interest. Only marginally significant results were found, for two of the outcome variables: Adolescents with overfits increased in time spent with peers more than adolescents with fits,

$\beta = -0.11$, $t(164) = -1.75$, $p < 0.10$; and adolescents with maturity gaps increased in conflict with their mothers more than adolescents with fits or overfits, $\beta = 0.14$, $t(164) = 1.88$, $p < 0.10$. In summary, there was not much evidence that adolescents' maturity representations was related to change in adjustment.

Discussion

In this study, we showed there are individual differences in maturity fits. Consistent with Moffitt's conceptualization of maturity gap, most adolescents in the sample had maturity gaps – they felt younger than they wanted to be. However, a significant number of adolescents also had overfits, feeling older than they wanted to be. In addition, we found age-related differences. Although there were no differences in maturity gap, younger adolescents were more likely to have fits and older adolescents were more likely to have overfits. The remaining question is why? We had predicted that both groups might have equal numbers of maturity gaps. We felt some younger adolescents would have gaps because pubertal development is so salient, but we also speculated that older adolescents might feel the press of adulthood. However, there is also another possibility. The older adolescents in this study were ninth graders who had recently made the transition to high school. Their reference group had changed from being "top" to "bottom" in terms of maturity. For some, this could make their desire for maturity more salient. For others, it could lead to the realization that more mature behavior is expected of them than they feel comfortable with. This would explain why there are equal numbers of adolescents with maturity gaps in sixth and ninth grade, but more overfits in ninth grade. This would also explain why there were not equal numbers of adolescents with maturity fits across grade. This, however, is speculation, awaiting further study.

As we expected, adolescents with maturity gaps differed significantly from adolescents with maturity fits or overfits. They disobeyed their parents more and were less psychosocially mature than their peers. There were also contextual differences: they had more deviant peers and experienced less paternal support than did their peers with maturity fits and overfits. Lastly, they also increased in conflict with mothers. These differences suggest that there is likely a connection between having a maturity gap and having a pseudomature profile, as they share many characteristics and behaviors. However, there is not complete overlap in results. Pseudomature adolescents had higher levels of substance use and antisocial behavior than their peers, whereas adolescents with maturity gaps did not differ in terms of these types of problem behavior. One reason for the difference in results is that the pseudomature profile may include both adolescence-limited and life-course persistent youth, whereas the group of adolescents with maturity gaps theoretically includes only individuals who are on an adolescence-limited trajectory of delinquency. Nonetheless, the similarity in profiles suggests that youth with maturity gaps may be on a different trajectory of adjustment than their agemates with maturity fits and overfits.

We also speculated that having a maturity overfit is not wholly positive. We found that adolescents with overfits disobeyed their parents more, had less consolidated identities, and lower work orientation than adolescents with maturity fits. This suggests that adolescents with overfits are not as behaviorally or psychologically as mature as those with a maturity fit. They were also higher on correlates of problem behavior. They were more behaviorally independent and increased in time spent with peers more so than their counterparts with maturity fits. One other tie to problem behavior was found: girls who were more physically mature than their peers were over-represented in the group with overfits. The girls who were more physically mature likely matured earlier than their peers, who typically engage in higher levels of problem behavior (Stattin and Magnusson, 1990). Early maturing girls also tend to feel older (Galambos *et al.*, 1999; Stattin and Magnusson, 1990). Our results linking an overfit to signs of adjustment difficulties suggest that although early maturers may feel older, this feeling may not be particularly desirable.

Although expected, we did not find much evidence that having a gap or an overfit drives adjustment problems. It may be that finding differences associated with change was precluded by rank-order stability in the adjustment measures. It may be, then that adjustment drives subjective feelings and presentations of maturity, rather than the other way around. This idea awaits testing with future research.

We note that although most of the linkages were found for both boys and girls, a few were specific only to girls: girls with overfits were more physically mature than those with fits, and girls with maturity gaps argued more intensely with their fathers than girls with fits or overfits. The first hints at intriguing possible avenues for how feeling older is related to problems for early maturing girls. There may be two trajectories for early maturing girls – one where feeling older, but not as old as they desire, drives the desire for more mature experiences, and another where being exposed to more experiences makes them feel older than they want to feel. The earlier has been assumed and substantiated in research examining the processes by which early maturation leads to more externalizing problems (Stattin *et al.*, 2010). The latter has not yet been explored.

Although we were able to show that there are differences in adolescents' maturity representations, studying these constructs using subjective and desired age may not be ideal. Moffitt's maturity gap is described as feeling a discrepancy between how mature one feels relative to how one is treated. We turn now to a study where we attempt to measure maturity fits, gaps, and overfits more directly.

STUDY 2

Having shown there are individual differences in fit between subjective and desired age, we then designed a measure that would directly assess individual differences in perceptions of fit. Using Harter's (1999) notion of *real* and *ideal* self as a template for the measures, two scales were constructed assessing the degree to which others are perceived as treating adolescents as mature (i.e., *real maturity treatment*) and the degree to which being treated as mature by others is important (i.e., *ideal maturity treatment*). The use of the two combined allows assessment of fit. Those who have a high ideal, but low real maturity treatment would have a maturity gap – they want to be treated more maturely than they feel they are. Conversely, low ideal and high real treatment would be indicative of an overfit – feeling they are being treated more maturely than they desire. Fit could be expressed in two ways: a *high fit* would be indicated by feeling treated and wanting to be treated more maturely, whereas a *low fit* would be indicated when adolescents feel they are treated less maturely, but also want to be treated less maturely.

As in Study 1, we examined externalizing and psychosocial maturity because of the expected similarities between pseudomaturity and having a maturity gap. In this study we also examined internalizing problems. Overall, we expected adolescents with overfits to internalize more than the other adolescents. If they feel they are treated more maturely than they desire because they are being thrust into experiences they do not feel prepared for, they might feel a loss of control, which is associated with depression.

In addition to adjustment, we also examined two aspects of parenting: support and psychological control. As before, we used the notion of stage-environment fit as a guide. We expected those with fits to feel more supported than those with gaps or overfits, as the latter are mismatches. We also speculated that the overuse of control might be associated with gaps or overfits, because of the links between psychological control and adjustment problems (Rogers, Buchanan, and Winchell, 2003).

We also examined whether these relationships were specific to girls. Given that girls are more prone to depression than boys, we expected any adjustment difficulties brought on by a mismatch between real and ideal maturity treatment to be manifested as internalizing for girls, but externalizing for boys. Given the finding in Study 1 that girls with maturity gaps also experience more conflict with their fathers than girls with maturity fits or overfits, it made sense to think that girls with gaps in this study might experience more negative parenting. We used gender, then, as a moderator of fit differences in adjustment and parenting. To summarize, we had the same three objectives, to see if there are gender or age-related differences in fit, if fit is related to adjustment or parenting, and if some differences are specific to girls.

Methods

Sample and procedures

The data for this study were collected from 101 12th grade adolescents (43 females, 57 males, 1 missing gender) ranging in age from 16 to 19 years ($M = 17.29$, $SD = 0.52$), attending two rural school districts in the northwestern

United States. The majority of participants (80.2%; $n = 81$) described their cultural background as European-American. The remaining adolescents reported themselves as Latino, North American Indian, or Asian. The homogeneity of the sample is consistent with the communities. Most of the adolescents in this sample lived with two parents (63.4%; $n = 64$); others lived with a parent and one step-parent (16.8%; $n = 17$), with one parent (17.8%; $n = 18$), or in other situations (2.0%, $n = 2$).

Measures

Ideal and Real Maturity Treatment   Real maturity treatment was assessed using 6 items: "My parents [My friends, Other adults] treat me as a mature person [do not treat me like a child]." The adolescents responded to these items using a 5-point Likert-type scale anchored by "Not at all true" (1), "Somewhat true" (3), and "Very true" (5). These items were then reworded to assess ideal maturity treatment, by adding "It is very important that..." to the beginning of each item. The same response format was used. Higher scores indicated adolescents felt they were treated more maturely (i.e., real maturity treatment, $\alpha = 0.86$) or wanted to be treated more maturely (i.e., ideal maturity treatment, $\alpha = 0.84$).

Internalizing Symptoms   To assess the extent to which adolescents internalized, we used the Center for Epidemiological Studies – Depression scale (CES-D, Radloff, 1977), a widely recognized measure of depressive symptoms. A sample item is "I felt that I could not shake off the blues even with help from my family and friends." The frequencies of behaviors or feelings for the past week are indicated on a 4-point Likert-type scale. Responses range from "rarely or none of the time (less than 1 day)" to "most or all of the time (5–7 days)." Internal consistency of the CES-D was 0.84.

Externalizing Symptoms   We used the same problem behavior measures as in Study 1, assessing disobeying parents, substance use, and antisocial behavior (Maggs et al., 1995). For this sample, the Cronbach alphas were 0.78 for disobeying parents, 0.87 for substance use, and 0.75 antisocial behavior.

Psychosocial Maturity   As before, we assessed self-reliance, identity, and work orientation using Greenberger and Bond's (1984) measure. Internal consistency for this sample was good (alphas were 0.71 for self-reliance, 0.78 for identity, and 0.71 for work orientation).

Parenting   Adolescents reported, separately for mothers and fathers, the amount of support provided by and psychological control used by their parents. For support, we used four items from the acceptance/support subscales of Schaefer's (1965) Child Report of Parenting Behavior Inventory (CRPBI). A sample item is "My mother/father feels affection for me." For control, four items from the CRPBI rejection/control subscale were administered (sample item reads "My mother/father is always trying to change me."). Cronbach alphas were good for both adolescent reports of mother (0.85 for support; 0.82 for control) and father (0.84 for support; 0.84 for control).

Results

As in Study 1, we sought first to determine if there were gender or age differences in adolescents' maturity representations. Using hierarchical regressions, we examined linear and interactive relationships of gender and age with *real* and *ideal* maturity treatment. No linear or interactive effects for gender or age were found for real maturity treatment. For ideal treatment, we found that girls felt that it was more important to be treated maturely than did boys, $R^2 = 0.06$, $F(2,96) = 3.05$, $p < 0.05$; $\beta = 0.25$, $t(97) = 2.46$, $p < 0.05$. This was moderated by age, $R^2\Delta = 0.05$, $F\Delta(1,95) = 5.78$, $\beta = 0.25$, $p < 0.05$. For boys, no significant relationship was found between age and ideal maturity treatment, $r = -0.09$, $p > 0.10$. In contrast, older girls felt it was more important to be treated maturely than did younger girls, $r = 0.43$, $p > 0.01$. It appears then, that girls, particularly older girls, feel it is important to be treated maturely. They may, then, be more apt to have maturity gaps than boys.

We next asked: are adolescents' real and ideal treatment related to their adjustment? We used hierarchical regressions, with adolescents' adjustment as the criterion, with four steps of predictors. In the first step, we entered youths' perceptions of their real and ideal maturity treatment with age and gender (girls = 1, boys = –1). This was followed by entering the interaction between real and ideal treatment in a second step, which allowed us to examine different types of fit. Adolescents with high levels of both real and ideal treatment would have maturity fits, as would those low on both. In order to distinguish between the two, we referred to them as *high fit* and *low fits*, respectively. Adolescents high in ideal but low in real treatment would have *maturity* gaps, whereas the opposite pattern – low in ideal, high in real, would indicate an *overfit*. After the step introducing the interaction of real and ideal, a third step added the two terms testing the interaction of real, ideal with age or gender. Finally, the interaction between real, ideal, age, and gender was entered. This allowed us to determine if the relationships were specific to girls or depended on both age and gender. We used the procedures outlined by Cohen *et al.* (2003) to examine the interaction of continuous variables (i.e., centering the continuous variables before creating the interaction term, probing by testing simple slopes). The results of the regressions are summarized in Table 2.3. For internalizing, the first block with the linear terms accounted for 17% of the variance, $F(4,92) = 4.65$, $p < 0.01$. Adolescents who felt they were treated less maturely reported more depressive symptoms than those who felt they were treated more maturely, $\beta = -0.34$, $t(95) = -2.67$, $p < 0.01$ and girls reported more depressive symptoms than boys, $\beta = 0.26$, $t(95) = 2.66$, $p < 0.01$. The interaction of ideal and real treatment with gender was significant, $R^2\Delta = 0.06$, $F\Delta(2,89) = 3.22$, $p < 0.05$; $\beta = -0.33$, $p < 0.05$. Probing showed that the relationships were not significant for boys. For girls, the relationships depended on ideal treatment. At high levels of ideal treatment, girls who felt treated maturely reported fewer symptoms than girls who felt they were treated less maturely ($\beta = -0.62$, $t(36) = -2.68$,

Table 2.3 Results of study 2 hierarchical regressions examining concurrent relations with ideal and real maturity treatment, age, and gender.

Standardized coefficients	Internalizing/Externalizing				Psychosocial maturity			Parenting			
	Depressive symptoms	Disobey parents	Substance use	Antisocial behavior	Self reliance	Identity	Work orient'	Maternal support	Paternal support	Maternal control	Paternal control
Step 1 R^2	0.17**	0.26***	0.07	0.15**	0.25***	0.30***	0.27***	0.38***	0.26***	0.27***	0.09†
Ideal	0.05	-0.16	-0.04	-0.32*	0.13	0.09	0.17	0.25*	-0.01	0.02	-0.02
Real	-0.34**	-0.37**	-0.01	-0.03	0.31*	0.45***	0.27*	0.43**	0.50***	-0.57***	-0.28*
Age	-0.04	0.00	0.08	-0.04	-0.07	0.13	0.16†	-0.05	-0.02	-0.01	-0.02
Gender	0.26**	-0.06	-0.23*	-0.11	0.23*	0.09	0.25**	-0.04	-0.12	0.00	0.01
Step 2 $R^2\Delta$	0.02	0.01	0.00	0.05*	0.02	0.03†	0.04*	0.00	0.00	0.04*	0.02
Fit: ideal × real	-0.15	-0.12	-0.05	-0.25*	0.14	0.18†	0.21*	0.04	0.02	-0.22*	-0.17
Step 3 $R^2\Delta$	0.06*	0.01	0.01	0.03	0.02	0.03	0.01	0.05*	0.00	0.00	0.01
Fit × age	-0.13	0.12	0.08	0.25†	0.21	0.25†	0.05	0.09	0.09	0.02	0.07
Fit × gender	-0.33*	-0.10	0.09	-0.01	-0.06	0.11	0.15	0.31**	0.04	-0.05	0.09
Step 4 $R^2\Delta$	0.00	0.00	0.00	0.00	0.00	0.01	0.02	0.00	0.01	0.02	0.01
Fit × age × gender	-0.06	-0.06	0.06	0.06	-0.01	0.14	-0.16	-0.03	-0.13	-0.19	-0.12
Model R^2	0.24***	0.28***	0.28***	0.23***	0.29***	0.36***	0.33***	0.43***	0.27***	0.33***	0.12†

Note: n ranges from 93 to 98.
†$p < 0.10$; *$p < 0.05$; **$p < 0.01$; ***$p < 0.001$.

$p < 0.05$. At low levels of ideal maturity, the relationship between real maturity treatment and depressive symptoms was not significant, $\beta = -0.11$, $t(36) = -0.37$, $p > 0.10$. These results show that the relationship of maturity treatment is specific to girls. Girls with maturity gaps (high ideal, low real maturity treatment) reported more depressive symptoms than girls with high maturity fits (high ideal and high real maturity treatment). This is consistent with our suggestion that girls with maturity gaps may be prone to internalizing.

For externalizing, significant relationships were found for disobeying parents and antisocial behavior. For disobeying parents, only the first step of predictors was significant, $R^2 = 0.26$, $F(4,93) = 7.96$, $p < 0.01$. Of the four linear terms, only real maturity treatment was a significant, unique predictor of disobeying parents, $\beta = -0.37$, $t(96) = -3.08$, $p < 0.01$. That is, adolescents who felt treated less maturely disobeyed their parents more than adolescents who felt treated more maturely.

For antisocial behavior, the first step of linear terms was significant, with 15% of the variance accounted for, $F(4,93) = 3.98$, $p < 0.01$, with ideal maturity treatment emerging as the sole predictor of antisocial behavior, $\beta = -0.32$, $t(96) = -2.38$, $p < 0.05$. Specifically, adolescents who felt that it was important to be treated maturely engaged in less antisocial behavior than those who felt it was less important. This relationship was moderated by ideal maturity treatment, $R^2\Delta = 0.05$, $F\Delta(1,92) = 5.71$, $\beta = -0.25$, $t(96) = -2.39$, $p < 0.05$. Although the probes revealed non-significant simple slopes, the relationships were reversed. At high levels of ideal treatment, those treated less maturely (i.e., gaps) engaged in higher levels of antisocial behavior than those treated less maturely (i.e., high maturity fits) ($\beta = -0.24$, $t[96] = -1.05$, $p > 0.10$); whereas at low levels the reverse was true ($\beta = 0.16$, $t[96] = 1.10$, $p > 0.10$). Thus, those with low fits (low ideal, low real) engaged in more antisocial behavior than adolescents with overfits (low ideal, high real treatment).

With respect to psychosocial maturity, significant models emerged for all three indices. For self reliance, only the first step explained a significant amount of variance, $R^2 = 0.25$, $F(4,92) = 7.80$, $p < 0.01$. Of the four linear terms, both gender, $\beta = 0.23$, $t(95) = 2.47$, $p < 0.05$; and real maturity treatment, $\beta = 0.31$, $t(95) = 2.58$, $p < 0.05$ were significant predictors. This indicates that girls were more self reliant than boys, and that adolescents who felt they were treated more maturely were more self reliant than adolescents who felt they were treated less maturely.

For identity, the first step was significant, with 30% of the variance explained by the linear terms, $F(4,92) = 9.72$, $p < 0.01$. Only real maturity treatment emerged as a significant, unique predictor of identity, such that adolescents who felt treated more maturely had more consolidated identities than those who felt treated less maturely, $\beta = 0.45$, $t(95) = 3.83$, $p < 0.01$. The second step, containing the interaction between ideal and real maturity treatment, was marginally significant, adding 3% to the variance explained, $F\Delta(1,91) = 3.31$, $\beta = 0.18$, $p < 0.10$. Probing showed that at high levels of ideal treatment, higher real maturity was associated with more consolidated identities than was lower real maturity, $\beta = 0.63$, $t[95] = 4.19$, $p < 0.01$; and at low levels of ideal treatment, higher levels of real treatment were associated with more consolidated identities than were lower levels, $\beta = 0.33$, $t[95] = 2.43$, $p < 0.05$. This suggests that adolescents with high maturity fits had more consolidated identities than those with gaps, and that adolescents with overfits have more consolidated identities than those with low maturity fits.

Similar results were found for work orientation, with the first and second steps accounting for significant amounts of incremental variance, $R^2 = 0.27$, $F(4,92) = 8.46$, $p < 0.01$ for Step 1; $R^2\Delta = 0.04$, $F\Delta(1,91) = 4.67$, $p < 0.05$ for Step 2. For Step 1, gender and real maturity treatment were significant, unique predictors. Girls had higher work orientations than boys, $\beta = 0.25$, $t(95) = 2.73$, $p < 0.05$; and adolescents who felt treated more maturely had higher work orientations than those who felt treated less maturely, $\beta = 0.27$, $t(95) = 2.22$, $p < 0.05$. In addition, older adolescents had marginally higher levels of work orientation than younger adolescents, $\beta = 0.16$, $t(95) = 1.79$, $p < 0.10$. For the interaction between ideal and real maturity treatment, probing suggested that at high levels of ideal maturity, adolescents who felt treated more maturely had stronger work orientations than those who felt treated less maturely, $\beta = 0.34$, $t(95) = 2.09$, $p < 0.05$. In contrast, the relationship at low levels of ideal maturity was not significant, $\beta = 0.10$, $t(95) = 0.69$, $p > 0.10$. This suggests that adolescents with maturity gaps have a lower work orientation than those with high maturity fits.

Taken together these results support some of our expectations. Those with maturity gaps appear to be somewhat less psychosocially mature than adolescents with high maturity fits (who both want to be and are treated more maturely). They had less consolidated identities and were less work-oriented than those with high maturity fits. Some other interesting patterns also emerged: those with overfits had more consolidated identities than those with low maturity fits – adolescents who were low on both ideal and real maturity treatment. In addition, real maturity treatment continued to consistently predict adjustment: adolescents who felt they were being treated more maturely were more self-reliant, had more consolidated identities, and had greater work orientation than adolescents who felt they were being treated less maturely.

We next examined parental support and control, expecting adolescents with gaps and overfits to experience less support and more psychological control than adolescents with maturity fits. Both parenting variables had significant relationships with the maturity treatment variables. For perceived maternal support, Step 1 was significant, $R^2 = 0.38$, $F(4,92) = 14.19$, $p < 0.01$, with both ideal, $\beta = 0.25$, $t(95) = 2.19$, $p < 0.05$; and real maturity treatment, $\beta = 0.43$, $t(95) = 3.80$, $p < 0.01$, emerging as significant, unique predictors of mothers' support. Adolescents who felt that they were treated more maturely felt more maternal support than those who felt treated less maturely. Similarly, those who felt being treated maturely was more important felt their mothers were more supportive than those who felt being treated maturely was less important. These relationships were both moderated, however, by gender, $\beta = 0.31$, $t(95) = 2.69$, $p < 0.01$; $R^2\Delta = 0.05$, $F\Delta(2,89) = 3.67$, $p < 0.05$. Probes suggest that for boys who felt it less important to be treated maturely, being treated more maturely was associated with more maternal support than being treated less maturely, $\beta = 0.34$, $t(53) = 2.53$, $p < 0.05$. For boys who expected to be treated more maturely (i.e., gaps and high fits), the relationship between real treatment and support was not significant, $\beta = 0.26$, $t(53) = 1.43$, $p > 0.10$. This suggests that boys with overfits (i.e., low ideal, high real) perceived their mothers as more supportive than boys with low maturity fits. The reverse was true for girls: no significant relationship emerged for those who felt it was less important to be treated maturely, $\beta = 0.13$, $t(40) = 0.47$, $p > 0.10$; but for those who felt it was more important, being treated more maturely was associated with feeling more maternal support, $\beta = 0.66$, $t(40) = 3.16$, $p < 0.01$. That is, girls with high maturity fits felt their mothers were more supportive than girls with maturity gaps. For paternal support, only the first step was significant, $R^2 = 0.26$, $F(4,88) = 7.51$, $p < 0.01$. Of the four terms, only real maturity treatment was a significant, unique predictor, $\beta = 0.50$, $t(91) = 4.03$, $p < 0.01$, suggesting that adolescents who felt treated more maturely also perceived their fathers as more supportive than those who felt treated less maturely. Where both parents are concerned, then, being treated more maturely was related to parents being more supportive. For mothers though, group differences depended on gender. Boys with overfits felt more supported than those with low fits and girls with high fits felt more supported than those with gaps.

Turning to psychological control, significant relationships were found for both mothers and fathers. For mothers, both the first and second steps were significant. In the first step, real treatment was the only significant predictor, showing that adolescents who felt they were treated less maturely felt less psychologically controlled than adolescents who felt they were treated more maturely $\beta = -0.57$, $t(95) = -4.33$, $p < 0.01$, $R^2 = 0.27$, $F(4,92) = 8.30$, $p < 0.01$. This relationship was qualified by ideal maturity treatment, $\beta = -0.22$, $t(95) = -2.29$, $p < 0.05$, $R^2\Delta = 0.04$, $F\Delta(1,91) = 5.25$, $p < 0.05$. Probing showed that at both low ($\beta = -0.67$, $t(95) = -4.54$, $p < 0.01$) and high levels ($\beta = -0.35$, $t(95) = -2.55$, $p < 0.05$) of ideal maturity, adolescents who felt treated less maturely felt their mothers were more psychologically controlling than adolescents who felt treated more maturely. The difference was more pronounced among those with higher ideal treatment. This means that adolescents with maturity gaps feel their mothers are more psychologically controlling than those with high maturity fits, and those with low maturity fits felt their mothers were more controlling than those with overfits. For fathers, Step 1 was marginally significant, $R^2 = 0.09$, $F(4,88) = 2.04$, $p < 0.10$. As with mothers, real maturity treatment was a significant, unique predictor of paternal control, $\beta = -0.28$, $t(91) = -2.15$, $p < 0.05$, such that adolescents who felt treated more maturely perceived their fathers as less psychologically controlling than adolescents who felt treated less maturely.

These findings support the expectation that adolescents with maturity gaps would experience more problems with their parents than those with maturity fits. However, contrary to what we expected, we found that adolescents with overfits experienced fewer problems with their parents than adolescents with low maturity fits.

Discussion

With this sample, we introduced a new measure designed to assess maturity fits and misfits. Its use offered new insight into adolescents' perceptions of maturity. Like fits or misfits with subjective age, real maturity treatment was consistently related to indices of adjustment, where feeling treated less maturely was related to more adjustment problems. Ideal maturity, by itself, predicted far less, but appeared to have the inverse relationship, where feeling it is important to be treated maturely was associated with better adjustment than feeling it is less important.

As expected, we found significant differences between adolescents with maturity gaps and those with high maturity fits. Adolescents with maturity gaps engaged in more antisocial behavior, had less consolidated identities, were less work oriented, and felt their mothers were more psychologically controlling than adolescents with high maturity fits. Unexpectedly, however, we found that having an overfit was largely positive. Adolescents with maturity overfits engaged in less antisocial behavior, had more consolidated identities, perceived less maternal control and more support (boys only) than adolescents with low maturity fits. Thus, these results may indicate that although adolescents with low ideal and low real maturity may also have a maturity fit, this may not be as positive as those whose maturity fit indicates high ideal and real maturity.

We looked to see if age or gender moderated these differences. We found little evidence of differences based on age. This is probably due, however, to the restricted variability in age with this sample. There was some moderation by gender, suggestive that maturity gaps may be especially challenging for girls. They reported more symptoms of depression and felt less support from their mothers than girls with high maturity fits. We note that this is the first evidence linking maturity gaps to internalizing problems.

These data, however, could not be used to infer causality. They leave open the question of whether adolescents who feel they are treated less maturely experience adjustment difficulties because of their treatment or are treated less maturely because they are already evincing adjustment difficulties. The latter is a distinct possibility, given evidence that parents tend to react negatively to adolescents' misbehavior or poor adjustment (Kerr and Stattin, 2003). Whether this is operating to create the differences we have seen in this study remains to be seen. It is an important issue to address, however, given Moffitt's (1993) suggestion that maturity gaps are largely a function of societal changes that have broadened the time frame of adolescence, rather than the result of contextual reactions to signs of adolescents' immaturity.

STUDY 3

In this final study, we continued to use the new measure of gap, assessing youths' maturity perceptions as *real* and *ideal* maturity treatment. In this study, we chose to look at some additional constructs that had been identified in research, but not available in the data for the second study. Specifically, prior research shows that pseudomature adolescents, who feel older, but want to be even older, are more oriented toward peers and pop culture (Galambos Barker, and Tilton-Weaver, 2003). Recall that in the first study, those with maturity gaps were had more deviant peers than the other adolescents and those with overfits increased in time spent with peers. In other research, adolescents describe some "more mature" youths as being focused on the privileges of adulthood. These descriptions were consistent with empirical accounts of pseudomaturity, depicting adolescents who were involved in problem behaviors and seemed to be interested in activities and experiences that would lend an air of maturity (Tilton-Weaver, Galambos, and Vitunski, 2001). For this reason, we suggest they might have reason to try to look more grown up and draw attention to this. We extended our examination to constructs tapping these issues, looking for differences between fits and misfits in the degree to which they have more deviant or less prosocial peers, and the extent to which they dress to appear more mature and to attract attention.

In addition to peer and presentational issues, we examined differences in their experiences with their parents. Not only does research suggest that pseudomature adolescents experience less than optimal relationships with their parents (Galambos and Tilton-Weaver, 2000), but we could see from the first study in this series that this was also the case for adolescents with maturity gaps. We also posited that overfits might have difficulties as well, because they are a type of stage-environment mismatch. Taking this into consideration, in this study we looked for differences in parent-adolescent attachment and psychological control.

In this study, we were also able to look at a broader age range, allowing us to determine if maturity fits and misfits operate in similar ways across adolescence. As we had already seen age differences in Studies 1 and 2, we suspected we would find them in these data as well. For example, because they are approaching adulthood, we thought that older adolescents with gaps might have more difficulties than younger adolescents with gaps (e.g., more deviant peers, perceive parents as more psychologically controlling).

To summarize, the goals of this study were to determine if the groups differed in peer orientation, motivations for self-presentation, or relationships with their parents, and to determine if these differences were modified by age.

As the focus of this book is also to examine problems specific to girls, we wanted to see if some differences were specific to girls.

Sample and Procedures

The data for this study were collected at a high school located in a large, western Canadian city. Students were administered surveys during classroom hours. Two waves of data are used here, separated by approximately two years. At initial data collection, 564 adolescents ranging in age from 12 to 19 years participated as part of a school-wide project. At the second data collection wave, 191 adolescents participated (113 females, 78 males; age range 13 to 18 years). Of those who participated, 103 provided data at both time points.

Measures

Maturity perceptions

We used the same measures of real and ideal maturity treatment, but created discrepancy scores by subtracting real maturity treatment items from their corresponding ideal items. The mean of the 6 items was then calculated, with positive scores indicating a maturity gap, 0 indicating a fit, and negative scores indicating an overfit (for Time 1, $M = 0.15$, $SD = 0.60$, $\alpha = 0.76$; for Time 2, $M = 0.14$, $SD = 0.61$, $\alpha = 0.80$). The scores were then divided into the three maturity types (based on scores that were positive, negative, and 0) and contrast codes were created. The first contrast code compared adolescents with overfits (−1) to adolescents with maturity fits (1). The second contrast code compared overfit and fit groups (−1) to adolescents with maturity gaps (2). The number of adolescents in each group is as follows: maturity fit, $n = 202$ (45.8%); maturity overfit, $n = 153$ (34.7%); maturity gap, $n = 86$ (19.5%).

Deviant/prosocial peers

The same two scales used in Studies 1 and 2 were used to measure deviant and prosocial friends. Cronbach alphas indicated good internal consistency: for prosocial peers, $\alpha = 0.67$ for Time 1, $\alpha = 0.77$ for Time 2; for deviant peers, $\alpha = 0.70$ for Time 1, $\alpha = 0.75$ for Time 2.

Self-presentational motives for clothing choices

We assessed two motives for selecting the type of clothing they wear: dressing to look more like an adult and to attract others' attention. A single item, designed by two of the authors, was used to assess adolescents' motivation to select clothes that make them look like an adult ("I buy clothing that makes me look more like an adult"). Dressing to attract attention (e.g., "Dressing to attract romantically interesting people to me is important") was the mean of three items modified from Chen-Yu and Seock's (2002) assessment of clothing purchase motivations. Responses to all items range from 1 (not true at all) to 5 (very true). Cronbach's alpha for dressing to attract attention was 0.81 at Time 1 and 0.85 at Time 2.

Parent–child attachment

West et al. (1998) developed the Adolescent Attachment Questionnaire (AAQ) as a brief self-report of adolescent attachment. Three subscales assess adolescents' perceptions of their parent: (1) confidence in the availability of the parent (Availability; "I'm confident that my mother/father will listen to me"); (2) anger towards the parent (Anger/Distress; "I often feel angry with my mother/father without knowing why"); and (3) empathy towards the needs of the parent (Goal-Directed Partnership; "It makes me feel good to be able to do things for my mother"). Responses to items are on a 5-point Likert-type scale ("strongly disagree" to "strongly agree"). Cronbach alphas for mothers and fathers ranged from 0.68 to 0.89.

Psychological control

The 8-item Psychological Control Scale – Youth Self-Report (Barber, 1996) was used to evaluate participants' perceptions of maternal and paternal intrusive parenting. A sample item is "My mother [father] is a person who is always trying to change how I feel or think about things." Item response was on a 5-point Likert-type scale with wording reflecting the target parent ("not like her [him]" to "a lot like her[him]"). The internal consistency was good (Time 1 $\alpha = 0.90$, Time 2 $\alpha = 0.88$ for mothers; Time 1 $\alpha = 0.89$, Time 2 $\alpha = 0.86$ for fathers).

Results

We first looked for age and gender differences in the distribution of maturity types and found no age differences. For gender, a marginally significant difference was found at Time 1, $\chi^2(2,437) = 5.40$, $p < 0.10$. The number of adolescents with maturity fits was relatively equal across gender (97 boys, 104 girls for 48.3% versus 51.7%), as was the number of adolescents with overfits (43 boys, 42 girls, for 50.6 and 49.4%, respectively). There were, however, more girls with gaps ($n = 95$, 62.1%) than boys ($n = 58$, 37.9%).

To examine differences in concurrent measures used hierarchical regressions. Five steps were entered. First, gender (effect coded, females = 1), and centered chronological age were entered, followed by the linear coded contrasts. These two steps were followed by the two-way interactions between the maturity codes and gender, the two-way interactions between the maturity codes and age, and three-way interactions between the maturity codes, gender, and age.

Table 2.4 Summary of Significant Fit Comparisons for Study 3.

Construct	Fit/Overfit versus gap[a]	By age	By gender	Change
Prosocial peers	F/OF more than MG	Older MG more than younger MG	—	Girls: MG decreased more than F/OF
Deviant peers	MG more than F/OF	—	Girls only: younger MG more than older MG	—
Dressing for maturity	MG more than F/OF	—	—	MG increased more than F/OF
Dressing for attention	MG more than F/OF	—	—	—
Maternal attachment				
Availability of mother	—	Younger F/OF more than older F/OF; Older MG more than younger MG		
Anger toward mother	MG more than F/OF	—	—	—
Paternal attachment				
Availability of father	F/OF more than MG	—	—	—
Anger toward father	MG more than F/OF	—	Boys only: MG more than F/OF	—
Empathy toward father	F/OF more than MG	—	Boys only: F/OF more than MG	Girls with MG: Older increase more than younger
Maternal psychological control	MG more than F/OF	—	—	—
Paternal psychological control	MG more than F/OF	Older MG more than younger MG	—	—

Note: F = fit, OF = overfit, MG = maturity gap. Change is residualized from T1 to T2.
[a] No significant differences were found between maturity fit and overfit, unless moderated.

We were primarily interested (and report here) the results of the contrast codes and the interactions. Significant comparisons are presented in Table 2.4.

We looked first at differences in peers, keeping in mind that in the first studies, adolescents with maturity gaps had more deviant peers. For prosocial peers, Step 1 was significant, $R^2 = 0.05$, $F(2,436) = 10.36$, $\beta = -0.20$, $p < 0.05$. Gender was the sole significant, unique predictor of prosocial peers, $\beta = 0.21$, $t(437) = 4.39$, $p < 0.01$, suggesting that girls reported having more prosocial peers than did boys. The second contrast code was marginally significant, $\beta = -0.08$, $t(437) = -1.69$, $p < 0.10$. This suggests that adolescents with maturity fits or overfits have more prosocial peers than adolescents with maturity gaps. This relationship, however, was moderated by age, $\beta = 0.15$, $t(437) = 2.89$, $p < 0.01$; $R^2\Delta = 0.02$, $F\Delta(2,429) = 4.19$, $p < 0.05$. Probing shows that there is no significant relationship between age and prosocial peers for individuals with maturity fits and overfits, $\beta = -0.02$, $t(283) = -0.36$, $p > 0.10$. In contrast, for those with maturity gaps, older adolescents had more prosocial peers than younger adolescents, $\beta = 0.23$, $t(151) = 2.96$, $p < 0.01$. For deviant peers, Step 1 was significant, $R^2\Delta = 0.02$, $F\Delta(2,436) = 3.08$, $p < 0.05$, with a significant, unique effect for gender, $\beta = -0.12$, $t(437) = -2.43$, $p < 0.05$. That is, girls reported having less deviant peers than did boys. Again, the second contrast code was significant, $\beta = 0.13$, $t(437) = 2.64$, $p < 0.01$, suggesting that adolescents with maturity fits and overfits reported having less deviant peers than did adolescents with maturity gaps. The final step with the 3-way interactions was also significant, $R^2\Delta = 0.02$, $F \Delta(2,427) = 4.24$, $p < 0.05$, with a significant interaction between the first contrast code, gender, and age, $\beta = 0.16$, $t(437) = 1.99$, $p < 0.05$. Probing showed that the only significant relationship between deviant peers and age was for girls with maturity gaps, for whom younger girls had more deviant peers than older girls, $\beta = -0.18$, $t(93) = -1.73$, $p < 0.10$. In short, adolescents with maturity gaps had more problematic peers than the other adolescents. This tended to be true primarily for younger adolescents with gaps. Moreover, issues specific to girls emerged: younger girls with maturity gaps had more deviant friends than older girls with maturity gaps.

Expecting adolescents with gaps to be motivated by a desire to look older and attract attention, we next looked at differences in motives. Only the second code was significant for both dressing to look older, $\beta = 0.09$, $t(434) = 1.81$, $p < 0.10$; and to attract attention, $\beta = 0.11$, $t(437) = 2.14$, $p < 0.05$. That is, adolescents with maturity gaps dressed to look more like adults and to attract attention than did adolescents with maturity fits or overfits. No other contrasts or interactions with gender or age were found. Thus, our expectations were largely supported.

Regarding relationships with parents, we examined differences on the three attachment constructs, analyzed separately for mothers and fathers. Recall that we expected adolescents with maturity gaps and overfits to have relationship difficulties. With respect to maternal attachment, a significant interaction for availability was found between the second code and age, $R^2\Delta = 0.02$, $F \Delta(2,426) = 3.55$, $p < 0.05$; $\beta = 0.14$, $t(434) = 2.62$, $p < 0.01$. Probing showed that younger adolescents with fits or overfits felt their mothers were more available than older adolescents with fits or overfits, $\beta = -0.10$, $t(280) = -01.74$, $p < 0.10$. In contrast younger adolescents with maturity gaps felt their mothers were less available than older adolescents with maturity gaps, $\beta = 0.18$, $t(151) = 2.16$, $p < 0.05$. For anger towards mothers, the second contrast was again significant, $\beta = 0.13$, $t(434) = 2.62$, $p < 0.01$, such that adolescents with maturity gaps felt more anger toward their mothers than did those with maturity fits or overfits. No maturity differences or interactions were found for empathy toward mothers. For attachment to fathers, there was a significant contrast for availability between gaps and overfits/fits, $\beta = -0.14$, $t(424) = -2.74$, $p < 0.01$. This suggests that adolescents with overfits/fits feel their fathers are more available than do those with maturity gaps. For attachment anger, the second code was also significant, $\beta = 0.13$, $t(424) = 2.64$, $p < 0.01$, with adolescents with gaps feeling more anger toward their fathers than did adolescents with fits or overfits. This was moderated by gender, however, $R^2\Delta = 0.01$, $F \Delta(2,418) = 2.38$, $p < 0.10$; $\beta = -0.16$, $t(424) = -2.08$, $p < 0.05$. For boys only, adolescents with gaps felt more anger toward their fathers than adolescents with fits or overfits, $\beta = 0.24$, $t(191) = 3.38$, $p < 0.01$. The second contrast was also significant for empathy toward fathers, $\beta = -0.10$, $t(424) = -2.05$, $p < 0.05$, such that adolescents with gaps responded less empathically to their fathers than did adolescents with fits or overfits. This was also moderated by gender, $R^2\Delta = 0.01$, $F \Delta(2,421) = 2.65$, $p < 0.10$; $\beta = 0.16$, $t(424) = 2.12$, $p < 0.05$. Again, the relationship was significant for boys only. Specifically, boys with maturity gaps responded less empathically to their fathers than did boys with fits or overfits, $\beta = -0.22$, $t(191) = -3.05$, $p < 0.01$.

In summary, our expectations were largely supported in terms of adolescents' attachment to their parents. Adolescents with gaps felt their parents were less available, felt more anger toward them, and responded less empathically to their fathers than did adolescents with fits or overfits. Some of these relationships were seen only for older adolescents with gaps (e.g., maternal availability), others were mainly for boys (e.g., more anger and less empathy toward fathers). There were few differences in attachment that were gender specific.

We then looked for differences in parents' use of psychological control. For maternal psychological control, only the second contrast code was significant, $\beta = 0.10$, $t(437) = 2.05$, $p < 0.05$. This suggests that adolescents who had maturity gaps reported that their mothers were more psychologically controlling than adolescents with maturity fits or overfits. No other predictors or interactions were significant. For paternal psychological control, the second contrast code was also significant, $\beta = 0.15$, $t(437) = 3.11$, $p < 0.01$, suggesting that like mothers, fathers of adolescents with maturity gaps were perceived as more psychologically controlling than fathers of adolescents with fits or overfits. This relationship was moderated by age, as indicated in Step 5, $R^2\Delta = 0.01$, $F \Delta(2,421) = 2.63$, $p < 0.10$; $\beta = 0.11$, $t(437) = 2.15$, $p < 0.05$. The probes showed that there was no significant relationship between age and fathers' psychological control for adolescents with maturity fits and overfits, $\beta = 0.02$,

$t(278) = 0.32$, $p > 0.10$. However, for those with maturity gaps, older adolescents reported feeling their fathers were more psychologically controlling than did younger adolescents, $\beta = 0.24$, $t(148) = 3.01$, $p < 0.01$. Again, these differences were largely what we expected for adolescents with gaps. In addition, our speculation that older adolescents with gaps might have more difficulties than younger adolescents with gaps was supported. We did not find differences between those with fits and overfits, either in psychological control or in attachment.

Lastly, we looked at change in the same set of constructs. If changes in peers, motives, or parent variables were related to fit, it would suggest that adolescents' feelings about their maturity could drive these differences. We found that adolescents with maturity gaps increased marginally in dressing to appear more adult-like than did adolescents with maturity fits or overfits, $\beta = 0.23$, $t(424) = 1.92$, $p < 0.10$. We also found that an interaction for prosocial peers, between the second code and gender, $R^2\Delta = 0.02$, $F \Delta(2,164) = 2.87$, $p < 0.10$; $\beta = -0.24$, $t(171) = -2.29$, $p < 0.05$. This time, the relationship was significant for girls only. That is, girls with gaps reported that their friends decreased in prosociality more than girls with fits or overfits, $\beta = -0.16$, $t(101) = -1.98$, $p < 0.10$. With respect to parent-adolescent attachment constructs, a significant 3-way interaction with the second contrast code was found for anger toward mothers, $R^2\Delta = 0.05$, $F \Delta(2,58) = 4.68$, $p < 0.05$; $\beta = 0.51$, $t(69) = 2.16$, $p < 0.05$. Probing showed no significant relationships once the file was split by gender and the second contrast code. However, boys with gaps had a stronger effect for age than any of the other three groups, $\beta = -0.23$. Although not significant, $t(69) = -1.22$, $p < 0.10$, the direction of the effect would suggest that younger boys with gaps increased in anger toward their mothers more than older boys with gaps. The 3-way interactions with the second code was also significant for empathy with fathers, $R^2\Delta = 0.05$, $F \Delta(2,57) = 5.07$, $p < 0.05$; $\beta = 0.54$, $t(68) = 2.25$, $p < 0.05$. The relationship between age and empathy for fathers was significant only for girls with gaps, $\beta = 0.26$, $t(35) = 1.99$, $p < 0.10$, such that older girls with gaps increased more in empathic responding toward their fathers than younger girls with gaps. No other differences or interactions were found for the attachment or parenting constructs. In short, there is some limited support that maturity gap is associated with increases in problems (less prosocial peers) for girls, maybe specifically for older girls.

Discussion

Like the other studies, we found that adolescents with maturity gaps were different than those with either maturity fits or overfits. Adolescents with maturity gaps had less desirable friends, dressed to look older and attract attention, and had more difficulties with parents than adolescents with fits or overfits. These findings are similar to those for pseudomaturity, reaffirming the idea that they might have similar profiles.

We note that although the majority of the sample had maturity fits, a substantial proportion had maturity gaps. We were somewhat surprised to find that more girls had maturity gaps than boys. This is only partially explained by the fact that more girls participated than boys. However, in the previous study we found that in comparison to boys, girls felt it was more important to be treated maturely, so perhaps it is not so surprising. This finding, however, suggests that it is important to pay attention to the way girls are treated, as these results also suggest that adolescents with maturity gaps may be at risk for developmental difficulties. Moreover, as with the other studies, we found evidence that there may be peer issues particular to girls, including having more deviant friends for younger girls, and having less prosocial friends over time for girls with gaps.

Fewer differences emerged between adolescents with fits and overfits, probably because of creating categories, rather than testing the interaction between real and ideal. We also may not be tapping all of the constructs on which adolescents with overfits differ from their peers. A more indepth, qualitative study of adolescents with overfits may provide insight as to what the causes and consequences of maturity overfits are.

Finally, age-related differences emerged, suggestive of developmental trends. For example, older adolescents with maturity gaps felt their fathers were more psychologically controlling than younger adolescents with gaps. Some of the differences were further moderated by the type of maturity fit. For those with overfits/fits, older adolescents felt their mothers were less available; for gaps, the opposite was found. If the phenomena of maturity gaps, fits, and overfits are to be properly understood, theoretical and empirical accounts will have to consider what happens over time. To date, we know of no one else who has attempted to address this issue.

General Conclusions

In this study, we aimed to measure adolescents' maturity representations and through them, to identify maturity fits and misfits. In doing so, we had three general aims: to identify individual differences in adolescents' perceptions of fit, to determine if their fits or misfits were related to their adjustment, and to see if there were differences in their peer and family contexts attributable to fit. Through how adolescents' fits and misfits were related to their age, gender, and adjustment, we were hoping to identify relationships specific to girls, in order to better understand girls' adjustment.

Behind these aims lie the intention of identifying adolescents with maturity gaps. We believe we succeeded, as the adolescents with maturity gaps were indeed engaged in more problem behavior, were more peer-oriented, and were motivated to appear older than other adolescents, as Moffitt (1993) has suggested. The differences we found in adjustment suggest that adolescents with maturity gaps are the most developmentally disadvantaged and bear further scrutiny. Indeed, they appear to be similar to pseudomature adolescents who have concerned researchers for decades. The question remains, however, whether fit drives adjustment, as suggested by Moffitt, or adjustment drives fit. In answering that question, we may also be able to determine if maturity gaps occur because of the extension of adolescence or because adolescents with gaps are already showing signs of being less mature and are being treated accordingly.

Although maturity gaps were identifiable and most prevalent in Study 1, there were also many adolescents with maturity fits and overfits. Indeed, these are the first studies in which adolescents with overfits were explicitly examined. Overall, the results suggest that having an overfit is more positive than negative. Measured using subjective and desired age, adolescents with overfits were engaged in more problem behavior and were less psychosocially mature than adolescents with maturity fits. However, when we used real and ideal maturity treatment, an overfit was more positive. Compared to those with low maturity fits, adolescents with overfits had more consolidated identities, and better perceptions of their mothers. Like the immature adolescents seen in the studies of Galambos and colleagues (Galambos and Tilton-Weaver, 2000; Galambos, Barker, and Tilton-Weaver, 2003), those with low fits may not feel ready to embark on the road to adulthood. Overfits, then appear to be in the middle somewhere, not as well adjusted as those with high fits, but not having as many difficulties as those with low fits. In short, overfits and low fits need more investigation.

These differences illustrate the systematic contextual and adjustment differences we found between fits and misfits. We also identified age and gender differences. The age differences we found (more younger adolescents with gaps, more older adolescents with overfits) suggest there are developmental trajectories that can be studied. Moreover, the meaning of having a fit or misfit may have different antecedents or consequences, depending on when they are experienced. For example, younger adolescents with gaps felt their mothers were less available, but older adolescents with gaps felt their fathers were more psychologically controlling.

HOW DO THESE FINDINGS HELP OUR UNDERSTANDING OF GIRLS' PROBLEM BEHAVIORS?

Although the majority of the findings apply to adolescents of both genders, we found signs that some relationships were specific to girls. Girls, more than boys, felt it was important to be treated maturely. This was particularly true for older girls, compared with younger girls. It was not surprising, then, to find that there are more girls than boys with gaps when gap is measured as a mismatch between real and ideal maturity treatment. Why should girls feel a gap more than boys? One possible explanation is that girls' environments do not afford them with opportunities to be treated as maturely as they desire. As we saw in this study, girls tend to be more psychosocially mature than boys, but they are not given as much behavioral autonomy (Fuligni, 1998; Ruble and Martin, 1998) and may be controlled more than boys (Pomerantz and Ruble, 1998). For girls, there may *be* a greater discrepancy between what they desire and how they are treated than for boys.

We had reasons to be concerned that there were more girls than boys with maturity gaps, not only because adolescents with gaps appear to have more adjustment difficulties than their peers, but some of the difficulties associated with having a maturity gap were specific to girls. Girls with gaps were more depressed than girls with fits or overfits. They also had greater difficulties with their parents, such as less maternal support and more intense conflict with their fathers than other girls. If problems in their environments drive their mismatch, the mismatch may, as Eccles has suggested, undermine their development and exacerbate already difficult relationships with parents.

We also found that girls who are more physically mature tended to feel they were treated more maturely than they desired. If these girls matured early, this is another indication that early maturation is not always a desirable experience. What the mismatch means for them over time, however, awaits more study. In addition, having an overfit is not wholly negative for girls, but it may not be optimal for their development either.

CONCLUSION

Many of the questions raised cannot be resolved with our data, but await clarification in future research. For example, does engagement in problem behaviors close the maturity gap? Moffitt's theory suggests that adolescents who do not initially engage in problem behaviors have maturity gaps. She further suggests that individuals on adolescence-limited trajectories will desist when their behaviors no longer lend an air of maturity, but interfere with the assumption of adult roles. This implies that engagement in problem behavior lends an air of maturity. It is not known, though, if the appearance of maturity closes the gap or drives an even stronger desire to reach adulthood and its concomitant privileges. Our results suggest it may be the latter. Curiosity drove us to conduct a post-hoc analysis examining the grouping of adolescents in the last sample at Time 1 and Time 2. Although not conclusive (because of attrition), the cross-tabs suggest that more than half of those who started with maturity gaps are categorized the same two years later (55%), with the other half either shifting to a maturity fit (30%) or to an overfit (15%). There are probably systematic differences between those who continue to have a maturity gap and those that do not. Future research can be directed at understanding what those differences are.

Although we found similar results across three samples, all of our participants were situated in US and Canadian cultural contexts. The extent to which the notion of a maturity gap or overfit holds cross-culturally is an open question. Collaborations have begun with researchers in South America and Asia, with the hope that we will soon know more about the nature of maturity perceptions in non-Western cultures.

Even so, the studies in this chapter show that there is utility in considering not only how adolescents view their own maturity levels, but also how their evaluation of their own maturity matches what they desire or feel is ideal. While confirming some ideas, such as the existence of maturity gaps and problems associated with them, these studies also generated new questions by revealing the considerable variation in adolescents' representations and evaluations of maturity. These questions draw attention to the importance of seeing development through the eyes of those who are experiencing it.

REFERENCES

Aiken, L. S., and West, S. G. (1991). *Multiple regression: Testing and interpreting interactions.* Newbury Park, CA: Sage.

Arbeau, K. J., Galambos, N. L., and Jansson, S. M. (2007). Dating, sex, and substance use as correlates of adolescents' subjective experience of age. *Journal of Adolescence, 30,* 435–447.

Barber, B. (1996). Parental psychological control: Revisiting a neglected construct. *Child Development, 67,* 3296–3319.

Brown, B. B., Clasen, D. R., and Eicher, S. A. (1986). Perceptions of peer pressure, peer conformity dispositions, and self-reported behavior among adolescents. *Developmental Psychology, 22,* 521–530.

Burger, G. K., and Armentrout, J. A. (1971). Comparative study of methods to estimate factor scores for reports of parental behaviors. *Proceedings of the 79th Annual Convention of the American Psychological Association, 6,* 149–150.

Chen-Yu, J. H., and Seock. Y. (2002). Adolescents' clothing purchase motivations, information sources, and store selection criteria: A comparison of male/female and impulse/nonimpulse shoppers. *Family and Consumer Sciences Research Journal, 31,* 50–77.

Cohen, J., Cohen, P., West, S., *et al.* (2003). *Applied Multiple Regression/Correlation Analysis for the Behavioral Sciences* (3rd ed.). Hillsdale, NJ: Lawrence Erlbaum.

Earley, L., and Cushway, D. (2002). The parentified child. *Clinical Child Psychology and Psychiatry, 7,* 163–178.

Eccles, J. S., Midgely, C., Wigfield, A., *et al.* (1993). Development during adolescence. The impact of stage-environment fit on young adolescents' experiences in schools and in families. *American Psychologist, 48,* 90–101.

Feldman, S. S., and Quatman, T. (1988). Factors influencing age expectations for adolescent autonomy: A study of early adolescents and parents. *Journal of Early Adolescence, 8,* 325–343.

Feldman, S. S., and Rosenthal, D. A. (1991). Age expectations of behavioral autonomy in Hong Kong, Australian and American youth: The influence of family variables and adolescents' values. *International Journal of Psychology, 26,* 1–23.

Fuligni, A. J. (1998). Authority, autonomy, and parent-adolescent conflict and cohesion: A study of adolescents from Mexican, Chinese, Filipino, and European backgrounds. *Developmental Psychology, 34,* 782–792.

Galambos, N. L., and Almeida, D. M. (1992). Does parent-adolescent conflict increase in early adolescence? *Journal of Marriage and the Family, 54,* 737–747.

Galambos, N. L., Kolaric, G. C., Sears, H. A., *et al.* (1999). Adolescents' subjective age: An indicator of perceived maturity. *Journal of Research on Adolescence, 9,* 309–337.

Galambos, N. L., and Tilton-Weaver, L. C. (2000). Adolescents' psychosocial maturity, subjective age, and problem behavior: In search of the adultoid. *Applied Developmental Science, 4,* 178–192.

Galambos, N. L., Barker, E. T., and Tilton-Weaver, L. C. (2003). Who gets caught at maturity gap? A study of pseudomature, immature, and mature adolescents. *The International Journal of Behavioral Development, 27,* 253–263.

Galambos, N. L., Turner, P. K., and Tilton-Weaver, L. C. (2005). Chronological and subjective age in emerging adulthood: The crossover effect. *Journal of Adolescent Research, 54,* 538–556.

Galambos, N. L., Albrecht, A. K., and Jansson, S. M. (2009). Dating, sex, and substance use predict increases in adolescents' subjective age across two years. *International Journal of Behavioral Development, 33,* 32–41.

Greenberger, E., and Bond, L. (1984). *User's Manual for the Psychosocial Maturity Inventory.* Irvine, CA: University of California.

Greenberger, E., and Steinberg, L. (1986). *When teenagers work: The psychological and social costs of adolescent employment.* New York: Basic Books.

Harter, S. (1999). *The Construction of Self: A Developmental Perspective.* New York, New York: Guildford Press.

Hubley, A. M., and Hultsch, D. F. (1994). The relationship of personality trait variables to subjective age identity in older adults. *Research on Aging, 16,* 415–439.

Jessor, R. (1992). Risk behavior in adolescence: A psychosocial framework for understanding and action. *Developmental Review, 12,* 374–390.

Koerner, S. S., Kenyon, D. B., and Rankin, L. A. (2006). Growing up faster? Post-divorce catalysts in the mother-adolescent relationship. *Journal of Divorce & Remarriage, 45,* 25–41.

Maggs, J. L., Almeida, D. M., and Galambos, N. L. (1995). Risky business: The paradoxical meaning of problem behavior for young adolescents. *Journal of Early Adolescence, 15,* 344–362.

Moffitt, T. E. (1993). Adolescence-limited and life-course-persistent antisocial behavior: A developmental taxonomy. *Psychological Review, 100,* 674–701.

Moffitt, T. E. (2006). Life-course-persistent versus adolescence-limited antisocial behavior. In D. Cicchetti, and D. J. Cohen (eds), *Developmental Psychopathology, Vol. 3: Risk, Disorder, and Adaptation* (2nd ed., pp. 570–598). Hoboken, NJ: John Wiley & Sons, Inc.

Montepare, J. M., and Lachman, M. E. (1989). "You're only as old as you feel": Self-perceptions of age, fears of aging, and life satisfaction from adolescence to old age. *Psychology and Aging, 4,* 73–78.

Montepare, J. M., Rierdon, J., Koff, E., *et al.* (1989). *The impact of biological events on females' subjective age identities.* Paper presented at the 8th Meeting of the Society for Menstrual Cycle Research, Salt Lake City, UT, May.

Petersen, A. C., Crockett, L., Richards, M., *et al.* (1988). A self-report measure of pubertal status: Reliability, validity, and initial norms. *Journal of Youth and Adolescence, 17,* 117–133.

Pomerantz, E. M., and Ruble, D. N. (1998). The multidimensional nature of control: Implications for the development of sex differences in self-evaluations. In J. Heckhausen and C. Dweck (eds), *Motivation and Self-regulation Across the Life-span* (pp. 159–184). Cambridge, UK: Cambridge University Press.

Prinz, R., Foster, S., Kent, R., *et al.* (1979). Multivariate assessment of conflict in distressed and nondistressed mother-adolescent dyads. *Journal of Applied Behavioral Analysis, 12,* 691–700.

Radloff, L. W. (1977). The CES-D Scale: A self-report depression scale for research in the general population. *Applied Psychological Measurement, 1,* 385–401.

Rogers, K. N., Buchanan, C. M., and Winchell, M. E. (2003). Psychological control during early adolescence: Links to adjustment in differing parent/adolescent dyads. *Journal of Early Adolescence, 23,* 349–383.

Ruble, D., and Martin, C. L. (1998). Gender development. In N. Eisenberg (ed.) and W. Damon (series ed.), *Handbook of Child Psychology: Vol. 3. Socialization, Emotional, and Personality Development* (5th ed., pp. 993–1016). New York: John Wiley & Sons, Inc.

Schaefer, E. (1965). Children's reports of parental behavior: An inventory. *Child Development, 36,* 413–424.

Simmons, R. G., and Blyth, D. A. (1987). *Moving into Adolescence: The Impact of Pubertal Change and School Context.* New York: Aldine.

Stattin, H., and Magnusson, D. (1990). *Pubertal maturation in female development.* Hillsdale, NJ: Lawrence Erlbaum Associates, Inc.

Stattin, H., Kerr, M., Skoog, T., *et al.* (2010). Early pubertal timing and girls' problem behavior: Explaining the mechanisms at different levels of social contexts. Under editorial review.

Tilton-Weaver, L. C., Galambos, N. L., and Vitunski, E. T. (2001). Five images of maturity in adolescence: What does "grown up" mean? *Journal of Adolescence, 24,* 143–158.

Turner, P. K., Runtz, M. G., and Galambos, N. L. (1999). Sexual abuse, pubertal timing, and subjective age in adolescent girls: A research note. *Journal of Reproductive and Infant Psychology, 71,* 111–118.

West, M., Rose, M.S., Spreng, S., *et al.* (1998). Adolescent attachment questionnaire: A brief assessment of attachment in adolescence. *Journal of Youth and Adolescence, 27,* 661–673.

CHAPTER 3

Physical Health in Adolescent Girls with Antisocial Behavior

Kathleen Pajer, Andrea Lourie, and Lisa Leininger
The Ohio State University College of Medicine, USA
Research Institute at Nationwide Children's Hospital, Columbus, OH, USA

This chapter will discuss several aspects of physical health in adolescent girls with a specific type of problem behavior – antisociality. Adolescent antisocial behavior can be defined legally (delinquency) or psychiatrically (conduct disorder). Both types of antisocial behavior exact high societal costs and cause significant suffering to the individuals and their families (Scott *et al.*, 2001; Jones *et al.*, 2002). For example, by the time youths with conduct disorder (CD) are 28 years old, it is estimated that the economic cost associated with them is 10 times higher than for youths who did not have any psychiatric disorder (Scott *et al.*, 2001). CD is one of the most difficult disorders to treat (Bourduin, Mann, and Cone, 1995; Campbell, Gonzalez, and Silva, 1992; Chiland and Young, 1994; Christ *et al.*, 1990; Haddad, Barocas, and Hollenbeck, 1991; Huizinga, Loeber, and Thornberry, 1994; Mendel, 1995; Offord and Bennett, 1994). Girls with CD or delinquency are particularly difficult to treat and do not respond well to the traditional interventions for boys, e.g., "boot camps" (Baines and Alder, 1996; Acoca, 1999).

Unfortunately, antisocial behavior in adolescent girls is increasingly prevalent. Between 1980 and 2003, arrest rates for assaults by girls increased 269% in the United States. In 2003, girls accounted for 24% of arrests for aggravated assault, 35% of forgery arrests, and 40% of embezzlement charges for American delinquents (Synder, 2005). Epidemiologic studies show that as many as 10% of 15–17 year-old girls in the general US population meet DSM-III, DSM-III-R, or DSM-IV criteria for CD (Kashani *et al.*, 1987; P. Cohen *et al.*, 1993; Costello *et al.*, 2003). In the United Kingdom, a population study of over 10 000 5–15 year-olds

Understanding Girls' Problem Behavior: How Girls' Delinquency Develops in the Context of Maturity and Health, Co-occurring Problems, and Relationships, Edited by Margaret Kerr, Håkan Stattin, Rutger C. M. E. Engels, Geertjan Overbeek and Anna-Karin Andershed © 2011 John Wiley & Sons, Ltd.

(90.8% Caucasian) reported that 3.5% of 15-year-old girls met criteria for DSM-IV criteria (5.5% of the boys the same age met criteria) (Maughan *et al.*, 2004). Two Canadian studies reported that 2.9-3.6% of 15 to 17-year-old girls met DSM-III-R criteria for CD (Breton *et al.*, 1999; Romano *et al.*, 2001). A large cohort study of New Zealand children followed from birth reported that 8% of the girls met DSM-IV criteria for CD at age 15 (Moffitt *et al.*, 2001). CD is the second most common psychiatric disorder in epidemiologic studies of adolescent girls in the United States, United Kingdom, and New Zealand (Rutter, Tizard, and Whitmore, 1970; P. Cohen *et al.*, 1987; Graham and Rutter, 1973; Kashani *et al.*, 1987; McGee *et al.*, 1990). Furthermore, such behavior in girls is not confined to problems in adolescence. A systematic cross-disciplinary and international literature review of studies done from 1900 to 1997 about the adult outcomes of girls with antisocial behavior fund that there were high rates of criminality, early mortality, depression, substance use, physical illness, health care utilization, and intergenerational transmission of antisocial behavior (Pajer, 1998).

At the time of the review, relatively little research had been done about female antisocial behavior at any age and none had been conducted to examine any biological mechanism. In contrast, a large body of research about boys and men with these problems existed, having started in the early twentieth century. This work included many large, longitudinal sociological studies, countless psychological investigations of putative psychological mechanisms, and numerous studies of the biological correlates of CD, delinquency, antisocial personality disorder (the adult analogue of CD), and criminality. The biological research in males was sometimes contradictory, but several findings were regularly reported across studies of boys and men. Among them were indications that stress response system function was blunted (Woodman, Hinton, and O'Neill, 1978; Tennes and Kreye, 1985; Tennes *et al.*, 1986; Van Goozen *et al.*, 1998a; McBurnett *et al.*, 1991; Vanyukov *et al.*, 1993; Moss, Vanyukov, and Martin, 1995; Vanyukov, and Martin, 1995; Flinn and England, 1997; McBurnett *et al.*, 2000) and that androgen hormone levels were higher (Mattson *et al.*, 1980; Nottelmann *et al.*, 1987; Susman *et al.*, 1987; Olweus *et al.*, 1988; Dabbs, Jurkovic, and Frady, 1991; Constantino *et al.*, 1993; Maras *et al.*, 2003; Scerbo and Kolko, 1994; Susman *et al.*, 1996; Van Goozen *et al.*, 1998b). Several theories about the mechanism of antisocial behavior were based on these data. However, given that there are gender differences in stress response system function and gonadal/adrenal hormone levels (the sources of androgens), we questioned whether these putative mechanisms would hold true for girls with antisocial disorder.

Therefore, our research program has spent the past ten years studying girls with antisocial behavior, the hypothalamic pituitary adrenal (HPA) axis arm of the stress response system, and gonadal and adrenal androgen hormone levels. Our findings further generated several hypotheses about physical health in these girls and we have more recently been investigating these research questions. This chapter summarizes our work on female adolescent antisocial behavior levels of cortisol (the primary biomarker of HPA axis function), and adrenal and gonadal hormones, presenting some of our new work on physical health. The remainder of the chapter is divided into five sections: (1) summary of studies about adrenal and gonadal hormone levels; (2) possible physical health consequences of these findings; (3) results from a systematic review of the literature on physical health of girls with adolescent antisocial behavior; (4) presentation of new findings from a study about self-reported physical health in this population; and (5) conclusions and directions for future research.

ADRENAL AND GONADAL HORMONE LEVELS

As mentioned above, biological studies of males with antisocial behavior indicate stress response system hypoactivity and elevated levels of androgens in this population. However, we cannot assume that these findings will pertain to girls and women because in the general population, there are important sex differences in these variables. However, the male data can guide us in hypothesis formation. Therefore, we hypothesized that girls with antisocial behavior would also demonstrated blunted HPA axis activity.

To test this hypothesis, we conducted two studies. The first examined morning plasma cortisol levels in 15–17-year-old girls with CD (n = 47) compared to girls without any psychiatric disorder who were the same age (n = 37). Three samples of blood were drawn in the morning over the course of 40 minutes from an in-dwelling catheter. All girls were in the early follicular stage of their menstrual cycles (Pajer et al., 2001b). Girls with CD had significantly lower cortisol levels than the comparison group at all three time points, even after adjusting for race, social class, and oral contraceptive usage.

Plasma cortisol levels measure the total amount of cortisol (bound plus free) in the blood. Saliva cortisol levels are a better estimate of free cortisol, i.e., the amount of biologically available steroid. Therefore, we conducted a second study to determine if morning saliva cortisol levels in 460 10–12-year-old girls and boys were associated with antisocial behaviors. In this study, antisocial behaviors were assessed with a multi-dimensional instrument that measured neurobehavioral disinhibition (Pajer et al., 2001a). Neurobehavioral disinhibition is defined as the inability to appropriately regulate affect and behavior. There is a high degree of overlap between neurobehavioral disinhibition and CD (Tarter et al., 2003).

Results differed for boys and girls. Morning saliva cortisol levels were significantly higher in girls than boys. Cortisol was significantly and negatively correlated with neurobehavioral disinhibition scores in girls, but not in boys. This association remained after adjusting for race, social class, and paternal substance use disorder, with morning saliva cortisol accounting for 24% of the variance in the girls' neurobehavioral disinhibition scores.

In summary, our hypothesis that girls with antisocial behavior would show evidence of HPA axis hypoactivity was supported. However, these findings only pertain to morning cortisol levels and our studies did not investigate possible mechanisms for this finding. To address these issues, we just completed a longitudinal study of girls who have CD that investigated additional aspects of HPA axis function and tested several mechanistic hypotheses. We are currently analyzing these data.

Based on data from males, we also hypothesized that androgen or gonadal hormone levels would be higher in girls with CD. To investigate this question, we measured morning plasma levels of testosterone, estradiol, androstenedione, dehydroepiandrosterone (DHEA), dehydroepiandrosterone-sulfate (DHEA-S), sex hormone binding globulin (SHBG), and cortisol in 47 girls with CD and 36 girls without any disorder (all were 15–17 years of age) (Pajer *et al.*, 2006a). Summary measures were the free estrogen index (FEI), the free testosterone index (FTI), index of hyperandrogenisim (IHA) and the cortisol to DHEA ratio. Girls with CD had significantly lower cortisol-to-DHEA ratios, but did not differ from non-disordered girls on any other hormone variable. However, girls with aggressive CD had significantly higher FTI's, lower SHBG levels, and lower cortisol-to-DHEA ratios than girls with non-aggressive CD. This suggests that the aggressive symptoms of CD may differentiate sub-groups of girls with CD.

IMPLICATIONS OF THE HORMONE DATA FOR PHYSICAL HEALTH

Mounting evidence indicates that HPA axis function, gonadal hormone levels, and adrenal androgen levels are all important etiologic factors in the physical health of adults. Specifically, low HPA axis activity has been associated with a shift in the T helper cell balance in the direction of predominance of T helper cell 1 (Th1) (Chrousos and Gold, 1992; Rook, 1999). This pattern of immune system function is associated with autoimmune diseases, allergic diseases, and chronic inflammation (Chrousos, 1995; Elenkov, *et al.*, 1999; Elenkov, Chrousos, and Wilder, 2000; Elenkov and Chrousos, 2006). Based on these studies and our findings from morning cortisol levels, we hypothesized that girls with antisocial behavior would have a Th1 shift. To test this, we measured IgG3:4 ratios as markers of Th1:Th2 ratios in 77 girls (42 CD and 35 non-disordered).

In support of our hypothesis, the IgG3:4 ratios in the CD group were significantly higher than the ratios in the non-disordered group. This result remained significant after controlling for the effects of oral contraceptive use, antidepressant use, socioeconomic status, race, smoking history, and substance use. Furthermore, IgG3:4 ratios were inversely correlated with the mean cortisol level. This study suggested that girls with CD may be less likely to contract acute viral or bacterial infections, but may be more vulnerable to chronic inflammation, auto-immune disorders, and disorders of chronic, unexplained pain, e.g., fibromyalgia.

In reviewing the literature further about health consequences of our previous studies on hormone levels, we also found that low SHBG levels, accompanied by high FTI (as found in the girls with aggressive CD symptoms) was associated with higher levels of glucose, greater insulin resistance, higher levels of inflammatory markers, and adverse lipid profiles in 3302 middle-aged pre- and post-menopausal women (Sutton-Tyrrell *et al.*, 2005) and in several other studies of adult women and men (Pugeat *et al.*, 1995; Bataille *et al.*., 2005; Heald *et al.*, 2005). In addition, low morning cortisol in men is associated with increased risk for cardiovascular disease (Rosmond and Bjorntorp, 2000).

These possible links between health and HPA axis function, immune system function, gonadal and androgen hormone levels suggested an explanation for a curious finding that was discovered in the systematic review about the adult outcomes of female adolescent antisocial behavior described in the Introduction. Several studies earlier in the twentieth century reported that the women with antisocial behavior had high rates of unexplained physical health complaints and significantly greater health care utilization than non-affected women. These findings were attributed to hysteria (Robins, 1966; Cloninger and Guze, 1970; Spalt, 1980), but the validity of this conclusion was undermined by significant limitations in the studies: small, non-representative samples, unstandardized methods of evaluating health complaints, and no analysis of other factors that could explain the findings, e.g., demographic characteristics. A newer study improved on some of these methodological shortcomings by using a population sample and the data revealed that young women who had CD or oppositional defiant disorder in adolescence had poorer health in young adulthood (Bardone *et al.*, 1998). However, the absolute number of girls who had true antisocial behavior, i.e., CD, was quite small and there was no standardized measure of health symptoms or health risk behaviors used.

Because of the methodological concerns in these studies, we conducted two studies to determine if women with past adolescent antisocial behavior (CD or delinquency) had poorer health outcomes than women without such a past history. The first study investigated health outcomes in the 1218 mothers of the boys who were subjects in the Pittsburgh Youth Study (Loeber *et al.*, 1998; Loeber *et al.*, 2002). Among these, 214 met our criteria for antisocial behavior and this group was nearly twice as likely to report long-term physical health problems, even after controlling for demographic characteristics (Pajer *et al.*, 2006b). The second study was a three-year longitudinal investigation into the young adult health outcomes of 93 girls, ages 15–17 years (52 with conduct disorder; 41 with no psychiatric illness), using a standardized health assessment instrument, the Child Health and Illness Profile (CHIP) (Starfield, Ensminger, and Green, 1995). In this study, we replicated the results of Bardone and colleagues (Bardone *et al.*, 1998) in that the young women with histories of CD had significantly worse health outcomes on nearly every aspect of health, with the exception of acute diseases and surgeries (Pajer *et al.*, 2007). This lends indirect support for our interpretation of the immune system study findings described above, i.e., HPA axis hypoactivity would be associated with lower rates of acute infectious illnesses, but equal or greater symptoms associated with chronic inflammation, chronic pain, or allergies.

We concluded that women with antisocial behavior do have poorer health status, but it is not clear when this association begins. Is it as early as adolescence? This is important to determine because childhood and adolescence are periods in which prevention and early treatment are more likely to be effective. Therefore, we conducted a systematic review of the literature to try to answer this question.

CD, DELINQUENCY, AND HEALTH: WHAT DO WE KNOW SO FAR?

To obtain the information for this new systematic review, we conducted a series of literature searches in PubMed, Sociological Abstracts, Psychological Abstracts, and Criminal Justice Abstracts. Our search terms were analogous, but depended on the unique requirements for each database: "conduct disorder" OR "delinquency/juvenile offenders/juvenile delinquents" AND "health status/health/physical health". Including the terms "female/girls" markedly reduced our yield, so they were dropped. To be used in our review, a study had to meet the following criteria: (1) have a sample of youths with CD or delinquency, (2) collect data on adolescent physical health; (3) include girls in the sample and present data on them. After obtaining an article, we back-searched from its reference list for any articles missed in the computerized search. Over 100 articles were examined, but only 19 met our criteria (Table 3.1). Ten additional articles examined adolescent health in samples of boys and girls (nine with delinquency, one with CD), but were not included because they provided no separate data about the girls. These citations are available from the first author.

In examining Table 3.1, it becomes apparent that sexually transmitted disease has been the main health focus for research about girls with antisocial behavior. This is consistent with the long-standing perspective that sexual transgressions are the most important antisocial behavior in girls (Glueck and Glueck, 1934; Schlossman and Wallach, 1978; Odem and Schlossman, 1991; Kunzel, 1993). A second problem is that few studies used comparison groups. However, the one study that examined health indicators other than gynecological infections or abnormalities and used comparison groups reported that health was worse in the both the delinquency groups than in the non-antisocial comparison group (Shanok and Lewis, 1981). The third limitation to these data is that no study investigated possible effects of other causal factors that could have explained the findings, e.g., minority race/ethnicity or social class, which are associated with both antisocial behavior and poor health (Baldwin, Harris, and Chambliss, 1997; Marmot and Wilkinson, 2000; Cohen, Doyle, and Baum, 2006a; Cohen et al., 2006b). Similarly, no study controlled for other psychiatric disorders, e.g., depression and anxiety that are well-known to have an association with health (Southard et al., 1986; Needham and Crosnoe, 2005).

In summary, the research reviewed did not answer our question about whether adolescent antisocial behavior in girls is associated with physical health status. One controlled study suggested that it is, but otherwise, the data were primarily from uncontrolled STD prevalence studies in the female juvenile justice population and none of these controlled for the effects of demographic

Table 3.1 Studies' of health in girls with antisocial behavior.

Authors, Date	Sample	Sites	Health Variables	Results
(Lofy et al., 2006)	Detainees N = 3593, Girls = 3593 Race = 61.1% Caucasian 23.9% African-American 9.7% Other Age range =< 12–17 yrs.	17 JDF's[1] (Washington)	C. trachomatis infection	• 18.7% girls infected • Rates higher in African-American or other race categories • Rates higher if >1 partner last 60 days • 27.2% infected girls had earlier (+) test
(Katz et al., 2004)	Detainees N = 101, Girls = 101 Race = ? Age range = 12–17 yrs.	1 JDF (Hawaii)	C. trachomatis infection N. gonorrhea infection	• 14% chlamydia • 6% gonorrhea • 3% both
(Mrus et al., 2003)	Detainees N = 588, Girls = 280 Race = ? Age range = 13–18 years	1 JDF (Ohio)	C. trachomatis infection	• 16.8% girls infected • 0.6% PID[2] • 0.18% chronic pelvic pain • 0.22% infertility • 0.08% ectopic pregnancy
(Broussard et al., 2002)	Detainees N = 5558, Girls = 529 Race$_{Girls}$ = 10.6% Caucasian 71.8% African-American 17.7% Other Mean age = 15.1 ± 1.1 yrs	1 JDF (Illinois)	C. trachomatis infection N. gonorrhea infection	• 32.5% Chlamydia • 13.6% gonorrhea
(Cromwell, Risser, and Risser, 2002)	Detainees N = 313, Girls = 313 Race = 32% Caucasian 37% African-American 30% Hispanic 1% Asian Mean age = 15.4 + 1.5 yrs	1 JDF (Texas)	Gynecological infections	• 71% chlamydia • 2% gonorrhea • 5% both • 3.9% PID

Table 3.1 (Cont'd)

Authors, Date	Sample	Sites	Health Variables	Results
(Mertzet et al., 2002)	Biological samples from incarcerated youth N = 50,073 Chlamydia tests; 40,529 gonorrhea test; 33,054 syphilis test Race = Caucasian, African-American, Hispanic Age range = 10–19 yrs.	12 JCF's[3] (U.S.)	*C. trachomati* *N. gonorrhea* *T. pallidem infection*	Medians across JCF's of infected girls: • chlamydia = 15.6% • gonorrhea = 5.2% • syphilis = 0.5%
(Risser et al., 2001)	Detainees N = 589, Girls = 139 Race = 23% Caucasian 43% African-American 26% Hispanic Age: Adolescents	1 JDF[1] (Texas)	*C. trachomatis* infection	• 13% girls < 14 yrs. Infected • 31% girls ≥ 14 yrs. infected
(Kelly et al., 2000)	Detainees N = 200, Girls = 65 Race$_{Girls}$ = 61.5% Hispanic 38.5% non-Hispanic Age range = 12–17 yrs	1 JDF (Texas)	*C. trachomatis* infection	• 22.2% girls infected • Rates higher in girls with IVDA[4]
(CDC, 1999)	Detainees N = 1135, Girls = 1135 Race = ? Age range = 9–17 yrs.	3 JDF's (Illinois, California, Alabama)	*C. trachomatis* infection *N. gonorrhea* infection	• 16–27% infected with chlamydia • 6–17% infected with gonorrhea
(Oh et al., 1998)	Detainees N = 263, Girls = 46 Race$_{Girls}$ = 30.4% Caucasian 69.6% African-American Mean age = 15.3 ± 1.3 yrs	JDF (Alabama)	*C. trachomatis* infection *N. gonorrhea* infection	• 28.3% girls infected with chlamydia • 13.1% girls infected with gonorrhea • 8.7% both

Study	Sample	Location	Focus	Findings
Hollis, 1999)	community girls N = 560, Girls = 560 JCF = 138, NC[5] = 422 Race$_{JCF}$ = 30% Caucasian 68% African-American 2% Hispanic or Asian Mean age = 15.5 ± 1.2 yrs Race$_{NC}$ = "primarily Caucasian" Age$_{NC}$ range = 11–16 yrs.			• JCF > NC all worries and fears about pain and illness • JCF = NC in health habits and treatment experiences
(Poulin et al., 1997)	Detainees/Incarcerated youth N = 453, Girls = 242 Race = ?	All JDF's and JCF's (Quebec, Canada)	C. trachomatis infection	• 10% girls infected
(Huerta et al., 1996)	Age range = 14–18 yrs. Detainees N = 135, Girls = 41 Race = 13% Caucasian 13% African-American 49% Hispanic 25% Other	1 JDF (California)	H. simplex – Type 2 infection	• 19.5% girls sero positive
(Forst, Harry, and Goddard, 1993)	Detainees and Homeless Shelter youth N = 405 Girls$_{JDF}$ = 70 Girls$_{Shelter}$ = 102 Race$_{JDF}$ = 10.6 Caucasian 571.% African-American 20.8% Latino, 11.4% other Race $_{Shelter}$ = 48.8% Caucasian 21.3% African-American 16.9% Latino, 13.1% other Mean age$_{JDF}$ = 16.3 yrs. Mean age$_{Shelter}$ = 16.6 yrs.	1 JDF and 1 Shelter (California)	All health problems	• JDF > Homeless girls for gynecological abnormalities

Table 3.1 (Cont'd)

Authors, Date	Sample	Sites	Health Variables	Results
(Alexander-Rodriquez and Vermund, 1987)	Detainees N = 2521, Girls = 285 Race = ?	1 JDF (New York)	*N. gonorrhea* infection *T. pallidum* infection	• 18.3% gonorrhea • 2.5% syphilis • 0.1% both

(Bell *et al.*, 1985)	Detainees
	N = 100, Girls = 100
	Race =
	  66% Caucasian
	  30% African-American
	  4% Other
	Mean age = 15.2 ± 1.3
		1 JDF (Washington)	Gynecological infections and abnormalities	• 81% vaginal discharge
				• 18% gonorrhea
				• 20% chlamydia
				• 48% trichomonas
				• 0% syphilis
				• 25% bacterial vaginitis
				• 15.5% abnormal PAP

(Shanok and Lewis, 1981)	Court Cases, incarcerated and community (NC) girls N = 84 Girls$_{Court}$ = 28 Girls$_{JCF}$ = 28 Girls$_{NC}$ = 28 Race = ? Age = ?	1 Juvenile court, 1 JCF local community (Connecticut)	All medical problems	• Court > NC in hospitalizations and clinic visits • Court > NC obstetrical and gynecological problems • JCF > Court > NC for head injuries, neurological symptoms
(Caloenescu *et al.*, 1973)	Detainees and CC[6] N = 1047, Girls = 1047 Race = 100% Caucasian Age range = 13–17 yrs.	1 JDF, Hospital clinic (Montreal, Canada)	Gynecological infections	• JD < CC gonorrhea • JD > CC trichomonas • JD > CC candida
(Gallagher, 1970)	Detainees N = 716, Girls = 176 Race = ? Age range = 14–17 yrs.	1 JDF (UK)	Gynecological infections	• 28.2% trichomonas • 8.8% gonorrhea • 6.7% vaginitis • 3.3% venereal warts • 0.5% syphilis

Notes:

[1] JDF: Juvenile Detention Facility.
[2] PID: Pelvic Inflammatory Disease.
[3] JCF: Juvenile Correctional Facility.
[4] IVDA: IV Drug Abuse.
[5] NC: Normal Control.

characteristics or psychiatric comorbidity. Answering these questions is not only important for elucidating the mechanisms underlying the predictive relationship between adolescent CD and adult poor health, but in caring for adolescents with antisocial behavior. Untreated adolescent medical problems can exacerbate problem behaviors, such as aggression, may complicate mental health treatment, and can adversely affect the next generation. This is a particularly salient issue for girls because adolescent antisocial behavior is associated with early pregnancies (Serbin et al., 1991; Kovacs, Krol and Voti, 1994; Kessler et al., 1997; Zoccolillo, Meyers, and Assiter, 1997; Woodward and Fergusson, 1999).

PRELIMINARY DATA ON PHYSICAL HEALTH IN GIRLS WITH CD

To investigate whether adolescent girls with antisocial behavior have health problems, we have undertaken a new project, for which we will present preliminary findings here. The specific questions to be answered with this study are: (1) Do girls with CD report worse health status than girls with no psychiatric disorder? (2) Does the self-reported health status in girls with CD differ from that in girls with depression or anxiety? (3) Is the full diagnosis of CD associated with poorer health than subclinlical CD (i.e., fewer problem behaviors or those displayed for shorter periods)? For all questions, we also are examining the effects of race and social class.

Methods

Participants

The sample to date, comprising 278 15–16-year old girls, is being recruited from the community, through newspaper and radio advertisements and posters. The target sample is 350 girls. When a girl or adult calls the study office to obtain information about the study, s/he is given a brief description of the protocol and the exclusion criteria. If the caller is still interested after this information, an intake appointment is scheduled with a girl and adult informant who knows her history. The majority of adult informants (91%) are parents. The girls are categorized into one of four diagnostic groups based on the results of a structured psychiatric interview (see below): 1) CD; 2) subclinical CD (SCD), defined as having symptoms of CD, but not meeting DSM-IV criteria; 3) psychiatric controls (PC), defined as having an anxiety or depressive disorder or both; and 4) non-affected control (NC) group, who have no disorder at all. Exclusion criteria for all groups are: age other than 15–16 years, pubertal stage < Tanner Stage V, IQ < 70, psychosis, or medical illness that could affect the hypothalamic pituitary adrenal (HPA) axis (e.g., Cushing's disease, thyroid disorders, diabetes). The last criterion was included because we are also studying HPA axis function in this sample. To be included in the PC or NC groups, girls cannot have any lifetime symptoms of CD or other externalizing disorders and girls in the NC group cannot have any lifetime history of a psychiatric disorder.

Protocol

The intake interview is conducted concurrently, but separately for each parent-girl dyad and collects data about the girl's race/ethnicity, family socioeconomic status (SES), psychiatric diagnosis, and self-reported health in the previous 12 months (girl only). The girl and parent each receive $20 for the interview. The protocol has been approved by the Institutional Review Boards of the Nationwide Children's Hospital and The Ohio State University.

Instruments

Demographics   Race/ethnicity is assessed by adolescent report. Family socio-economic status (SES) is determined by the four-factor Hollingshead Scale (Hollingshead, 1975).

Psychiatric diagnosis   Psychiatric diagnoses are determined from the compu-terized version of the Diagnostic Interview Schedule for Children (C-DISC), Parent and Youth Versions (Shaffer *et al.*, 1996; Shaffer *et al.*, 2000). Reliability of this instrument is fair to good, depending on the diagnosis; CD has the high-est test-retest reliability and the highest parent-youth agreement of all the diagnoses (Fisher *et al.*, 1997). CD has the highest validity of the Parent-reported diagnoses (0.77) and the second to highest validity score on the Youth report (0.72) (Schwab-Stone *et al.*, 1996).

Whether the DSM-IV criteria for CD in girls are valid is controversial. Unlike boys, the age of onset for many girls with CD is older than 12 years and most girls with CD do not repeatedly initiate fights (Zoccolillo, 1993; Zoccolillo, Tremblay, and Vitaro, 1996; Delligatti, Akin-Little, and Little, 2003; Ohan and Johnston, 2005). Therefore, CD criteria were slightly modified to ensure that girls with persistent antisocial behaviors were enrolled, but those girls who had not started their symptoms until after 13 were not missed. We rephrased the DISC questions about fighting to: "Do you often *get into* fights?" rather than "Do you often *start* fights?" Second, our diagnostic algorithm required that antisocial behaviors be demonstrated for at least one year before the interview instead of onset before age 13.

All diagnoses are made based on meeting criteria from the youth *or* parent DISC. Adolescents may not reveal the behaviors to their parents (a false nega-tive on DISC-Parent Version) or they may minimize their antisocial behavior on report to us (a false negative on DISC-Youth Version) (Andrews *et al.*, 1993). Therefore, we use all data as equally valid (de los Reyes and Kazdin, 2004).

Health status   The Child Health and Illness Profile-Adolescent Edition (CHIP-AE) is used to collect self-report data about health in the previous 12 months (Starfield *et al.*, 1995). This instrument yields scores for six domains of health: Satisfaction (general feeling of health and well-being), Discomfort (pain, fatigue, etc.), Disorders (major and minor disorders in the past and within the past 12 months; includes surgical history), Risks (health risk behaviors), Resilience (health promotion behaviors and features of the home environment conducive to health), and Achievement (functioning in school and, if relevant, at a job). It has been standardized in a multi-site study on 3,451 urban and rural children and adolescents, ages 11–17 years (Starfield *et al.*, 1993). Reliability is good, with Cronbach's α ranging from 0.42 (only two subdomain scales) to 0.93, the majority of the results in the 0.70 to 0.80 range. Convergent and divergent discrimination were good on all sub-domains in the original standardization testing.

Data analysis

Univariate analyses for this preliminary presentation of results were conducted with Chi-square, ANOVA, or Pearson's *r*, depending on the types of variables. We used MANOVA or MANCOVA to determine if there were overall group effects on the six health domains, with and without adjustment for demographic variables. *Post-hoc* analyses were conducted with the Games-Howell test because the groups were unequal in size. Univariate analyses in follow-up to the MANCOVA used a Bonferroni correction. All tests were two-tailed; statistical significance was set at $p < 0.05$ and SPSS-PC, Version 14 was used for the analyses.

Results

Participant characteristics are displayed in Table 3.2. Because these are preliminary data from a study in which recruitment has not been completed, the groups are unequal in size. The mean ages do not differ by group, but race and social class are different. Specifically, the NC and PC groups have higher proportions of Caucasian and upper class girls than do the CD and SCD groups.

Table 3.3 displays the means and standard deviations by group for each of the six health domains. Note that higher scores indicate better health for all domains. There was a significant overall effect of group on health.

(1) Is the self-reported health of girls with CD worse than that of girls in the NC group?

Post-hoc analyses (Table 3.3) indicate that the answer to this is yes. The scores for girls with antisocial behavior indicted poorer health than the girls without any psychiatric disorder on *every* domain of the CHIP-AE; the statistical significance for the comparison of NC and CD groups on every domain was $p < 0.001$.

Table 3.2 Sample characteristics: conduct disorder (CD), psychiatric controls (PC), subclinical CD (SCD), and no disorder (NC).

Variables	CD (n = 121)	PC (n = 30)	SCD (n = 81)	NC (n = 46)	p value
Age in years (mean ± SD)	15.85 ± 0.56	15.73 ± 0.53	16.00 ± 0.54	15.91 ± 0.60	0.135
Race					0.025
Caucasian	41 (35.0%)	18 (62.1%)	23 (28.0%)	27 (57.4%)	
African-American	72 (61.5%)	6 (20.7%)	49 (59.8%)	15 (31.9%)	
Other	4 (3.4%)	5 (20.7%)	10 (12.2%)	5 (10.6%)	
SES					0.005
High	40 (34.2%)	15 (51.7%)	38 (46.3%)	30 (63.8%)	
Low	77 (65.8%)	14 (48.3%)	44 (53.7%)	17 (36.2%)	

Table 3.3 Group means for health domains.

Domains (means ± SD)	CD (n = 121)	PC (n = 30)	SCD (n = 81)	NC (n = 46)	F	p value
Satisfaction[1]	2.93 ± 0.57	2.79 ± 0.54	2.86 ± 0.54	3.32 ± 0.39	9.14	<0.001
Discomfort[2]	4.14 ± 0.48	4.26 ± 0.50	4.34 ± 0.47	4.60 ± 0.24	12.47	<0.001
Resilience[3]	3.05 ± 0.43	3.40 ± 0.44	3.22 ± 0.36	3.64 ± 0.42	25.43	<0.001
Risks[4]	3.44 ± 0.48	4.18 ± 0.30	3.93 ± 0.35	4.28 ± 0.24	69.30	<0.001
Disorders[5]	4.43 ± 0.38	4.63 ± 0.18	4.60 ± 0.20	4.66 ± 0.15	11.29	<0.001
Achievement[6]	2.26 ± 0.69	2.86 ± 0.69	2.66 ± 0.66	3.01 ± 0.65	18.02	<0.001

Notes: Overall F (18,813) = 11.65; Pillai's trace: $p < 0.001$.
[1] NC > PC = SCD = CD.
[2] NC > PC = SCD > CD.
[3] NC = PC = SCD > CD.
[4] NC = PC > SCD > CD.
[5] NC = PC = SCD > CD.
[6] NC = PC > SCD > CD.

(2) Is there any difference between the health reported by girls with CD and girls who have internalizing disorders?

Girls who met criteria for anxiety or depression reported satisfaction with overall health and levels of discomfort that were not statistically different from those in the CD group: Satisfaction ($p = 0.606$) and Discomfort ($p = 0.675$). However, the PC group scores on health risks, resilience, disorders, and achievement indicated better health status than the CD group: Resilience ($p = 0.001$); Risks ($p < 0.001$); Disorders ($p < 0.001$); Achievement ($p < 0.001$).

Table 3.4 Race and health domains.

Domains (means ± SD)	Caucasian (n = 110)	African-American (n = 143)	Other[1] (n = 25)	F	p value
Satisfaction	2.93 ± 0.57	2.79 ± 0.54	2.86 ± 0.54	1.27	0.281
Discomfort	4.14 ± 0.48	4.26 ± 0.50	4.34 ± 0.47	1.10	0.362
Resilience[2]	3.05 ± 0.43	3.40 ± 0.44	3.22 ± 0.36	10.88	<0.001
Risks	3.44 ± 0.48	4.18 ± 0.30	3.93 ± 0.35	0.753	0.472
Disorders	4.43 ± 0.38	4.63 ± 0.18	4.60 ± 0.20	0.664	0.515
Achievement	2.26 ± 0.69	2.86 ± 0.69	2.66 ± 0.66	1.64	0.196

Overall F (12,542) = 3.14; Pillai's trace: $p < 0.001$.
[1] Other = Hispanic and Asian.
[2] Caucasian > Other > African-American.

(3) Do girls with CD report worse health than girls who have problem behaviors, but do not meet the criteria for CD?

There was no significant difference between the perceived overall health and well-being between girls with CD and those with subclinical CD ($p = 0.835$). However, on all other domains, the CD group scores were significantly worse than those of the girls with subclinical CD: Discomfort ($p = 0.014$); Resilience ($p = 0.014$); Risks ($p < 0.001$); Disorders ($p < 0.001$); Achievement ($p < 0.001$).

We next examined the question of how race and SES affect health in adolescent girls. Table 3.4 presents the mean score for each domain by race. The overall model was significant, but this difference was the result of differences in the Resilience domain, with the mean score of the group significantly worse than either the Caucasian or Other race categories (between which there was no significant difference). We used the primary supporting parent's raw score (or the highest score of two parents living together) from the Hollingshead calculations for SES. This continuous score for SES was significantly correlated with every domain, except Disorders ($r = 0.077$; $p = 0.098$): Satisfaction ($r = 0.149$; $p = 0.02$); Discomfort ($r = 0.222$; $p < 0.001$); Resilience ($r = 0.321$; $p < 0.001$); Risks ($r = 0.159$; $p = 0.007$); Achievement ($r = 0.188$; $p = 0.001$).

To determine if accounting for the effects of race and SES changed the results for each of our questions, we used MANCOVA for three separate analyses: CD vs. NC; CD vs. PC; and CD vs. SCD. We again used Pillai's trace as the criterion to determine if the combined dependent variables (the six health domains) were affected by each of the three group pairings, controlling for demographic factors. Our results from the unadjusted data for the CD-NC group contrasts used to answer Question 1 did not markedly change (Table 3.5). The overall F (6,155) = 11.83; Pillai's Trace indicated $p < 0.001$ for group; for race, F (12,312) = 2.00, $p = 0.023$; and for SES, F (6,155) = 2.24, $p = 0.042$. Univariate analyses of the effect of group on each domain revealed that when accounting for demographic factor effects, girls with CD did not score significantly worse than the NC group

Table 3.5   Adjusted[1] effects of group on health domains for questions 1–3.

Questions/Domains	Mean square	df	F	p value
Question 1: CD vs. NC				
Satisfaction[2]	2.77	1	10.21	0.002
Discomfort	2.04	1	11.49	0.001
Resilience	2.82	1	17.24	<0.001
Risks	10.91	1	62.61	<0.001
Achievement	5.78	1	12.76	<0.001
Question 2: CD vs. PC				
Resilience	1.61	1	8.76	0.004
Risks	8.25	1	43.40	<0.001
Achievement	6.88	1	14.43	<0.001
Question 3: CD vs. SCD				
Risks	3.84	1	21.35	<0.001
Achievement	3.86	1	8.35	0.004

Notes:
[1] Adjusted for race and SES.
[2] Only statistically significant effects (Bonferroni correction) presented in the table.

girls in the Disorders domain. CD group scores indicated worse health status than the NC group on all other domains.

Results for Question 2 did change after adjusting for demographic factors. The overall $F_{(6,139)} = 10.53$, $p < 0.001$ for group; there were no significant effects of race and SES: race, $F_{(12,280)} = 1.11$, $p = 0.351$; and for SES, $F_{(6,139)} = 1.11$, $p = 0.360$. However, the univariate analyses demonstrated that after accounting for race and SES, mean scores in the CD group were only worse than scores for the PC group on Resilience, Risks, and Achievement. The answers to Question 3 also changed with the MANCOVA analysis. The overall $F_{(6,190)} = 5.27$, $p < 0.001$ for group; but, again there were no significant effects of race and SES: race, $F_{(12,382)} = 1.66$, $p = 0.073$; and for SES, $F_{(6,190)} = 1.92$, $p = 0.080$. Univariate analyses for group indicated that only Risks and Achievement were significantly worse in the CD group, compared to the SCD group, if demographic factors were taken into account.

Conclusions

These preliminary data demonstrate that girls with CD have worse self-reported health on every domain measured by the CHIP-AE than girls who do not have any psychiatric disorder. This multi-faceted difference in health was present even when the effects of demographic factors, well-known to affect health outcomes, were taken into account. However, when comparing scores from the CD group to scores from girls with internalizing disorders or problem behaviors not meeting full DSM-IV criteria, the interpretations are more complicated.

Girls with CD scored worse than girls in the PC and SCD groups on Risks and Achievement, even after adjusting for effects of race and SES. Items in these two domains collect data that focus more on the behaviors of the individual, i.e., health risk behaviors and function at school and work. Some of the items in the Risks domain overlap with CD criteria (e.g., fighting); this might partially explain the much higher scores for this group. However, if that was the entire explanation, the SCD group should not have been significantly lower than the CD group. We speculate that when girls are troubled enough to meet full criteria for CD, many of them may also engage in high rates of additional health risk behaviors that do not overlap with the symptoms of CD (e.g., eating large amounts of fatty foods). Differences in the Achievement domain may be the result of the myriad social adjustment and neuropsychological problems that girls with CD display. In another study of adolescent girls with CD and a comparison group without any psychiatric illness, we found that the CD group had social difficulties that had first appeared in elementary school and neuropsychological deficits that could make academic or work achievement difficult (Pajer *et al.*, 2008). The data from our new study tentatively support the results from our previous work. Moreover, although these problems may be due to health complaints, the reverse is also possible. Repeated difficulties in daily function may compromise long-term health by leading to a chronic level of stress from failure or inter-personal struggles.

It would be misleading, however, to simply conclude that girls with CD have poorer health than girls with internalizing disorders or SCD. Our data suggest that the overall satisfaction with health and levels of discomfort experienced on a regular basis were no different in the CD, PC, or SCD groups, but that all were significantly worse than the scores in the NC group. Lower satisfaction with health and high levels of discomfort have frequently been reported to predict higher rates of later morbidity and mortality, even without higher rates of disorders at baseline (Idler and Benyamini, 1997; Manor, Matthews, and Power, 2001). However, correlates of self-reported poor global health ratings in adults and adolescents are depression and health risk behaviors (Krause and Jay, 1994; Shields and Shooshtari, 2001; Tremblay, Dahinten, and Kohen, 2003). Our data are consistent with these findings. If our results persist when we re-analyze the data with a larger sample of PC and NC girls, it will suggest that those who provide care for adolescents should evaluate overall health and discomfort and take steps to improve these perceptions.

There are several limitations of our study. First, and most important, is that we have not completed recruitment of the PC and NC samples. Therefore, our results are preliminary. Second, we did not do physical or laboratory examinations of the girls. Doing so may have diagnosed unrecognized diseases or conditions that were the source of general perceptions of poor health. Therefore, our data may be biased in the direction of underestimating the effect of CD on health, but we do not think the lack of physical exam or lab data explains the findings. Third, our study does not have a large enough sample of Hispanic or Asian girls to draw conclusions about these race/ethnicity categories, psychopathology, and health.

CONCLUSION

The studies reviewed in this chapter and the new data presented converge on one major point: many girls with antisocial behavior have physical health problems and this association persists into adulthood. Why would CD or delinquency be associated with poor health in multiple domains? At least two theories could explain this relationship. First, it may be due to high rates of health risk behaviors manifested by girls with antisocial behavior (Donovan, Jessor, and Costa, 1985; Huizinga, Loeber, and Thornberry, 1993; Forrest *et al.*, 2000). Smoking, drinking, drug use, poor diet, little exercise, and poor oral care have all been associated with health problems in (Millstein *et al.*, 1992; Astrom, 1998; Nelson, *et al.*, 2006). Substance abuse has both direct (higher rates of acute and chronic illness) and indirect (fatigue, poor concentration) effects on health (Arria *et al.* 1995). Sub-standard diet and lack of exercise contribute to unhealthy weight, muscle weakness, and chronic diseases. Poor oral hygiene is associated with higher rates of acute and chronic diseases (Herzberg and Meyer, 1996).

Second, a factor common to both antisocial behavior and poor health could explain the association. Exposure to abuse or neglect may be such a factor. Many studies have demonstrated that rates of early maltreatment are high in girls with CD or delinquency (Green *et al.*, 1999; Keenan, Loeber, and Green, 1999; Herrera and McCloskey, 2003; Dixon, Howie, and Starling, 2005). Exposure to maltreatment has also been associated with poor physical health in adulthood (Walker *et al.*, 1999; Arnow, 2004; Batten *et al.*, 2004) and adolescence (Nelson, Higginson, and Grant-Worley, 1995; Diaz, Simantov, and Rickert, 2002). The mechanisms underlying maltreatment and antisocial behavior or poor health are not well-defined, but animal data suggest that maltreatment may alter brain function in ways that affect both behavior and physical health (McEwen, 2003); one of the most important systems disrupted is the hypothalamic pituitary adrenal (HPA) axis. Dysregulation of the hypothalamic pituitary adrenal (HPA) of the type that we have identified in this population is associated with alterations in pain perception (Fries *et al.*, 2005; Rief and Barsky, 2005) and metabolic disturbances (Taylor *et al.*, 2004; Chen and Paterson, 2006). This may explain some of our findings on poorer health in this group.

Both of these theories may be true and they may be mediated by the biological findings we report here. Halfon and colleagues have incorporated these factors and others into a new model of health that links childhood and adult health, called the Life Course Health Development Model (Halfon and Hochstein, 2002; see also Worthman and Kuzara, 2005). Future research efforts aimed at disentangling the multiple causes of poor health in girls and women with antisocial behavior should consider using this model.

In conclusion, girls with antisocial behavior have worse health than girls without any psychopathology; they may also have more health problems than girls with other types of psychopathology, such as depression. These problems have significant ramifications for adult health and for the health of the next generation. More research is needed to fully understand the mechanisms of these findings. However, possible biological explanations are dysregulation of the HPA axis and immune system and possible psychosocial mechanisms may be health risk behaviors or exposure to maltreatment. Research based on the Life Course Health Development Model as applied to this population may yield critical mechanistic data needed for the development of prevention and early intervention programs.

REFERENCES

Acoca, L. (1999). Investing in girls: A 21st century strategy. *Juvenile Justice, 6*, 3–13.

Alexander-Rodriquez, T., and Vermund, S. H. (1987). Gonorrhea and syphilis in incarcerated urban adolescents: Prevalence and physical signs. *Pediatrics, 80*, 561–564.

Andrews, V. C., Garrison, C. Z., Jackson, K. L., *et al.* (1993). Mother-adolescent agreement on the symptoms and diagnoses of adolescent depression and conduct disorders. *J Am Acad Child Adolesc Psychiatry, 32*, 869–877.

Arnow, B. A. (2004). Relationships between childhood maltreatment, adult health and psychiatric outcomes, and medical utilization. *J Clin Psychiatry, 65 Suppl 12*, 10–15.

Arria, A., Dohey, M., Mezzich, A., *et al.* (1995). Self-reported health problems and physical symptomatology in adolescent alcohol abusers. *J Adolesc Health, 16*, 226–231.

Astrom, A. (1998). Parental influences on adolescents' oral health behavior: Two-year follow-up of the Norwegian Longitudinal Health Behavior Study participants. *Eur J Oral Sciences, 106*, 922–930.

Baines, M., and Alder, C. (1996). Are girls more difficult to work with? Youth workers' perspectives in juvenile justice and related areas. *Crime Del, 42*, 476–485.

Baldwin, D., Harris, S., and Chambliss, L. (1997). Stress and illness in adolescence: Issues of race and gender. *Adolescence, 32*, 839–853.

Bardone, A. M., Moffitt, T. E., Caspi, A., *et al.* (1998). Adult physical health outcomes of adolescent girls with conduct disorder, depression, and anxiety. *J Am Acad Child Adolesc Psychiatry, 37*, 594–601.

Bataille, V., Perret, B., Evans, A., *et al.* (2005). Sex hormone-binding globulin is a major determinant of the lipid profile: the PRIME study. *Atherosclerosis, 179*, 369–373.

Batten, S. V., Aslan, M., Maciejewski, P. K., *et al.* (2004). Childhood maltreatment as a risk factor for adult cardiovascular disease and depression. *J Clin Psychiatry, 65*, 249–254.

Bell, T. A., Farrow, J. A., Stamm, W. E., *et al.* (1985). Sexually transmitted diseases in females in a juvenile detention center. *Sex Trans Dis, 12*, 140–144.

Bourduin, C., Mann, B., Cone, L., *et al.* (1995). Multisystematic treatment of serious juvenile offenders: long-term prevention of criminality and violence. *J Consult Clin Psychol, 63*, 569–578.

Breton, J. J., Bergeron, L., Valla, J. P., *et al.* (1999). Quebec child mental health survey: prevalence of DSM-III-R mental health disorders. *J Child Psychol Psychiatry, 40*, 375–384.

Broussard, D., Leichliter, J. S., Evans, A., *et al.* (2002). Screening adolescents in a juvenile detention center for gonorrhea and chlamydia: Prevalence and reinfection rates. *Prison J, 82*, 8–18.

Caloenescu, M., Larose, G., Birry, A., *et al.* (1973). Genital infection in juvenile delinquent females. *Br J Vener Dis, 49*, 72–77.

Campbell, M., Gonzalez, N. M., and Silva, R. R. (1992). The pharmacologic treatment of conduct disorders and rage outbursts. *Pediatric Psychopharmacol, 15*, 69–85.

CDC (1999). High prevalence of chlamydial and gonococcal infection in women entering jails and juvenile detention centers – Chicago, Birmingham, and San Francisco, 1998. *MMWR, 48*, 793–796.

Chen, E., and Paterson, L. Q. (2006). Neighborhood, family, and subjective socioeconomic status: How do they relate to adolescent health? *Health Psychol, 25*, 704–714.

Chiland, C., and Young, J. (1994). *Children and Violence*. Northvale, NJ: Jason Aronson.

Christ, M., Lahey, B., Frick, P., *et al.* (1990). Serious conduct problems in the children of adolescent mothers: Disentangling confounded correlations. *J Consult Clin Psychol, 58*, 840–844.

Chrousos, G. P., and Gold, P. W. (1992). The concepts of stress and stress system disorders: Overview of physical and behavioral homeostasis. *JAMA, 267*, 1244–1252.

Chrousos, G. P. (1995). The hypothalamic-pituitary-adrenal axis and immune-mediated inflammation. *NEJM, 333*, 942–943.

Cloninger, C., and Guze, S. (1970). Psychiatric illness and female criminality: The role of sociopathy and hysteria in the antisocial woman. *Am J Psychiatry, 127*, 303–311.

Cohen, P., Cohen, J., Kasen, S., *et al.* (1993). An epidemiological study of disorders in the late childhood and adolescence: I. Age and gender-specific prevalence. *J Child Psychol Psychiatry Allied Disciplines, 34*, 851–867.

Cohen, P., Velez, N., Kohn, M., *et al.* (1987). Child psychiatric diagnosis by computer algorithm: theoretical issues and empirical tests. *J Am Acad Child Adolesc Psychiatry, 26*, 631–638.

Cohen, S., Doyle, W., and Baum, A. (2006a). Socioeconomic status is associated with stress hormones. *Psychosom Med, 68*, 414–420.

Cohen, S., Schwartz, J., Epel, E., *et al.* (2006b). Socioeconomic status, race, and diurnal cortisol decline in the Coronary Artery Risk Development in Young Adults (CARDIA) Study. *Psychosom Med, 68*, 41–50.

Constantino, J. N., Grosz, D., Saenger, P., *et al.* (1993). Testosterone and aggression in children. *J Am Acad Child Adolesc Psychiatry, 32*, 1217–1222.

Costello, E. J., Mustillo, S., Erkanli, A., *et al.* (2003). Prevalence and development of psychiatric disorders in childhood and adolescence. *Arch Gen Psychiatry, 60*, 837–844.

Cromwell, P. F., Risser, W. L., and Risser, J. M. (2002). Prevalence and incidence of pelvic inflammatory disease in incarcerated adolescents. *Sex Trans Dis, 29*, 391–396.

Dabbs, J. M. J., Jurkovic, G. J., and Frady, R. L. (1991). Salivary testosterone and cortisol among late adolescent male offenders. *J Ab Child Psychol, 19*, 469–478.

de los Reyes, A., and Kazdin, A. E. (2004). Measuring informant discrepancies in clinical child research. *Psychol Assess, 16*, 330–334.

Delligatti, N., Akin-Little, A., and Little, S. G. (2003). Conduct disorder in girls: Diagnostic and intervention issues. *Psychol Schools, 40*, 183–192.

Diaz, A., Simantov, E., and Rickert, V. I. (2002). Effect of abuse on health: Results of a national survey. *Arch Pediatr Adolesc Med, 156*, 811–817.

Dixon, A., Howie, P., and Starling, J. (2005). Trauma exposure, posttraumatic stress, and psychiatric comorbidity in female juvenile offenders. *J Am Acad Child Adolesc Psychiatry, 44*(8), 798–806.

Donovan, J., Jessor, R., and Costa, F. (1985). The syndrome of problem behavior in adolescence: A replication. *J Consult Clin Psychol, 5*, 762–765.

Elenkov, I., Webster, E., Torpy, D., *et al.* (1999). Stress, corticotrophin-releasing hormone, glucocorticoids, and the immune/inflammatory response: Acute and chronic effects. *Ann NY Acad Sci, 876*, 1–13.

Elenkov, I., Chrousos, G., and Wilder, R. (2000). Neuroendocrine regulation of IL-12 and TNF-alpha/IL-10 balance. Clinical implications. *Ann NY Acad Sci, 917*, 94–105.

Elenkov, I., and Chrousos, G. (2006). Stress system – organization, physiology and immunoregulation. *Neuroimmunomodulation, 13*, 257–267.

Fisher, P., Lucas, C., Shaffer, D., *et al.* (1997). *Diagnostic interview schedule for children, version IV (DISC-IV): Test-restest reliability in a clinical sample*. Paper presented at the American Academy of Child and Adolescent Psychiatry, Toronto.

Flinn, M. V., and England, B. G. (1997). Social economics of childhood glucocorticoid stress response and health. *Am J Phys Anthropol, 102*, 33–53.

Forrest, C. B., Tambor, E., Riley, A. W., *et al.* (2000). The health profile of incarcerated male youths. *Pediatrics, 105,* 286–291.

Forst, M. L., Harry, J., and Goddard, P. A. (1993). A health-profile comparison of delinquent and homeless youths. *J Health Care Poor Underserved, 4,* 386–400.

Fries, E., Hesse, J., Hellhammer, J., *et al.* (2005). A new view on hypocortisolism. *Psychoneuroendocrinol, 30,* 1010–1016.

Gallagher, E. (1970). Genital infection in young delinquent girls. *Br J Vener Dis, 46*(2), 129–131.

Glueck, S., and Glueck, E. T. (1934). *Five Hundred Delinquent Women.* New York: Alfred A. Knopf.

Graham, P., and Rutter, M. (1973). Psychiatric disorder in the young adolescent: a follow-up study. *Proc Royal Soc Med, 66,* 1226–1229.

Green, S. M., Russo, M. F., Navratil, J. L., *et al.* (1999). Sexual and physical abuse among adolescent girls with disruptive behavior problems. *J Child Fam Studies, 8,* 151–168.

Haddad, J., Barocas, R., and Hollenbeck, A. (1991). Family organization and parent attitudes of children with conduct disorder. *J Clin Child Psychol, 20,* 152–161.

Halfon, N., and Hochstein, M. (2002). Life course health development: An integrated framework for developing health, policy, and research. *Milbank Q, 80,* 433–479.

Heald, A. H., Anderson, S. G., Ivison, F., *et al.* (2005). Low sex hormone binding globulin is a potential marker for the metabolic syndrome in different ethnic groups. *Exp Clin Endocrinol Diabetes, 113,* 522–528.

Herrera, V. M., and McCloskey, L. A. (2003). Sexual abuse, family violence, and female delinquency: findings from a longitudinal study. *Violence Vict, 18,* 319–334.

Herzberg, M. C., and Meyer, M. W. (1996). Effects of oral flora on platelets: possible consequences in cardiovascular disease. *J Periodontol, 67,* 1138–1142.

Huerta, K., Berkelhamer, S., Klein, J., *et al.* (1996). Epidemiology of herpes simplex virus type 2 infections in a high-risk adolescent population. *J Adolesc Health, 18,* 384–386.

Huizinga, D., Loeber, R., and Thornberry, T. (1993). Longitudinal study of delinquency, drug use, sexual activity, and pregnancy among children and youth in three cities. *Pub Health Rep, 108 (Suppl 1),* 90–96.

Huizinga, D., Loeber, R., and Thornberry, T. (1994). *Urban delinquency and substance abuse. Research Summary.* Washington, DC: Publication of the Office of Juvenile Justice and Delinquency Prevention.

Idler, E. L., and Benyamini, Y. (1997). Self-rated health and mortality: a review of twenty-seven community studies. *J Health Soc Behav, 38,* 21–37.

Jones, D., Dodge, K. A., Foster, E. M., *et al.* (2002). Early identification of children at risk for costly mental health service use. *Prev Sci, 3,* 247–256.

Kashani, J., Beck, N., Hoeper, E., *et al.* (1987). Psychiatric disorders in a community sample of adolescents. *Am J Psychiatry, 144,* 584–589.

Katz, A. R., Lee, M. V. C., Ohye, R. G., *et al.* (2004). Prevalence of chlamydial and gonorrheal infections among females in a juvenile detention facility, Honolulu, Hawaii. *J Comm Health, 29,* 265–269.

Keenan, K., Loeber, R., and Green, S. (1999). Conduct disorder in girls: A review of the literature. *Clin Child Fam Psychol Rev, 2,* 3–19.

Kelly, P. J., Blair, R., Baillargeon, J., *et al.* (2000). Risk behaviors and the prevalence of chlamydia in a juvenile detention center. *Clin Ped, 39,* 521–527.

Kessler, R. C., Berglund, P. A., Foster, C. L., *et al.* (1997). Social consequences of psychiatric disorders, II: Teenage parenthood. *Am J Psychiatry, 154*(10), 1405–1411.

Kovacs, M., Krol, R. S. M., and Voti, L. (1994). Early onset psychopathology and the risk for teenage pregnancy among clinically referred girls. *J Am Acad Child Adolesc Psychiatry, 33,* 106–113.

Krause, N. M., and Jay, G. M. (1994). What do global self-rated health items measure? *Med Care, 32,* 930–942.

Kunzel, R. G. (1993). *Problem girls: Unmarried Mothers and the Professionalization of Social Work, 1890–1945.* New Haven, Conn.: Yale University Press.

Loeber, R., Farrington, D., Stouthamer-Loeber, M., *et al.* (1998). *Antisocial Behavior and Mental Health Problems: Explanatory Factors in Childhood and Adolescence.* Mahwah, NJ: Lawrence Erlbaum Associates, Publishers.

Loeber, R., Stouthamer-Loeber, M., Farrington, D., *et al.* (2002). Three longitudinal studies of children's development in Pittsburgh: the Developmental Trends Study, the Pittsburgh Youth Study, and the Pittsburgh Girls Study. *Crim Behav Mental Health, 12*, 1–23.

Lofy, K. H., Hofmann, J., Mosure, D. J., *et al.* (2006). Chlamydial infections among female adolescents screened in juvenile detention centers in Washington State, 1998–2002. *Sex Trans Dis, 33*, 63–67.

McBurnett, K., Lahey, B., Frick, P., *et al.* (1991). Anxiety, inhibition, and conduct disorder in children: II. Relation to salivary cortisol. *J Am Acad Child Adolesc Psychiatry, 30*(2), 192–196.

McBurnett, K., Lahey, B., Rathouz, P., *et al.* (2000). Low salivary control and persistent aggression in boys referred for disruptive behavior. *Arch Gen Psychiatry, 57*, 38–43.

McEwen, B. S. (2003). Early life influences on life-long patterns of behavior and health. *Ment Retard Dev Disabil Res Rev, 9*, 149–154.

McGee, R., Feehan, M., Williams, S., *et al.* (1990). DSM-III disorders in a large sample of adolescents. *J Am Acad Child Adolesc Psychiatry, 29*, 611–619.

Manor, O., Matthews, S., and Power, C. (2001). Self-rated health and limiting longstanding illness: inter-relationships with morbidity in early adulthood. *Int J Epidemiol, 30*, 600–607.

Maras, A., Laucht, M., Gerdes, D., *et al.* (2003). Association of testosterone and dihydrotestosterone with externalizing behavior in adolescent boys and girls. *Psychoneuroendocrinol, 28*, 932–940.

Marmot, M., and Wilkinson, R. (2000). *Social Determinants of Health.* Oxford: Oxford University Press.

Mattson, A., Schalling, D., Olweus, D., *et al.* (1980). Plasma testosterone, aggressive behavior, and personality dimensions in young male delinquents. *J Am Acad Child Psychiatry, 19*, 476–490.

Maughan, B., Rowe, R., Messer, J., *et al.* (2004). Conduct disorder and oppositional defiant disorder in a national sample: Developmental epidemiology. *J Child Psychol Psychiatry, 45*, 609–621.

Mendel, R. (1995). *Prevention or pork? A hard-headed look at youth-oriented anti-crime programs.* Washington, DC: American Youth Policy Forum.

Mertz, K., Voigt, R., Hutchins, K., *et al.* (2002). Findings from STD screening of adolescents and adults entering corrections facilities: Implications for STD control strategies. *Sex Trans Dis, 29*, 834–839.

Millstein, S., Irwin, C. J., Adler, N., *et al.* (1992). Health-risk behaviors and health concerns among young adolescents. *Pediatrics, 89*, 422–428.

Moffitt, T. E., Caspi, A., Rutter, M., *et al.* (2001). *Sex Differences in Antisocial Behaviour.* New York: Cambridge University Press.

Moss, H. B., Vanyukov, M. M., and Martin, C. S. (1995). Salivary cortisol responses and the risk for substance abuse in prepubertal boys. *Biol Psychiatry, 38*, 547–555.

Mrus, J. M., Biro, F. M., Huang, B., *et al.* (2003). Evaluating adolescents in juvenile detention facilities for urogenital chlamydial infection. *Arch Pediatr Adolesc Med, 157*, 696–702.

Needham, B. L., and Crosnoe, R. (2005). Overweight status and depressive symptoms during adolescence. *J Adolesc Health, 36*, 48–55.

Nelson, D., Higginson, G., and Grant-Worley, J. (1995). Physical abuse among high school students: Prevalence and correlation with other health behaviors. *Arch Ped Adolesc Med, 149*, 1254–1258.

Nelson, M., Gordon-Larsen, P., North, K., *et al.* (2006). Body mass index gain, fast food, and physical activity: effects of shared environments over time. *Obesity 14*, 701–709.

Nottelmann, E., Susman, E., Dorn, L., *et al.* (1987). Developmental processes in early adolescence. relations among chronologic age, pubertal stage, height, weight, and serum levels of gonadotropins, sex steriods, and adrenal androgens. *J Adolesc Health Care, 8,* 246–260.

Odem, M., and Schlossman, S. (1991). Guardians of virture: The juvenile court and female delinquency in early 20th-century Los Angeles. *Crime Del, 37,* 186–203.

Offord, D. R., and Bennett, K. J. (1994). Conduct disorder: Long-term outcomes and intervention effectiveness. *J Am Acad Child Adolesc Psychiatry, 33,* 1069–1078.

Oh, M. K., Smith, K. R., O'Cain, M., *et al.* (1998). Urine-based screening of adolescents in detention to guide treatment for gonococcal and chlamydial infections. Translating research into intervention. *Arch Ped Adolesc Med, 152,* 52–56.

Ohan, J. L., and Johnston, C. (2005). Gender appropriateness of symptom criteria for attention-deficit/hyperactivity disorder, oppositional-defiant disorder, and conduct disorder. *Child Psychiatry Hum Dev, 35,* 359–381.

Olweus, D., Mattsson, A., Schalling, D., *et al.* (1988). Circulating testosterone levels and aggression in adolescent males: A causal analysis. *Psychosom Med, 50,* 261–272.

Pajer, K. (1998). What happens to "bad" girls? A review of the adult outcomes of antisocial adolescent girls. *Am J Psychiatry, 155,* 862–870.

Pajer, K., Gardner, W., Kirillova, G., *et al.* (2001a). Sex differences in cortisol level and neurobehavioral disinhibition in children of substance abusers. *J Child Adolesc Subs Abuse, 10,* 65–76.

Pajer, K., Gardner, W., Rubin, R., *et al.* (2001b). Decreased cortisol levels in adolescent girls with conduct disorder. *Arch Gen Psychiatry, 58,* 297–302.

Pajer, K., Tabbah, R., Gardner, W., *et al.* (2006a). Adrenal androgen and gonadal hormone levels in adolescent girls with conduct disorder. *Psychoneuroendocrinol, 31,* 1245–1256.

Pajer, K., Stouthamer-Loeber, M., Gardner, W., *et al.* (2006b). Women with antisocial behavior: Long-term health disability and help-seeking for emotional problems. *Crim Behav Mental Health, 16,* 29–42.

Pajer, K., Kazmi, A., Gardner, W., *et al.* (2007). Female conduct disorder: health status in young adulthood. *J Adolesc Health, 40,* 84.e81–84.e87.

Pajer, K., Chung, J., Leininger, L., *et al.* (2008). Neuropsychological function in adolescent girls with conduct disorder. *J Am Acad Child Adolesc Psychiatry, 47,* 416–425.

Poulin, C., Alary, M., Ringuet, J., *et al.* (1997). Prevalence of chlamydial infection and frequency of risk behaviours for STDs and HIV infection among adolescents in public juvenile facilities in the province of Quebec. *Can J Pub Health, 88,* 266–270.

Pugeat, M., Moulin, P., Cousin, P., *et al.* (1995). Interrelations between Sex Hormone-Binding Globulin (SHBG), plasma lipoproteings and cardiovascular sisk. *J Steroid Biochem Molec Biol, 53,* 567–572.

Rief, W., and Barsky, A. J. (2005). Psychobiological perspectives on somatoform disorders. *Psychoneuroendocrinol, 30,* 996–1002.

Risser, J. M., Risser, W. L., Gefter, L. R., *et al.* (2001). Implementation of a screening program for chlamydial infection in incarcerated adolescents. *Sex Trans Dis, 28,* 43–46.

Robins, L. (1966). *Deviant Children Grown Up: A Sociological and Psychiatric Study of Sociopathic Personality.* Baltimore: Williams & Wilkins.

Romano, E., Tremblay, R. E., Vitaro, F., *et al.* (2001). Prevalence of psychiatric diagnoses and the role of perceived impairment: Findings from an adolescent community sample. *J Child Psychol Psychiatry, 42,* 451–461.

Rook, G. A. (1999). Glucocorticoids and immune function. *Baillieres Best Pract Res Clin Endocrinol Metab, 13*(4), 567–581.

Rosmond, R., and Bjorntorp, P. (2000). The hypothalamic-pituitary-adrenal axis activity as a predictor of cardiovascular disease, type 2 diabetes and stroke. *J Intern Med, 247,* 188–197.

Rutter, M., Tizard, J., and Whitmore, K. (1970). *Education, Health, and Behaviour.* London: Longmans.

Scerbo, A. S., and Kolko, D. J. (1994). Salivary testosterone and cortisol in disruptive children: Relationship to aggressive, hyperactive, and internalizing behaviors. *J Am Acad Child Adolesc Psychiatry, 33,* 1174–1184.

Schlossman, S., and Wallach, S. (1978). The crime of precocious sexuality: Female juvenile delinquency in the progressive era. *Harvard Ed Rev, 48,* 65–94.

Schwab-Stone, M., Shaffer, D., *et al.* (1996). Criterion validity of the NIMH Diagnostic Interview Schedule for Children Version 2.3 (DISC-2.3). *J Am Acad Child Adolesc Psychiatry, 35,* 865–877.

Scott, S., Knapp, M., Henderson, J., and Maughn, B. (2001). Financial cost of social exclusion: follow up study of children into adulthood. *BMJ, 323,* 191–198.

Serbin, L. A., Peters, P. L., McAffer, V. J., *et al.* (1991). Childhood aggression and withdrawal as predictors of adolescent pregnancy, early parenthood, and environmental risk for the next generation. *Can J Behav Sci, 23,* 318–331.

Shaffer, D., Fisher, P., Dulcan, M. K., *et al.* (1996). The NIMH Diagnostic Interview Schedule for Children Version 2.3 (DISC-2.3): description, acceptability, prevalence rates, and performance in the MECA Study. Methods for the Epidemiology of Child and Adolescent Mental Disorders Study. *J Am Acad Child Adolesc Psychiatry, 35,* 865–877.

Shaffer, D., Fisher, P., Lucas, C. P., *et al.* (2000). NIMH Diagnostic Interview Schedule for Children Version IV (NIMH DISC-IV): Description, differences from previous versions, and reliability of some common diagnoses. *J Am Acad Child Adolesc Psychiatry, 39,* 28–38.

Shanok, S. S., and Lewis, D. O. (1981). Medical histories of female delinquents. Clinical and epidemiologic findings. *Arch Gen Psychiatry, 38,* 211–213.

Shields, M., and Shooshtari, S. (2001). Determinants of self-perceived health. *Health Rep, 13,* 35–52.

Southard, D. R., Coates, T. J., Kolodner, K., *et al.* (1986). Relationship between mood and blood pressure in the natural environment: an adolescent population. *Health Psychol, 5,* 469–480.

Spalt, L. (1980). Hysteria and antisocial personality. A single disorder? *J Nerv Ment Dis, 168,* 456–464.

Starfield, B., Bregner, M., Einsminger, M., *et al.* (1993). Adolescent health status measurement. Development of the Child Health and Illness Profile. *Pediatrics, 91,* 430–435.

Starfield, B., Ensminger, M., and Green, B. (1995). *Manual for the Child Health and Illness Profile-Adolescent Edition (CHIP-AE).* Baltimore, MD: The Johns Hopkins University Press.

Susman, E., Granger, D., Murowchick, E., *et al.* (1996). Gonadal and adrenal hormones. Developmental transitions and aggressive behavior. *Ann NY Acad Sci, 794,* 18–30.

Susman, E., Inoff-Germain, G., Nottelmann, E., *et al.* (1987). Hormones, emotional dispositions, and aggressive attributes in young adolescents. *Child Dev, 58,* 1114–1134.

Sutton-Tyrrell, K., Wildman, R. P., Matthews, K. A., *et al.* (2005). Sex-hormone-binding globulin and the free androgen index are related to cardiovascular risk factors in multiethnic premenopausal and perimenopausal women enrolled in the Study of Women Across the Nation (SWAN). *Circulation, 111,* 1242–1249.

Synder, H. M. (2005). *Juvenile Arrests 2003.* Washington, D.C.: Office of Juvenile Justice and Delinquency Prevention.

Tarter, R. E., Kirisci, L., Mezzich, A., *et al.* (2003). Neurobehavioral disinhibition in childhood predicts early age at onset of substance use disorder. *Am J Psychiatry, 160,* 1078–1085.

Taylor, S. E., Lerner, J. S., Sage, R. M., *et al.* (2004). Early environment, emotions, responses to stress, and health. *J Personality, 72,* 1365–1393.

Tennes, K., and Kreye, M. (1985). Children's adrenocortical responses to classroom activities and tests in elementary school. *Psychosom Med, 47,* 451–460.

Tennes, K., Kreye, M., Avitable, N., *et al.* (1986). Behavioral correlates of excreted cate-cholamines and cortisol in second grade children. *J Am Acad Child Psychiatry, 25,* 764–770.

Tremblay, S., Dahinten, S., and Kohen, D. (2003). Factors related to adolescents' self-perceived health. *Health Rep, 14 Suppl,* 7–16.

Van Goozen, S., Matthys, W., Cohen-Kettenis, P., *et al.* (1998a). Salivary cortisol and car-diovascular activity during stress in oppositional-defiant disorder boys and normal controls. *Biol Psychiatry, 43,* 531–539.

Van Goozen, S. H., Matthys, W., Cohen-Kettenis, P. T., *et al.* (1998b). Adrenal androgens and aggression in conduct disorder prepubertal boys and normal controls. *Biol Psychiatry, 43,* 156–158.

Vanyukov, M., Moss, H., Plail, J., *et al.* (1993). Antisocial symptoms in preadolescent boys and in their parents: Associations with cortisol. *Psychiatry Res, 46,* 9–17.

Walker, E. A., Gelfand, A., Katon, W. J., *et al.* (1999). Adult health status of women with histories of childhood abuse and neglect. *Am J Med, 107,* 332–339.

Williams, R. A., and Hollis, H. M. (1999). Health beliefs and reported symptoms among a sample of incarcerated adolescent females. *J Adolesc Health, 24,* 21–27.

Woodman, D. D., Hinton, J. W., and O'Neill, M. T. (1978). Cortisol secretion and stress in maximum security hospital patients. *J Psychosom Res, 22,* 133–136.

Woodward, L. J., and Fergusson, D. M. (1999). Early conduct problems and later risk of teenage pregnancy in girls. *Dev Psychopathol, 11,* 127–141.

Worthman, C. M., and Kuzara, J. (2005). Life history and the early origins of health dif-ferentials. *Am J Hum Biol, 17,* 95–112.

Zoccolillo, M. (1993). Gender and the development of conduct disorder. *Dev Psychopath, 5,* 65–78.

Zoccolillo, M., Tremblay, R., and Vitaro, F. (1996). DSM-III-R and DSM-III criteria for conduct disorder in preadolescent girls: Specific but insensitive. *J Am Acad Child Adolesc Psychiatry, 35,* 461–470.

Zoccolillo, M., Meyers, J., and Assiter, S. (1997). Conduct disorder, substance depen-dence, and adolescent motherhood. *Am J Orthopsychiatry, 67,* 152–157.

PART 2

Co-occurring Problems

CHAPTER 4

Using Girls' Voices and Words to Study Their Problems

Joanne Belknap
University of Colorado at Boulder, USA

Emily Gaarder
University of Minnesota-Duluth, USA

Kristi Holsinger
University of Missouri-Kansas City, USA

Cathy McDaniels Wilson
Xavier University-Cincinnati, USA

Bonnie Cady
Colorado Division of Youth Corrections, USA

One of the most common needs delinquent girls report to researchers is the desire to be listened to and understood. This should come as no surprise, given the many ways problem girls have been misrepresented, judged, and blamed for their own victimization. Although the study of girls' problem behaviors has existed for some time (e.g., Lombroso and Ferrero, 1895; Thomas, 1923, 1967; Cohen, 1955; Cloward and Ohlin, 1960; Konopka, 1966; Cowie, Cowie, and Slater, 1968; Vedder and Sommerville, 1970), the data have historically often been interpreted through a sexist, classist, and racist lens (see Smart, 1976; Klein, 1980; Mann, 1984; Naffine, 1987; Chesney-Lind and Hagedorn, 1999; Rafter and Gibson, 2004; Belknap, 2007). Some early scholars assumed that girls' biggest strains in life were finding boyfriends, dates, and husbands (e.g., Cohen, 1955; Cloward and Ohlin, 1960) and there was a practice by many of these early researchers to view girls' (and women's) offending/deviance and sexuality as one in the same (e.g., Lombroso and Ferrero, 1895; Thomas, [1923]

Understanding Girls' Problem Behavior: How Girls' Delinquency Develops in the Context of Maturity and Health, Co-occurring Problems, and Relationships, Edited by Margaret Kerr, Håkan Stattin, Rutger C. M. E. Engels, Geertjan Overbeek and Anna-Karin Andershed © 2011 John Wiley & Sons, Ltd.

1967; Cohen, 1955), a practice never used in the analyses of boys' problem behaviors. Indeed, participating in consensual sex was viewed as a behavioral problem for girls, while ignored or lauded for boys (see Chesney-Lind and Sheldon, 1981; Heidensohn, 1985; Naffine, 1987; Belknap, 2007). Even girls' rape *victimizations* have been used to portray them as deviant and even delinquent (e.g., Odem, 1995; Hagedorn, 1999).

Amidst these shallow and biased interpretations, there were a handful of studies offering more insight. Ruth Morris's (1964) work posited that girls were less delinquent than boys because they experienced less subcultural support and more disapproval for delinquency and other problem behaviors than boys. Sandhu and Allen's (1969) study reported that girls' delinquency was unrelated to their efforts to find boyfriends and husbands.

With the second wave of the women's movement in the 1970s, a number of feminist scholars tackled the male-centered status quo in criminology, pointing out the overt and covert sexism in the canon (e.g., Chesney-Lind, 1974; Rasche, 1975; Klein and Kress, 1976; Smart, 1976). In the 1980s, the body of feminist analyses chastising mainstream criminology, sometimes referred to as 'male-stream' criminology, grew rapidly (e.g., Klein, 1980; Smart, 1981, 1982, 1989; Leonard, 1982; Chesney-Lind and Rodriguez, 1983; Mann, 1984; Rafter, 1985; Morris, 1987; Naffine, 1987; Daly and Chesney-Lind, 1988; Simpson, 1989).

In their review of the research on girls in gangs in the United States from 1927 to 1977, Chesney-Lind and Hagedorn (1999, p. 6) attributed the lack of theory and abundance of sexism and racism in these writings to 'beginning attempts by white male social scientists, social workers, and journalists to describe a phenomenon in which they had little interest.' Similarly, in a classic article called "Feminism and criminology," Daly and Chesney-Lind (1988) refer to the phenomenon of trying to "fit" girls and women into studies and theories designed to explain boys' and men's problem behaviors as the 'add-women-and-stir' approach.

In short, over a century of male-centered criminology conducted almost exclusively by male researchers until the 1970s had a two-fold result: invisibility *or* biased representations. More specifically, both girls and women were virtually ignored (invisible), *or* if made visible, their far-fetched depictions were often made through distorted lenses based on classed, raced, and sexed stereotypes. At the same time that we acknowledge girls' invisibility and, when visible, the troubling portrayals, the renowned Australian feminist legal scholar, Ngaire Naffine, points out the necessity of also recognizing the significant and powerful contribution of feminist criminologists:

> [F]eminist criminology is a healthy, robust and rich oeuvre which poses some of the more difficult and interesting questions about the nature of (criminological) knowledge. A hallmark of feminist criminology and of feminism generally, is its willingness to put itself to precisely the sort of critical scrutiny it has

applied to others. The work of feminists consistently displays sensitivity to its working assumptions and a willingness to subject them to revision. (Naffine, 1996, pp. 4–5)

The purpose of this chapter is to highlight the significant impact of feminist criminology on the larger field of criminology, most specifically in the qualitative methods used to garner data on girls' and women's "own words," and in regard to the development of the pathways perspective in studying the etiology of problem behaviors. We will begin with a brief overview of the contributions of feminist and qualitative research, and then provide specific examples of our own and others' work on girls' problem behaviors in light of the pathways perspective. The pathways perspective is described in more detail later in this chapter, but the major tenet of the pathways perspective is to examine events, often traumatic events, which seem to increase an individual's risk of offending or being labeled "offender." The pathways approach is similar in some respects to the life-course perspective, in that both approaches attempt to determine the succession of events that lead to offending. They differ in that the life-course data collection is prospective (longitudinal) in nature while the pathways research is retrospective (collected at one point in time about past occurrences); the life-course model is a far more expensive means of data collection (due to the prospective method) compared to the pathways approach; the majority of the life-course research data has been conducted on boys while pathways research is almost exclusively on girls; and, finally, the pathways approach has focused more heavily on traumatic life events than the life-course perspective has.

FEMINIST AND QUALITATIVE METHODS

Hesse-Biber, Leavy, and Yaiser (2004, p. 3) view feminist scholarship as "challenging hierarchical modes of creating and distributing knowledge." Similarly, Harding (2004, p. 39) emphasizes the need for feminist scholars to "create research that is *for* women in the sense that it provides less partial and distorted answers to questions that arise from women's lives and are not only about those lives but also about the rest of nature and social relations." Although "feminist methods" per se does not offer any new methods, it does grapple with such topics of changing the hierarchy between the researcher and the researched, rejecting an androcentric (male-centered) bias, and understanding the process of "othering" by which researchers detach from their participants. Hesse-Biber and her colleagues (2004, p. 12) describe the "othering" process and provide reasons why it is fundamental to acknowledge othering when conducting feminist research:

> Positivist science assumes a subject-object split where the researcher is taken for granted as the knowing party. The researcher and researched, or, knower and

knowable, are on different planes within the research process. By privileging the researcher as the knowing party a hierarchy paralleling that of patriarchal culture is reproduced. Unequal power relations between the researcher and the research participants serve to transform the research subject into an object.

Following this, a primary goal of much of feminist scholarship is to allow the participants to be the "experts" on their own lives, reporting and interpreting their own experiences. This does not mean that the researcher does not provide critical and careful analyses and interpretations of the data (be they quantitative or qualitative). Rather, the researcher considers his or her own interpretations alongside those of the participant, sometimes even asking research participants to review and comment on interview transcriptions or draft manuscripts.

Ramazanoğlu and Holland (2002, p. 15) point out that "[t]here is no research technique that is distinctively feminist," rather feminist researchers have "developed, and experimented with, qualitative, politically sensitive research styles and fieldwork relationships, because this suits their purpose of making diverse women's voices and experiences heard." They state that feminist research can also be quantitative and use additional techniques, and, indeed, may require approaches such as quantitative methods depending on the research question. They conclude: "There is no research method that is consistently or specifically feminist" (Ramazanoğlu and Holland, 2002, p. 15). Rather, the goal is to address the power relations between the researcher and the researched, and when necessary, to allow women's and girls' voices, so that they are able to define and describe their own experiences.

There are certainly feminist-friendly or feminist-informed studies that use quantitative methods, such as those exploring girls' arrest and incarceration rates, how girls' demographic characteristics are related to their likelihood of victimization and offending or the length of their sentences. Yet there has also been a need to 'step back' from quantitative studies, particularly when the researcher is unsure of which questions to start asking. Certainly, many of the authors in this chapter have used quantitative studies to examine such feminist criminology topics as the gendered nature of girls' and boys' delinquency risk factors (Belknap and Holsinger, 2006) and the sexual abuse histories of incarcerated women (McDaniels-Wilson and Belknap, 2008).

The remainder of this chapter will be an examination of significant studies addressing the risk factors for girls' problem behaviors, most commonly childhood traumas, previously missing in the delinquency theories on girls' *or boys'* offending. We refer to these as the pathways perspective. Many of the studies first reporting these childhood traumas as precursors to girls' problem behaviors started by using girls' voices to study their problem behaviors (often prostitution).[1] This section is followed by reports about our own research where we drew on girls and women's reports about their childhood traumas. We also discuss how the authors used qualitative research to collect information on troubled girls, or information about the troubled childhoods of adult women prisoners.

A BRIEF HISTORY OF THE PATHWAYS PERSPECTIVE ON OFFENDING

As stated in the last section, feminist research is not restricted to qualitative methods, but it is certainly encouraging of qualitative research when the goal is to capture the researched individuals' voices and when the work is significantly exploratory in nature. Given that most of the early studies on girls' (and women's) problem behaviors were fraught with demonizing, sexualizing, and otherwise misrepresenting them in sexist, racist and classist manners, it is hardly surprising that the early feminist studies beginning with the second wave of the women's movement (particularly research in the 1970s and 1980s) tended to employ qualitative methods. To our knowledge, there is no definitive study or scholar that identified the 'pathways perspective' in examining girls' roads to problem behaviors. Rather, the studies that attempted to examine delinquent girls and offending women's histories that found significant childhood traumas (and often adulthood traumas as well) preceding problem behaviors, started referring to this trajectory from trauma victim to offender as "feminist pathways research," "the pathways perspective," or simply "pathways research" (see Belknap, 2007, p. 71).

The first study consistent with the pathways perspective that we know of was conducted by James and Meyerding (1977). They used multi-methods techniques, which included ethnographic field observations, interviews and questionnaires, to study prostitutes (sex workers), many of whom were adolescent street walkers. James and Meyerding's (1977) study is astounding in many ways, not the least of which was their approach to collect data using multi-methods, a practice so rare at that time but lauded as ideal more recently (e.g., Hantrais, 2005). James and Meyerding (1977) were also remarkable in their design and interpretations, as they used none of the traditional voyeuristic and debasing manners to study girls' (and women's) problem behaviors. But perhaps most notable about James and Meyerding (1977) are their findings, which would not have been possible if data were collected in the more traditional means: They found extraordinarily high rates of incest and other sexual abuses, something that was never included in the risks for delinquent or adult offending behaviors for either girls/women or boys/men. Given the incredible contribution of this study to knowledge in the etiology of crime/delinquency and the stature of the journal (*American Journal of Psychiatry*) in which it was published, it is astonishing that this study was only cited once in the 1970s, and 46 times each in the 1980s and 1990s.[2]

Four years later, Silbert and Pines (1981) published their study (consistent with the pathways perspective), using public service announcements and word of mouth to recruit 200 current and former prostitutes (sex workers) in the San

Francisco Bay area. They also found alarming levels of self-reported child sexual abuse, often perpetrated by fathers or father figures (e.g., step-fathers, foster fathers, etc.). Then two years later Chesney-Lind and Rodriguez (1983) published an article that also found severe and prevalent child abuse experienced by 16 incarcerated women with whom they conducted in-depth one-on-one interviews. Significantly, all three of these studies reported running away from home as a major coping strategy to escape family-perpetrated abuse, only to encounter additional abuse on the streets (James and Meyerding, 1977; Silbert and Pines, 1981; Chesney-Lind and Rodriguez, 1983).

Four studies published in the early 1990s are also consistent with the pathways perspective. Arnold's (1990) interviews with 60 incarcerated African American women and found that their resistance to their childhood victimizations resulted in them being officially processed as delinquents. Fox and Sugar's (1990) interviews with 39 Aboriginal Canadian incarcerated women found extensive violent victimizations in their childhood histories that were frequently tied to their marginalization by gender, race/ethnicity, and age. In addition to abuses perpetrated against them in their homes, many reported the trauma of abuses perpetrated by foster home guardians and officials working in juvenile delinquent facilities (Fox and Sugar, 1990). Shaw's (1991) survey of incarcerated women in Canada reported extraordinarily high rates of physical and sexual abuse compared to the general (non-incarcerated) population. Gilfus (1992) conducted 20 in-depth interviews with incarcerated women who reported that their entries into street crime offending were often a response to survival strategies of running away from home. Like many of the other girls and women in pathways studies, they ran away from home to escape sexual and physical abuse, only to be encounter additional abuse living on the streets. Since the mid-1990s numerous other studies document findings consistent with the pathways approach, providing more evidence for the harsh realities of offending girls' and women's childhoods before they were incarcerated (e.g., Daly, 1992; Lake, 1993; Klein and Chao, 1995; Singer et al., 1995; Comack, 1996; Richie, 1996; Coker *et al.*, 1998; Girshick, 1999; Owen, 1998; Browne, Miller, and Maguin, 1999; Belknap and Holsinger, 2006).

This section briefly reviewed the research documenting the pathways perspective on female problem behaviors. Again, the pathways perspective views traumatic and other troubling antecedent events as significant risk factors in girls' subsequent deviance and offending behaviors.[3] It is probably apparent to the reader that the majority of the studies reported in this section drew on data garnered from in-depth interviews or ethnographies. However, some were quantitative in nature as well.

The remainder of this chapter reports on our own research where we used girls' voices and words to inform us. Most of us have also used quantitative methods in our research, including research on the topics reported herein. The point of this chapter, however, is to familiarize the reader with the power and contribution of girls' reports on their own experiences (and adult women's reports on their childhood experiences) when they are not limited to checking boxes on a survey, or having an interviewer do this for them.

THE POWER OF GIRLS' WORDS AND VOICES

In this section, where we report on the studies we have conducted using girls' and women's verbal and written reports to us, we will describe a variety of studies. What these studies have in common is that they used solely or at least partially, girls' (and sometimes adult women's) words and voices about their experiences prior to being processed as delinquents and/or adult offenders. Additionally, the studies described in this section are related because the first author, Joanne Belknap, was involved as a co-author/ researcher in all of the studies. When the words 'I' or 'my' are used, they will be to refer to Joanne Belknap. This section will be divided into subsections based on the studies.

The Ohio Focus Group Study (Data Collected in 1996)[4]

As a result of the 1992 Reauthorization of the Juvenile Justice and Delinquency Prevention Act of 1974, the US Congress provided funding to a number of states to conduct research on gender-specific services and needs for delinquent girls. The Ohio Office of Criminal Justice Services applied for and oversaw the portion of these federal monies acquired by Ohio, and brought together 19 individuals committed to improving responses to delinquent girls, known as the Gender Specific Services Work Group (GSSWG). After numerous meetings to brainstorm approaches to study the needs of Ohio's delinquent girls, the GSSWG determined that focus groups would be the ideal method to meet with incarcerated and otherwise detained girls to learn of their experiences. Focus groups allow a more relaxed setting to collect data, where the participants can respond to a variety of questions in less formal or official setting, where the researched outnumber the researchers (see Wilkinson, 2004).

In September and October of 1996, Kristi Holsinger and I conducted six focus groups with delinquent girls across Ohio (N = 58 girls) who were in group homes, on probation, in detention, on house arrest, or in a diversion program. They ranged in age from 13 to 20 years old and reported that they ranged from 4 to 17 years old when they were first officially processed by the juvenile justice system. Approximately three fourths of the girls were African American or biracial, and the remainder were White. We also held six focus groups with professionals who work with delinquent girls, such as social workers, institutional 'corrections' officers, psychologists, and probation officers.

In the first focus group a very young looking girl told us the following story after we asked "What happened that you got into trouble the first time?" She described being about seven years old when her father died, murdered by her uncle. She not only witnessed the murder, but she was the only witness and her father died with his head in the girl's lap. Her uncle subsequently went to prison. After describing this tragedy, with almost no affect other than a tired-sounding voice, she reported: "I don't know. Everything just went downhill after that." When we asked if she had received any counseling or help at school or elsewhere to recover from her father's death/murder, she told us there was nothing for her, no one asked to help. Here are some other statements from the girls during the focus groups:

- "When I was 11, I saw my father get killed. I had a lot of anger."
- "It's hard to get off pot when you smell it and your parents are doing it in front of you."
- "I had no structure. My older brother brought me up. My parents divorced when I was two, and my mom was gone a lot. If mom could have sat down and talked with me and told me what I should or shouldn't be doing...."
- "HIV– I have two girlfriends and tons of guy friends with HIV. One's 12 [years old]."
- "My mom sold pot and some coke and turned tricks. I started to steal from my mom's stash to give to my older friends."
- "My mother and my father abused me physically and verbally. My father raped my sister. I didn't have anyone."
- "My problems with physical-sexual abuse built up and I let them build up. I never talked to anyone, because going to counseling sounds like you're crazy."
- "Trouble runs in family, everyone in my family has been in trouble except my mom, my brother was suicidal, I saw so much violence."
- "I wanted someone to love me ... to talk to me ... to tell me right from wrong ... someone to help me with my homework and just be there for me. They (her parents) did not have time. They did not talk to me in an appropriate manner. They were always yelling and hitting."

The Colorado Focus Group Study (Data Collected in 2000)[5]

I moved to the University of Colorado in 1998, and in the Spring of 2000, Bonnie Cady, a client manager with the Colorado Department of Youth Corrections with over two decades of experience working with delinquent girls, attended a research presentation I was giving about the Ohio focus group study. Almost immediately we decided we wanted to work together and met regularly to plan a focus group study of Colorado girls. Like the Ohio focus group study, the Colorado focus group study was collaborative, also known as practitioner-informed, where Cady and I met routinely with ten others invested in and working with delinquent girls in the state of Colorado in a group we called the Young Women's Research Group (YWRG).

The main difference in method between this and the Ohio focus group study was that we added focus groups with pre-adjudicated girls. That is, in addition to the focus groups in each of five regions in Colorado with committed girls (already processed as delinquents) and with professionals who worked with delinquent girls, we also conducted focus groups with pre-adjudicated girls (girls currently on the trajectory to becoming committed delinquents but not officially judged as delinquents). This was due to a suggestion by the practitioners, and ended up being very important as it documented what they suspected: Girls with harsh lives fraught traumas, including victimizations, must be adjudicated before they can get help (e.g., drug addiction treatment, sexual abuse recovery work, etc.). Thirty girls took part in the five focus groups for committed delinquents across Colorado, and another 33 girls took part in the five focus groups for pre-adjudicated girls that took place across Colorado. They ranged in age from 13 to 17 years old and their ages at the time of their first involvement with the juvenile justice system ranged from age seven to 17 years old. What follows are some of the girls' words when asked what they thought led to them getting in trouble in the first place:

- "I was sexually and emotionally abused at home a lot ... that was why I kept leaving. I didn't want to be home with the abuse."
- "My brother's death. He was 20."
- "My father sexually abused me when I was six. When I got older I started doing drugs, gangs, getting pregnant, running away from home, mostly drugs. I started going to detention facilities and all that. I've been in and out for so long it's hard for them to find placement for me."
- "My mother's death when I was 13."
- "My dad's in prison for life."
- "My step-dad's on death row."
- "My mom and dad were too busy doing crack. They used to beat on me. It was hard for me."
- "I wasn't raised with my biological family – some of them were in gangs and stuff. I wanted to be like my adoptive brother and be in trouble all the time."

In some of the other focus groups questions, girls reported the following:

- "My stepdad used to hit us, and they said he didn't have rights to hit us. They sent us away for six months. They took us away from our mom."
- [What are your goals for the future?] "I want to be a lawyer, send my mom to jail."
- "My family said you ain't gonna make it, you're going to be a criminal just like your brother. He's sitting on death row right now for killing three people. I know I don't want my daughter to grow up like I did. I love her so much. My dad was never there for me; my mom was a drug addict, alcoholic, living everywhere."
- "I lost my baby because my dad beat me, and the stress of foster care. This has been the hardest time of my life."
- "My dad was in prison all my life. Sometimes things happen when people are young."

The Study of Girls Waived to Adult Court and Serving Sentences in a Women's Prison (Data Collected in 1998 and 1999)[6]

In the summer of 1997, Emily Gaarder and I wrote a proposal to study girls who had been convicted of crimes in adult court and were serving their sentences in an adult women's prison in the Midwest. Acquiring approval to do this study was arduous because the prison wanted to 'protect their rights as minors.' This seemed more than a bit ironic to us since their status as minors had already been stripped away by the court system. Furthermore, we had crafted an extremely careful research proposal that was designed to minimize any negative impact on the girls and protect their confidentiality. One of the ways we sought to minimize the negative effects of participating in the interviews was to avoid asking direct questions about any sexual abuse and assault the girls may have experienced during their lifetime. We felt that the link between sexual abuse and girls' delinquency was already well established, and we did not want to re-traumatize them, especially since we knew the girls had limited access to psychological services in the prison. Indeed, the prison did not even offer the girls access to the support group for survivors of abuse (only the adult women were allowed to attend).[7]

After many months of negotiations, we were finally allowed to interview some of the young women who had come into the prison as minors but were now 18 or older. After we conducted these interviews with seemingly no problems, the prison administration and corrections research office for the state allowed us to interview all of the girls/women in the prison who had come in as minors, even if they were still minors.[8]

Between July 1998 and August 1999 we conducted interviews with 22 young women who had convictions for their cases waived to adult court and were serving time in the large state women's prison. The women ranged from 16 to 19 years old at the time of the interviews. At the time of the offense for which they were incarcerated, three of the girls were 15 years old, six were 16 years old, and 13 were 17 years old. According to their self-identifications of race/ethnicity, half of the girls were white, six were African-American, one was Latina, and four were bi-racial (one was Mexican-American and African-American, and three were White and American Indian).

The first girl that I interviewed identified as White and was 16 when she was tried and convicted as an adult. She had been arrested several times for running away. She had spent overnights in juvenile detention, and had been in foster home placements. However, she had nothing in terms of a serious offense history prior to the crime for which she was incarcerated. When I first talked to her and asked her, as an ice-breaker, what kind of person she was, she told me she was someone who really liked other people, and that she enjoyed interacting with others, including the other girls in the girls' wing of the women's prison. Then she said wistfully: "I'm a people person.

It's hard to be a people person in prison." This seemed like the understatement of the century given that these young study participants almost all talked about how they felt like their humanity was stripped from them. (Girls were discouraged from forming close friendships with each other in the prison, and the guards were told to avoid engaging in 'personal' conversation with the girls (and women) they supervised. Indeed, the guards only called the girls by their last names.)

When I asked the same girl to talk about the crime for which she was now serving time, she reported that a male acquaintance, significantly older, lent her his car for a few hours while he was visiting a friend. She drove around to visit all of her friends. When she was leaving one friend's house she saw a police car pull up behind her, putting the flashing lights on that signaled for her to stay in the stopped car. She waited for the officers to get almost to her car and then she took off in what ended up being a high-speed chase. She struck an adult male pedestrian at a crosswalk, hitting the pole holding the stop light for the intersection (as well as the pedestrian). She awoke the next day from a coma in the hospital and her grandmother told her what she had done. She was convicted of involuntary manslaughter, resisting arrest, and aggravated vehicular homicide.

She appeared to be genuinely and thoroughly remorseful for her crimes. When I was leaving she asked if I would like to see a poem she had written in her cell the night before. After I read it, I asked if I could type it into my computer. She seemed flattered that I wanted to have it for the study. This is the poem she wrote:

I have walked the darkness, seen the death, the dying the lost souls.
I have reached my heart out to some, helped take the pride and faith away from others.
I have lied, cheated, and stole, but I have loved, been honest, given everything I have to offer.
I have struggled to obtain goals that I was told I'd never achieve. I've done things so shameful to have ever been thought of.
I've experienced pain and misery; also happiness and love. I've been lonely but never really alone.
I've had someone to turn to yet, and no one I felt I could trust.
I've had people see me eye to eye, and then not understand me at all.
I've cried so many tears, fought my many fears, and have struggled throughout the years to survive.
I've been locked away from society, but I'll have my freedom someday. May be soon?
I've learned there's not just black and white but gray in between but I see that others are blind to this.
I have had faith and have lost hope. I have felt lost and been found. I'm young, but I am old beyond my years. My mind is open but is strong, cleared and yet cluttered through everything, every change, every emotion of

thought; I've experienced another and then found a brighter side. With
every darkness there is light, just time can really take time.
But I will survive!

I have read this poem on many occasions when giving talks about this study, as it captures so many aspects of this girl and many other girls who have been in my studies. First, I did not realize until I started doing the interviews that I was assuming that the girls would not be very smart. Instead, we encountered many girls with uncanny insights into not only their own lives, but the hypocrisy of the prison (e.g., some were in for drug possession or use, yet they were encouraged to use psychotropic drugs by the health professionals in the prison).

Second, the range of emotions captured in this poem, from very positive and hopeful to very negative and devastated, was very consistent with the quantitative findings from a survey of institutionalized delinquent boys and girls in Ohio on a project Kristi Holsinger and I designed. Girls reported very high levels of both positive *and* negative self-esteem items, and while there were no gender differences in reporting measures of high self-esteem, the girls were significantly more likely than the boys to report the measures of low self-esteem (Belknap and Holsinger, 2006).

Almost all of the girls in this study reported horrific experiences. One girl reported that her mother 'prostituted her out' in exchange for drugs. When she moved to her father's house to escape this, she was sexually abused by a male friend of her father's who lived in the home. Her father refused to believe her (but allowed that if it had happened, then it was her fault). She was sent to a foster home, while the man who had abused her remained in her home. She ran from the foster home a week later and conducted a drive-by shooting of her father's home with a boy she knew. As a result, the man the girl reported as raping her was paralyzed from the waist down. The girl's father then went around their community to collect signatures in support of trying his daughter as an adult. (The boy who was the co-offender was also tried and convicted as an adult and is serving time in a men's prison.)

Emily Gaarder came up with the title of our first article: 'Tenuous borders.' I love this title because it captures the twisted questions: 'Are these girls children, or are they adults? Are they offenders, or are they victims?' It was clear that in none of the cases did the girls have their traumatic victimizations responded to by the state. Yet when they offended they were convicted at the deepest end of the criminal legal system for youth: being tried and convicted as an adult and serving a sentence in an adult prison. Most of the girls had mild to moderate offending histories. In fact, five had no prior record, and ten had never been placed in foster care, residential treatment, or a long-term juvenile correctional program before being sentenced to adult prison. Many of these girls had never been given a chance to succeed in the juvenile justice system before being subject to adult sanctions.

A Study of Incarcerated Women's Sexual Abuse Histories (Data Collected in 1996)[9]

In the mid-1990s, Cathy McDaniels-Wilson put together what I believe is the most extensive set of survey questions for incarcerated women (or anyone else, for that matter) on their sexual abuse histories, accounting for the age at the time of the abuse, the type of abuse (ranging from ogling to rape), and a variety of victim-offender-relationships (e.g., neighbor, father, step-father, mother's boyfriend, minister, teacher, cousin, etc.). In addition to collecting 391 usable surveys completed by the women, McDaniels-Wilson conducted intensive one-on-one, face-to-face interviews with ten women who wrote on the surveys that they would be willing to be interviewed about their sexual abuse histories (thus employing multiple methods for the data collection).

The sexual abuse findings from these surveys are truly staggering: seventy percent of the women report at least one event that is legally considered rape in most states in the United States, and most victims have multiple rape victimizations by a variety of perpetrators (McDaniels-Wilson and Belknap, 2008). Many of the women described the effects of child-sexual victimization on them in the one-on-one interviews:

- "I get angry – I mean, just to think that somebody was supposed to care about you, be a part of your family. I get angry, I get hurt, but I try not to think about it because I don't like the feeling."
- "Oh-h, when it first started happening, I can remember stealing liquor from my mother, and then I graduated from the liquor, and I started taking pills– I took a lot of pills. I remember one time it happened, I took 15 valium–I didn't know what they were, but I took them, and I wound up in the hospital."
- "It's hard. For one thing, I have come to realize it wasn't my fault, and I have no reason to dislike me for something somebody else did. I've done learned not to claim their problems; I have to deal with my own. I just try to be real and accept that it happened. The only thing that upsets me is that the person that did it died and I didn't get to confront him about it, and the only regret that I have is that they died since I've been here, and I had built up to the point where I told my mother. I don't think she believed me, but that's okay too. And, I'm mad, I'm pissed off because I never, ever, never, got to confront him about what he did to me! And, when we were growing up, he was always parading around like he was the most favorite uncle–always giving, giving, giving, but nobody realized what he was taking. That's what, oh-h-h, really gets to me."
- "You know, it all started happening to me at such a young age, I don't really know if I ever felt good about myself, because I never really had a chance to. It was just like –I'm a little girl, and then I just feel – I don't know how to explain it – it's just, just – one minute you're clean, and the next minute, you just feel so dirty, you feel worthless, like 'why is this happening to me?' And,

it is possible, you know, because once I took that first drink, it was over – it just got worse and worse and worse. And once the alcohol didn't give me the feeling I wanted, I went searching for something else. And once I got tired of that feeling, I wanted another feeling, I went to something else. And, you know, when my one means ran out of me being able to get it, like when my mother got hip to me stealing her medication, I would start stealing some-body else's; then I started stealing out of the stores; then I started selling my body; and then it just went downhill from there. I can remember a point in time in my life where I actually got a job and had my own place, had my family, and, you know, I felt good about myself. But, in reality, I think it was just a cover-up for the way I was really feeling, not admitting to what hap-pened, not accepting what happened – but just dealing with it day by day."

CONCLUSION

This chapter provides a historical overview of the studies on delinquent girls (and incarcerated women) that from the late 1800s to the 1960s were conducted almost exclusively *by* men *about* girls and women who were typically several economic classes below them, and often a different race/ethnicity. Such studies are ripe with sexist, racist, and classed assumptions. The advent of more women attending graduate schools and bringing a feminist focus to their studies' designs and their interpretation of the data resulted in findings on girls and women with problem behaviors that were radically different from the early studies. More specifically, the studies on the etiology of both females' and males' problem behaviors failed to take into account childhood traumas, includ-ing the traumas of child abuse, rape, loss of a parent, experiencing extreme racism, and so on.

The feminist pathways perspective, starting in the late 1970s, identified the often traumatic and even violent childhoods of many delinquent girls and incarcerated women. Many of these cases were girls abused and neglected by their parents or other legal guardians. Indeed, many abused girls run away from home in a survival or help-seeking mode. Often the help-seeking behav-iors were themselves criminalized, such as running away (a status offense[10]), turning to prostitution for survival (for food and shelter), and turning to drugs for self-medication. While life-course research has yielded valuable informa-tion, it often fails to capture serious traumas in youths' lives, and it is more likely to be focused on boys.

The pathways approach, then, provides a significant contribution to the research on risks for delinquent behaviors. More than any other theoretical approach, it examines childhood traumas as risk factors, and how these combine with such injustices as sexism, racism, and classism. Pathways helps us under-stand real youths' lives, and in their own words. The pathways perspective has proven crucial not only to provide a better understanding of girls' problem behav-iors, but also of boys' problem behaviors (e.g., Dodge, Bates, and Pettit, 1990;

Dembo, Williams, and Schmeidler, 1993; Belknap and Holsinger, 2006). More specifically, to truly understand the risk factors for youths' problem behaviors, whether they are girls *or* boys, it is necessary to account for childhood traumas.

Pathways research mostly adds to existing research, rather than negating findings from different theoretical approaches. In particular, the pathways approach documents the significant victimizations, other traumas, and challenges many incarcerated girls and women experienced in childhood. But the pathways findings have also made significant departures from the traditional findings. The pathways perspective portrays delinquent girls as far more dynamic, resilient, and interesting than the boring, hapless, and spineless characterizations of delinquent girls in much of the classic delinquency research (as noted so clearly by Naffine, 1987).

Although some of the pathways research has been quantitative in method, most of it has been qualitative, typically involving lengthy interviews of the participants, but also including written statements and ethnographic data collection. The advantage of such an approach allows the researcher to gather information that s/he may never have thought to ask. For example, when Kristi Holsinger and I attended our first focus group and heard the story of a girl who witnessed her father being murdered by her uncle, we realized the need to ask about the loss of a parent (which seems obvious, yet was rarely asked about in existing studies) when assessing risk factors. We also heard many girls in the focus groups talk about being abandoned by a parent and the pain this involved. Thus, when we devised a survey to compare girls' and boys' pathways, we knew to ask on the survey about parental death and abandonment (Belknap and Holsinger, 2006).

This chapter briefly describes four studies where we used offending girls' and women's voices about their childhood traumas. In two of the studies we used focus groups with girls with problem behaviors, one study in Ohio (Belknap, Holsinger and Dunn, 1997) and one in Colorado (Belknap, Winter, and Cady, 2003; Belknap and Cady, 2007). This allowed the girls the 'power of numbers,' where they were the dominant number of people in the room, outnumbering the researchers, and they were treated as the experts they were on their own lives and experiences. They could respond to each other as well as to the researchers. To watch these focus groups was often to experience how the girls related to their many harsh experiences, how they negotiated them, and how they viewed them with each other. These data would have been impossible to collect on a survey. The other two studies of ours that we reported in more detail in this chapter included in-depth interviews with 22 girls tried and convicted as adults serving their sentences in an adult women's prison (Gaarder and Belknap, 2002, 2004), and in-depth interviews with incarcerated adult women about their sexual abuse histories, which included questions about their childhood sexual abuse victimizations and how it affected their lives (McDaniels-Wilson and Belknap, 2008).

Many of the cases in the research projects we include in this chapter include harrowing and heart-breaking stories that would be difficult to account for in a survey. For example, in one study a girl was charged with carrying a weapon after she started carrying a knife to school – the school and her parents were indifferent to an older boy stalking her to and from school daily. In another study an incarcerated women reported that when she was young her family was part of a religious cult that routinely and repeatedly raped the girls in the sect's families, including her. There was also a girl who was found abandoned at the age of two in an apartment with no food, piles of dog feces on the floor, and a diaper she had been wearing for at least a day. Anyone who works with these girls or does this type of research could provide many more examples, and so could we from our own work.

We are not arguing that there is no place for quantitative research, nor that quantitative research cannot be "feminist." Rather, in this chapter we are hoping to document the power of girls' voices and words about themselves, and how this provides an insight into their lives that cannot necessarily be captured through quantitative research. Certainly quantitative studies typically have better external validity and are far better equipped to document the rates of such important events as the childhood traumas of delinquent girls. But it is also undeniable that girls' own words offer a more human and careful picture of the real lives and experiences of girls with problem behaviors.

NOTES

1   Some of these studies were on adult women in prison asking them about their lives, where most of them reported childhood traumas.
2   The authors thank Lindy Schultz, librarian at the University of Colorado for finding these citation numbers.
3   It is worth noting that some of the studies on boys/men indicate that the pathways approach is an important aspect of explaining boys'/men's problem behaviors (e.g., Dodge, Bates, and Pettit, 1990; Dembo, Williams, and Schmeidler, 1993; Belknap and Holsinger, 2006).
4   This study was published in whole as Belknap, Holsinger, and Dunn (1997).
5   Findings from this study have been published in Belknap, Winter, and Cady (2003) and Belknap and Cady (2007).
6   These findings have been published in Gaarder and Belknap (2002, 2004).
7   Despite our concerns that the interviews would stir up painful memories for the girls, almost all of them reported by the end that they were glad to have taken part. One of the youngest girls we interviewed cried off and on throughout the interview. The interviewer repeatedly asked her if she would like to stop the interview and apologized that it was upsetting. The girl plugged through, but chose not to answer some questions, particularly about her childhood and her mother being shot. At the end of the interview, when the interviewer apologized again, the girl smiled and said she was glad she had done the interview because it was "sort of like releasing a weight from me."
8   Part of our negotiations with the prison and state to collect the data was that we do not identify the actual prison, except as a large women's prison in a Midwestern state.
9   The article publishing these findings, McDaniels-Wilson and Belknap (2008), won the Best Article of 2008 in the journal *Violence Against Women*.
10 A status offense is an offense that only applies to youth, such as running away from home and truancy from school.

REFERENCES

Arnold, R. A. (1990). Women of color: Processes of victimization and criminalization of black women. *Social Justice, 17*, 153–166.

Belknap, J., Holsinger, K. and Dunn, M. (1997). Understanding incarcerated girls: The results of a focus group study. *Prison Journal, 77*(4), 381–404.

Belknap, J., Winter, E., and Cady, B. (2003). Professionals' assessments of the needs of delinquent girls: The results of a focus group study. In B. E. Bloom (ed.), *Gendered Justice* (pp. 209–240). Durham, NC: Carolina Academic Press.

Belknap, J., and Holsinger, K. (2006). The gendered nature of risk factors for delinquency. *Feminist Criminology, 1*(1), 48–71.

Belknap, J. (2007). *The Invisible Woman: Gender, Crime, and Justice*, 3rd ed. Belmont, CA. Wadsworth Publishing Company.

Belknap, J, and Cady, B. (2007). Pre-adjudicated and adjudicated girls' reports on their lives before and during detention and incarceration. In Ruth T. Zaplin (ed.), *Female Crime and Delinquency: Critical Perspectives and Effective Interventions*, 2nd ed. Boston, MA: Jones & Bartlett Publishers.

Browne, A., Miller, B., and Maguin, E. (1999). Prevalence and severity of lifetime physical and sexual victimization among incarcerated women. *International Journal of Law and Psychiatry, 22*(3–4), 301–322.

Chesney-Lind, M. (1974). Juvenile delinquency: The sexualization of female crime. *Psychology Today,* (July), 43–46.

Chesney-Lind, M., and Rodriguez, N. (1983). Women under lock and key. *Prison Journal, 63*(2), 47–65.

Chesney-Lind, M., and Hagedorn, J. M. (eds) (1999). Introduction: Present but invisible. In *Female Gangs in America: Essays on Girls, Gangs and Gender,* Chesney Lind, M. and Hagedorn, J. M. (eds), pp. 6–9. Chicago: Lakeview Press.

Cloward, R. A., and Ohlin, L. E. (1960). *Delinquency and Opportunity: A Theory of Delinquent Gangs.* New York: Free Press.

Cohen, A. K. (1955). *Delinquent boys: The Culture of the Gang.* New York: Free Press.

Coker, A. L., Patel, N. J., Krishnaswami, S., *et al.* (1998). Childhood forced sex and cervical dysplasia among women prison inmates. *Violence Against Women, 4*(5), 595–608.

Comack, E. (1996). *Women in Trouble: Connecting Women's Law Violations to Their Histories of Abuse.* Halifax, NS: Fernwood Publishing.

Cowie, J., Cowie, V., and Slater, E. (1968). *Delinquency in Girls.* London: Heinemann.

Daly, K. (1992). Women's pathways to felony court: Feminist theories of lawbreaking and problems of representation. *Review of Law & Women's Studies, 2*, 11–52.

Daly, K., and Chesney-Lind, M. (1988). Feminism and criminology. *Justice Quarterly, 5*, 497–538.

Dembo, R., Williams, L., and Schmeidler, J. (1993). Gender differences in mental health service needs among youth entering a juvenile detention center. *Journal of Prison and Jail Health, 12*, 73–101.

Dodge, K. A., Bates, J. G., and Pettit, G. S. (1990). Mechanisms in the cycle of violence. *Science, 250*, 1678–1683.

Fox, L., and Sugar, F. (1990). Survey of federally sentenced aboriginal women in the community. Canada: Correctional Service of Canada, 16 pp (or available at http://www.csc-scc.gc.ca/text/prgrm/fsw/nativesurvey/toce_e.shtml).

Gaarder, E., and Belknap, J. (2002). Tenuous borders: Girls transferred to adult court. *Criminology, 40*: 481–517.

Gaarder, E. and Belknap, J. (2004). Little women: Girls in adult prison. *Women & Criminal Justice, 15*(2), 51–80.

Gilfus, M. E. (1992). From victims to survivors to offenders: Women's routes of entry and immersion into street crime. *Women & Criminal Justice, 4*, 63–90.

Girshick, L. B. (1999). *No Safe Haven: Stories of Women in Prison.* Boston, MA: Northeastern University Press.

Hantrais, L. (2005). Combining methods: A key to understanding complexity in European societies? *European Societies, 7*(3), 399–421.

Harding, S. (2004). Rethinking standpoint epistemology, in S. N. Hesse-Biber and M. L. Yaiser (eds), *Feminist Perspectives on Social Research,* pp. 39–64. New York, NY: OUP.

Heidensohn, F. M. (1985). *Women and crime: The life of the female offender.* New York, NY: New York University Press.

Hesse-Biber, S. N., Leavy, P., and Yaiser, M. L. (2004). Feminist approaches to research as a process: Reconceptualizing epistemology, methodology, and method. In S. N. Hesse-Biber and M. L. Yaiser (eds), *Feminist Perspectives on Social Research* (pp. 3–26). New York, NY: OUP.

James, J., and Meyerding, J. (1977). Early sexual experiences and prostitution. *American Journal of Psychiatry, 134*(12), 1381–1385.

Klein, D. (1980). The etiology of female crime: A review of the literature. In S. K. Datesman and F. R. Scarpitti (eds), *Women, Crime, and Justice* (pp. 70–105). New York, NY: OUP.

Klein, D., and Kress, J. (1976). Any woman's blues: A critical overview of women, crime, and the criminal justice system. *Crime and Social Justice, 5*, 34–49.

Klein, H, and Chao, B. S. (1995). Sexual abuse during childhood and adolescence as predictors of HIV-related sexual risk during adulthood among female sexual partners of drug users. *Violence Against Women, 1*(1), 55–76.

Konopka, G. (1966). *The Adolescent Girl in Conflict.* Englewood Cliffs, NJ: Prentice Hall.

Lake, E. S. (1993). An exploration of the violent victim experiences of female offenders. *Violence and Victims, 8*(1), 41–51.

Leonard, E. B. (1982). *Women, Crime, and Society: A Critique of Criminology Theory.* New York, NY: Longman.

Lombroso, C. and Ferrero, W. (1895). *The Female Offender.* London: Fisher Unwin.

McDaniels-Wilson, C., and Belknap, J. (2008). The extensive sexual violation and sexual abuse histories of incarcerated women. *Violence Against Women, 14*(10), 1090–1127.

Mann, C. R. (1984). *Female Crime and Delinquency.* Montgomery, AL: University of Alabama Press.

Morris, R. R. (1964). Female delinquency and relational problems. *Social Forces, 43*(1), 82–88.

Morris, A. (1987). *Women, Crime and Criminal Justice.* Oxford: Basil Blackwell. Naffine, N. (1987). *Female Crime: The Construction of Women in Criminology.* Sydney, Australia: Allen & Unwin.

Naffine, N. (1996). *Feminism and Criminology.* Philadelphia: Temple University Press.

Odem, M. E. (1995). *Delinquent Daughters: Protecting and Policing Adolescent Female Sexuality in the United States, 1885–1920.* Chapel Hill, NC: The University of North Carolina Press.

Owen, B. (1998). *In the Mix: Struggle and Survival in a Women's Prison.* Albany, NY: State University of New York Press.

Rafter, N. H. (1985). *Partial Justice: Women in State Prisons 1800–1935.* Boston, MA: Northeaster Press.

Rafter, N. H., and Gibson, M. (2004). Editors' introduction (pp. 3–33) in *Criminal Woman, the Prostitute, and the Normal Woman* (translated by Nicole Hahn Rafter and Mary Gibson). Durham, NC: Duke University Press.

Ramazanoğlu, C., with Holland, J. (2002). Introduction. In C. R. Ramazanoğlu and J. Holland (eds), *Feminist Methodology: Challenges and Choices,* (pp. 1–22). London: Sage Publications.

Rasche, C. (1975). The female offender as an object of criminological research. In A. M. Brodsky (ed.), *The Female Offender* (pp. 9–28). Beverly Hills, CA: Sage.

Richie, B. E. (1996). *Compelled to Crime: The Gender Entrapment of Battered Black Women*. New York, NY: Routledge.

Sandhu, H. S., and Allen, D. E. (1969). Female delinquency: Goal obstruction and anomie. *Canadian Review of Sociology and Anthropology 5,* 107–110.

Shaw, M. (1991). *Survey of Federally Sentenced Women: Report to the Task Force on Federally Sentenced Women on the Prison Survey*. (User Report 1991–4: Ottawa, Ministry of the Solicitor General).

Shelden, R. G. (1981). Sex discrimination in the juvenile justice system: Memphis, Tennessee, 1900–1917. In M. Q. Warren (ed.), *Comparing Female and Male Offenders* (pp. 55–72). Beverly Hills, CA: Sage.

Silbert, M. H., and Pines, A. M. (1981). Sexual abuse as an antecedent to prostitution. *Child Abuse and Neglect, 5*(4), 407–411.

Simpson, S. S. (1989). Feminist theory, crime, and justice. *Criminology, 27*(4), 605–630.

Singer, M. I., Bussey, J., Song, L., *et al.* (1995). The psychosocial issues of women serving time in jail. *Social Work, 40*(1), 103–113.

Smart, C. (1976). *Women, crime and criminology: A feminist critique*. London: Routledge & Kegan Paul.

Smart, C. (1981). Criminological theory: Its ideology and implications concerning women. L. H. Bowker (ed.), *Women and crime in America* (pp. 6–17). New York, NY: Macmillan.

Smart, C. (1982). The new female offender: Reality or myth? In B. R. Price and N. J. Sokoloff (eds), *The Criminal Justice System and Women* (pp. 105–116). New York, NY: Clark Boardman.

Smart, C. (1989). *Feminism and the Power of Law*. London: Routledge & Kegan Paul.

Thomas, W. [1923] (1967). *The Unadjusted Girl: With Cases and Standpoint for Behavior*. New York, NY: Harper & Row.

Vedder, C. and Sommerville, D. (1970). *The Delinquent Girl*. Springfield, IL: Charles C. Thomas.

Wilkinson, S. (2004). Focus groups: A feminist method. In S. N. Hesse-Biber and M. L. Yaiser (eds), *Feminist Perspectives on Social Research*, New York, NY: OUP.

CHAPTER 5

Developmental Comorbidity of Depression and Conduct Problems in Girls

Kate Keenan
University of Chicago, USA

Xin Feng
The Ohio State University, USA

Dara Babinski
University of Buffalo, USA

Alison Hipwell, Amanda Hinze, Rolf Loeber, and Magda Stouthamer-Loeber
University of Pittsburgh, USA

The authors would like to thank the participants in the Hot Topics Conference: Understanding Girls' Problem Behavior, at the University of Örebro. This work was supported by grants R01 MH66167 and R01 MH56630 from the National Institute of Mental Health.

By the time girls reach late adolescence there is a 1 in 5 chance of their experiencing a major depressive episode. This is twice the rate of depression in males, and represents the most common and disabling disorder for women. There has been very little effort at identifying precursors to depression, however, and as a result, there are few existing programs aimed at preventing this major public health problem.

Understanding the development of comorbid psychopathology also is highly relevant for females. Beginning in adolescence, females are more likely than males to exhibit co-occurring symptoms and disorders (Costello *et al.*, 2003), and functional disability is increased by the presence of comorbidities

Understanding Girls' Problem Behavior: How Girls' Delinquency Develops in the Context of Maturity and Health, Co-occurring Problems, and Relationships, Edited by Margaret Kerr, Håkan Stattin, Rutger C. M. E. Engels, Geertjan Overbeek and Anna-Karin Andershed   © 2011 John Wiley & Sons, Ltd.

(de Graaf *et al.* 2004). Decades of research have supported an increased rate of the most common DSM-IV Axis I disorders among females with a history of conduct problems (Robins, 1986; Teplin, Abram, and McClelland, 1997; Zoccolillo, 1993). Given that MDD is the most common form of psychopathology among females it is not surprising that disorders often co-occur with MDD (Costello *et al.*, 2003). Thus, identifying and perhaps differentiating the preadolescent correlates of MDD from those associated with the comorbidity of MDD and CD has significant implications for understanding the development of disorders that cause the greatest amount of morbidity among adolescent females and contribute the largest portion to the global burden of disease among women (Murray and Lopez. 1997).

In this chapter, we review the existing research on the developmental comorbidity of depression and conduct problems in females. The goals are to describe what is known about the common pathways to comorbidity and the possible contributing factors to the etiology of this comorbidity. We also use data from an ongoing study to examine the overlap of MDD and CD symptoms in the preadolescent period and explore whether impairment and deficits in emotion regulation during preadolescence are differentiated by comorbid MDD and CD as compared to MDD or CD symptoms alone.

OVERVIEW OF NOSOLOGY AND EPIDEMIOLOGY OF DEPRESSION AND CONDUCT DISORDER

As defined in the American Psychiatric Association's *Diagnostic and Statistical Manual* (American Psychiatric Association, 1994, 4th edition), conduct disorder (CD) is a disorder of childhood that is characterized by aggression and violation of rules (e.g., stealing) and social norms (e.g., lying to con). CD is more common among males than females, and this is true regardless of sampling design and age at assessment: in community based samples the rate of CD in girls in approximately 2% in childhood and 4–5% in adolescence (Maughan *et al.*, 2004). The developmental pattern of CD in girls is still not well documented, but cross-sectional studies suggest an increase in the rate of DSM-IV CD among girls in the teen-age years, with the most common symptoms including aggressive symptoms and rule violations (e.g., staying out late), which is similar to the most commonly endorsed symptoms for boys (Maughan *et al.*, 2004). There are no data on predictors of persistence or impairment in females, but among males, covert symptoms of CD (e.g., lying and stealing) as opposed to overt symptoms (e.g., fighting and bullying) are predictive of continued antisocial behavior in adulthood (Lahey *et al.*, 2005). As adults, females with a history of CD are more likely to have problems with mental and physical health, even after controlling for sociodemographic factors (Pajer, 1998; Pajer *et al.*, 2007).

Major depressive disorder, as defined by *DSM-IV* (1994) requires a disturbance in mood (in children this can be manifest as dysphoria or irritability) or anhedonia, and four other symptoms that can include disturbances in sleep, appetite, or concentration, feelings of guilt or hopelessness, and suicidal thoughts or behaviors. Specific symptoms of depression have been shown to be associated with chronicity and impairment in adolescents and adults including suicidal ideation, hopelessness, and worthlessness (Moos and Cronkite, 1999; Laukkanen *et al.*, 2001; Stewart *et al.*, 2005; McCarty, Vander Stoep, and McCauley, 2007).

In contrast to CD, depressive disorders, including major depression, minor depression (still an experimental diagnosis) and dysthymia, are more common among females. In females, the rate of depression is approximately 1–2% in childhood and increases to approximately 15–20% in adolescence (Birmaher *et al.*, 1996). Prior to the 1980s, depression was thought to be very rare in children and adolescents. With the advent of structured methods of assessing depressive symptoms, the prevalence of depression in children and adolescents began to be examined more systematically (Puig-Antich, 1982; Chambers *et al.*, 1985). To date, however, the data on epidemiology and developmental phenomenology of *childhood* depression are still fairly limited.

The study of CD in females and MDD in children is characterized by several nosological controversies. In the case of CD, the debate centers on whether there are additional, female-sensitive symptoms to be included such as relational forms of aggression (e.g., overtly excluding someone from play; see Crick and Grotpeter, 1995; Galen and Underwood, 1997; Xie, Cairns, and Cairns, 2002; Crick, Ostrov, and Werner, 2006) and indirect aggression (e.g., spreading rumors; Bjorkqvist, Lagerspetz, and Kaukiainen, 1992). Further, there are debates about whether symptoms of the corresponding adult disorder, Antisocial Personality Disorder, such as callous-unemotional behavior need to be incorporated in the defining symptoms of childhood CD for both sexes (Lynam, 1997; Frick, Bodin, and Barry, 2000; Pardini, Obradovic, and Loeber, 2006; Schrum and Salekin, 2006). In the case of MDD, there is debate on whether early symptoms in childhood are different from those seen in adolescence and adulthood (Weiss*et al.*, 1992), and whether the inclusion of irritability as a manifestation of "depressed" mood clarifies or confuses the diagnosis.

On the other hand, there are data supporting the use of the current DSM-IV system in a reliable and valid way for females and children for both CD and MDD (Lahey *et al.*, 2000; Keenan *et al.* 2004; Keenan, Coyne, and Lahey, 2008). This is not to say that the current nosology needs no further improvement. There is sufficient support, however, for continued use of the current diagnostic framework for females, and during the period of early childhood and preadoelscence.

Both CD and MDD are highly impairing disorders. Impairment is especially evident in interpersonal relationships with family members, peers and romantic partners, and in academic problems (Gotlib and Hammen, 1991; Harrington, 2004). CD and MDD are associated with an increased risk of early childbearing. And offspring of young mothers with these forms of psychopathology are in turn at heightened risk for developing behavior problems and depression (e.g. Cassidy, Zoccolillo, and Hughes, 1996; Conseur et al., 1997). CD and MDD in girls are also costly in terms of service delivery systems. Estimates based on medical expenditures among children in a Medicaid population (age 3–15) show that CD and depression rank among the most costly of childhood disorders (Mandell et al., 2003).

The comorbidity of CD and MDD is of particular concern because the types of impairments that result are significant in terms of mortality and morbidity. A long-term follow-up of individuals with juvenile depression demonstrated that adults who were diagnosed with comorbid depression and conduct disorders as youth had higher rates of suicidal behaviors and evidenced greater social dysfunction in every domain assessed (e.g., work, friendships, etc) than those diagnosed with depression only (Fombonne et al., 2001). This increased risk for poor outcomes among youth with comorbid MDD and CD may be particularly true for girls. For example, in the Ontario Child Health Study, Joffe, Offord, and Boyle (1988) reported that the odds of manifesting suicidal behavior (including ideation) for girls with CD were 8.6. This risk was higher than that observed for boys with CD (odds ratio = 5.6), despite the fact that the prevalence of suicide is higher in adolescent males than females (Shaffer, 1988). Similarly, Cairns, Peterson, and Neckerman (1988) found that rate of attempted suicide among highly aggressive adolescent females (age 14–15 years) was three times the observed rate of aggressive boys. Thus, co-occurring MDD and CD in girls appears to be have more than simply an additive effect on functioning (the more symptoms the worse the impairment), rather the combination yields an increased risk for very serious outcomes and poor long-term prognosis for general social functioning.

DEVELOPMENTAL COMORBIDITY OF DEPRESSION AND CONDUCT DISORDER IN FEMALES

Relatively little is known about the developmental phenomenology of comorbid CD and MDD in girls. This is mostly due to a lack of sufficiently powered and representative studies that have begun early enough in development to reveal the developmental unfolding of these two conditions. In the Great Smoky Mountains Study the cumulative prevalence of any depressive disorder for girls up through the age of 16 was 11.7% and the prevalence of CD was 3.8%. The risk of concurrent comorbidity of depressive disorders and CD were 10.6 for girls; whereas there was no increase in the odds of co-occurring CD and depressive disorder in boys. However, there was not sufficient data to test whether one disorder was more likely to precede the other (Costello et al., 2003).

There are three common pathways to comorbid MDD and CD that one would hypothesize for girls: CD precedes the onset of MDD, MDD precedes the onset of CD, or the two disorders co-vary over time. There are theoretically based hypotheses to support each pathway, which are not mutually exclusive. In the case of CD preceding MDD, Capaldi (1991) posited that problems arising from CD behaviors leading to feelings of rejection and worthlessness, which in turn place the child at risk for depression. There is some support for this pathway for boys (Capaldi, 1991). Kovacs and colleagues (1988) proposed that depressogenic ways of interacting with other could lead to negative interactions with others, which could increase the risk for conduct problems. CD and MDD could also reflect shared underlying etiology and therefore could wax and wane in concert over time, as has been shown for boys (Lahey *et al.*, 2002).

Results from the existing studies indicate that the highest period of co-occurrence of CD and MDD in girls is in adolescence (Costello *et al.*, 2003; Storvoll and Wichstrøm, 2003). The nature of the developmental timing between CD and MDD however, is still unknown. Although there are retrospective reports of age of onset (e.g., Nock *et al.*, 2006), such studies are not highly useful for determining temporal ordering. Of the existing prospective studies, each possible pathway is supported. Findings from the Dunedin Longitudinal Study (Moffitt *et al.*, 2001) indicate that MDD typically emerges *after* the onset of CD in girls. In contrast, results from the Ontario Child Health Study demonstrate that the co-occurrence of CD and depression appears to be already higher for girls than boys during preadolescence: at ages 4–11, 31.3% of girls with CD had a comorbid emotional disorder and this increased to 48.1% in adolescence. Kovacs and colleagues (2003) have provided quite a bit of data on the course of depression in clinic-referred children. Girls who were depressed during early adolescence had fairly high rates of recurrence of depression ranging from 59.2% at ages 13–15 years to 43.5% at 19–21 years. Comorbid disruptive behavior disorders, which in this study included CD, ODD and ADHD, among girls who were depressed during early adolescence, reached a high of 19.4% at ages 13–15 and decreased to 7.3% at ages 19–21. Thus, the rate of co-occurring disruptive disorders among depressed girls was higher than one would expect in the general population, although the vast majority of girls who were depressed in late childhood/early adolescence did not manifest comorbid CD, and the rate of comorbid MDD and CD in girls was much lower than that observed for boys (Kovacs *et al.*, 2003). In addition, there was a trend toward a decrease in the risk of girls developing comorbid disruptive behavior disorders if the onset of depression was before the age of 10 (Kovacs, Obrosky, and Sherrill, 2003). The authors concluded that among girls, early onset depression appears to be a purer form of affective disorder than later onset depression.

Thus, the developmental phenomenology of comorbid depression and conduct problems appears to vary significantly as a function of sample characteristics (e.g., clinic-referred versus community-based), age of onset of depression, and demographic characteristics. Recently, Wolf and Ollendick (2006) tackled the conundrum of the co-occurrence of MDD and CD and proposed four possible explanations for comorbidity. First, the apparent comorbidity may be an artifact of measurement and sampling. Many studies of comorbidity rely on clinic-referred samples, which is partly due to the feasibility of assessing low base rate symptoms. Thus, the rate may be inflated in these settings in comparison to the population at large. Second, there may be symptom overlap that results in a high rate of comorbidity. This is especially a problem when symptoms of oppositional defiant disorder, such as irritability, are included in the operational definition of conduct problems. Third, one disorder may increase the risk of the other disorder, as in the aforementioned theories posited by Capaldi (1991) and Kovacs *et al.* (1988). Fourth, MDD and CD may co-occur because of shared etiology such as deficits emotion regulation.

Wolf and Ollendick (2006) provided a solid framework upon which to organize research questions aimed at providing useful data on the developmental comorbidity of MDD and CD. We avoid struggling with the first two explanations for comorbidity of MDD and CD by using a community-based sample, which was over-sampled on measures designed to increase the rate of CD and MDD, and by assessing DSM-IV symptoms of MDD and CD specifically. Instead we focus on revealing potential clues about the nature of the association between CD and MDD in the preadolescent period. Six questions are posed:

1. What is the rate of DSM-IV symptoms of MDD and CD during preadolesence?
2. What is the overlap between conduct disorder symptoms and depression symptoms during preadolescence?
3. Does depression increase the risk for specific symptoms of CD and vice-versa, and are these symptoms among those known to be most impairing?
4. Do depression symptoms, conduct symptoms, and/or the interaction of the two account for current levels of impairment?
5. Is the co-occurrence of conduct and depression symptoms associated with deficits in emotion regulation?
6. What is the nature of association between depression and conduct symptoms in the stability of symptoms and the prediction to disorder one year later?

Providing answers to these questions will not resolve the debate on the developmental relationship between MDD and CD in girls, but will provide clues about the nature of this relationship. Symptom endorsement and diagnostic overlap will shed some light on the developmental ordering of the two disorders. If symptoms of one disorder are more common than the other, then it is likely that that disorder precedes the onset of the other disorder. If the overlap of MDD and CD, or even symptoms of MDD and CD is quite high during preadolescence, then there would be some support for the hypothesis that these symptoms and disorders co-vary over time and, for at least some girls, may reflect shared etiology. Similarly, if depression increases the risk for specific symptoms of CD that are impairing, or if the reverse is true, depression increases the risk for impairing symptoms of CD, then there may be evidence that one disorder is paving the way for the increases risk for impairment that is observed among adolescents and adults who experienced comorbid CD and MDD as youth. Examining deficits in emotion regulation may reveal clues about possible shared etiology. Finally, the relative effects of CD and MDD symptoms on the short-term stability and predictive utility to disorders one year later will provide preliminary data on the temporal ordering of these two disorders.

We provide answers to these questions using data from the *Preadolescent precursors to depression in girls study*, an ongoing longitudinal study of 232 9-year-old girls. As described below, this is a sample that has some unique advantages for exploring the development interface of MDD and CD in girls.

PREADOLESCENT PRECURSORS TO DEPRESSION IN GIRLS STUDY

The preadolescent precursors to depression in girls study (PGS-E), is a sub-study to the Pittsburgh Girls Study (PGS). The sampling strategy for the PGS-E study provides a unique opportunity for studying the emergence of comorbid conduct problems and depression. The aim of the PGS is to describe the development of conduct disorder in girls from early childhood through late adolescence. In order to achieve this aim, a stratified, random household sample with over-sampling of households in low-income neighborhoods of girls who were between the ages of 5 and 8 years of age was used to increase the sample of girls at risk for developing conduct disorder. Neighborhoods in which at least 25% of the families were living at or below the poverty line were fully enumerated (i.e., all homes were contacted to determine if the household contained an eligible girl) and a random selection of 50% of the households in non-risk neighborhoods were enumerated. This process identified 3974 separate households in which an eligible girl resided. From these households, families moving out of the state, families in which two girls were enumerated, and families in which girls were too old or too young by the start of the study were excluded. The participation rate for the remaining eligible sample was 87%, (N = 2451).

The aim of the PGS-E is to identify precursors to depression. The first goal for the recruitment of the PGS-E, therefore, was to include girls who did not already meet criteria for major depression so that precursors could be studied. We also needed to select a sample that contained enough girls at high and low risk for later depression to generate adequate power to test the proposed hypotheses. Based on our preliminary studies and the existing literature on the prevalence and onset of depression in girls, we elected to over-sample girls who were already showing the emergence of depressive symptoms on the CSI (maternal report) or the Short Moods and Feeling Questionnaire (child report) at age 8. Girls scoring in the upper quartile by either informant or who scored in the 3rd quartile by both informants were identified as eligible and an equal number from the remaining girls was randomly selected. There were significantly more African American than European American girls in the screen high group. Thus, the girls selected from the remainder ($n = 136$) were matched to the screen high group on race. Of the 263 girls identified for recruitment into the PGS-E and eligible for recruitment (i.e., residing with the biological mother in Allegheny County) 232 (88%) participated in Year 01 data collection. Thus, girls in the PGS-E were sampled to increase the risk of *both* conduct problems and depression. In addition, the data that we present here, when the girls are 9 years of age, allow us to test whether comorbid conduct problems and depression are actually emerging prior to adolescence.

Girls and their mothers completed a laboratory assessment during which DSM-IV symptoms of depression were assessed and questionnaires were administered. Symptoms of depression were measured using the *Schedule for Affective Disorders for School- Age Children-Epidemiological 5th version* (K-SADS; see Kaufman *et al.*, 1997), a semi-structured diagnostic interview administered to both the girls and their mothers. We assessed all symptoms of depression, regardless of whether disturbance in mood (i.e., sadness or irritability) or anhedonia were endorsed. Minor and major depressive disorders were generated according to *DSM-IV* (1994) criteria. A second interviewer listened to and coded responses from the digital video of the K-SADS-PL interview to assess interrater agreement ($n = 42$). Intraclass correlation coefficients for total number of symptoms were 0.92, and the kappa coefficient for minor/major depressive disorders were 0.77.

Conduct problems were assessed using child reports on the Child Symptom Inventory (CSI-4, see Gadow and Sprafkin, 1994). The CSI-4 includes *DSM-IV* (1994) symptoms of Conduct Disorder (CD) scored on 4-point scale (0 = "never" to 3 = "very often"). Adequate concurrent validity, and sensitivity and specificity of CD symptom scores to clinicians' diagnoses are reported for the CSI (Gadow and Sprafkin, 1994). In the present study, the internal consistency coefficients for the CD items was adequate $\alpha = 0.69$. To generate symptom levels that corresponded to the frequency threshold for DSM-IV symptoms of CD, endorsement at the level of often or very often was required for bullying, fighting and lying, and endorsement at the level of 'sometimes', 'often', or 'very often' was required for the remaining items.

Deficits in emotion expression were assessed via child report using the *Children's Sadness/Anger Management Scale* (CSMS/CAMS) and the Emotion Expressive Scale (EESC; see Penza-Clyve and Zeman, 2002). The CSMS/CAMS are 12-item self-report measures designed for elementary school-age children. Each item is rated on a 3-point scale, yielding scores on three factors: inhibition, regulation, and dysregulation (alphas = 0.77, 0.62, and 0.60, respectively). Adequate validity has been reported (Zeman, Shipman, and Penza-Clyve, 2001). For the purposes of the present study, scores on inhibited (e.g., I get mad inside but I don't show it), and dysregulated (e.g., "I cry and carry on when I'm mad") sadness and anger were used to measure inhibition and disinhibition, respectively.

The EESC is a 16-item self-report measure yielding scores on two factors: poor awareness and expressive reluctance. Each item is rated on a 5-point scale.

The scale was validated using 9–12-year-old children and has demonstrated internal consistency, test-retest reliability, and construct validity (Penza-Clyve and Zeman, 2002). In the present study, scores on the expressive reluctance factor (e.g., "I do not like to talk about how I feel"; "I prefer to keep my feelings to myself") were used as a broad measure of reluctance to express emotions.

The *Child-Global Assessment Scale* (C-GAS; see Setterberg *et al.*, 1992) is a measure of impairment developed for children 4–18 years of age, which was completed by the caregiver. Scores on the C-GAS range from 1 to 100 with each decile containing a description of the severity of symptomatology in terms of the impact the symptoms have on school, family, and peer relations. Inter-rater agreement on 42 cases of interviewer-generated C-GAS ratings following the child K-SADS was very high: intra-class correlation coefficient (ICC) = 0.91.

RATE OF DSM-IV SYMPTOMS OF MDD AND CD

By youth report, having at least one symptom of depression was more common than having no symptoms. Eighty-four girls (36.2%) reported no symptoms of depression, 51 (22.0%) reported one symptom, 39 (16.8%) reported two symptoms, 38 (16.4%) reported three or four symptoms, and 20 girls (8.6%) reported five or more symptoms. Maternal report of girls' symptoms produced lower rates: 99 (42.7%) girls had no symptoms of depression, 54 (23.3.0%) had 1 symptom, 40 (17.2%) had 2 symptoms, 33 (14.2%) had 3–4 symptoms and 6 (2.6%) had 5 or symptoms. The distribution in depression symptoms by informant was significantly different (Spearman's *rho* = 0.33, $p < 0.001$).

As shown in Table 5.1, the most commonly endorsed symptoms of depression by youth report were the symptoms of appetite disturbance (32.3%), concentration (33.6%) and sleep disturbance (26.3%). Appetite disturbance (32.3%) and concentration (30.2%) were also among the most commonly endorsed symptoms by maternal report.

In this sample, CD symptoms were less commonly report by girls than MDD symptoms: 197 girls (85.3%) reported no symptoms of CD, 22 (9.5%) reported 1 symptom, 5 (2.2%) reported two symptoms, 3 (1.3%) reported 3-4 symptoms, and 4 girls (1.7%) reported 5 or more symptoms. Maternal report of girls' CD symptoms produced comparable rates: 192 (83.1%) girls had no symptoms of CD, 22 (9.5%) had 1 symptom, 8 (3.5%) had 2 symptoms, 6 (2.6%) had 3-4 symptoms, and 3 (1.3%) had 5 or symptoms. The distribution in CD symptoms by informant was not significantly different (Spearman's *rho* = 0.08, $p > 0.05$), and this is due to the majority of girls having no symptoms by both informants. The most commonly endorsed CD symptoms by youth report were stealing (6.4%), cruel to others (4.7%) and destroying property (3.8%). Destroying property (10.4%), stealing (7.9%) and cruel to others (5.2%) were among the most commonly endorsed symptoms by maternal report (Table 5.2).

Table 5.1 Rate of DSM-IV symptoms of depression by informant.

Symptom	Child		Mother		Combined	
	N	%	N	%	N	%
Depressed mood	22	9.5	15	6.5	34	14.7
Anhedonia	16	6.9	10	4.4	25	10.8
Suicidal ideation	24	10.3	2	0.9	26	11.2
Sleep disturbance	61	26.3	18	7.8	71	30.6
Appetite disturbance	75	32.3	75	32.3	124	53.4
Motor disturbance	36	15.5	41	17.7	67	28.9
Concentration	78	33.6	70	30.2	118	50.9
Fatigue/low energy level	24	10.3	3	1.3	26	11.2
Guilt	43	18.5	38	16.4	69	29.7

Table 5.2 Rate of DSM-IV symptoms of conduct disorder by informant.

Symptom	Child		Mother		Combined	
	N	%	N	%	N	%
Destroys property	9	3.8	24	10.4	31	13.4
Steals	15	6.4	18	7.9	31	13.4
Cruel to others	11	4.7	12	5.2	23	9.9
Bullies	7	3.0	6	2.6	12	5.2
Lies	4	1.7	7	3.1	11	4.7
Starts fights	5	2.2	3	1.3	8	3.4
Weapon use	3	1.3	2	0.9	5	2.2
Stealing with confrontation	2	0.8	3	1.3	5	2.2
Cruel to animals	4	1.7	0	0.0	4	1.7
Truancy	2	0.9	0	0.0	2	0.9
Stays out late	5	2.1	0	0.0	5	2.1

As is standard in research on conduct disorder, we combined informants such that a positive endorsement by either informant was sufficient for a symptom to be counted as present. Although research on combining informants for generating depressive symptoms is less well developed, we used the same approach for depression symptoms. Using combined informants, over 70% of nine-year old girls had no symptoms of CD, and the distribution across symptom level declined is a fairly linear pattern from 1 to 5 or more symptoms. The reverse was true for MDD: over 70% of girls had at least 1 symptom of MDD, and the distribution across symptoms level (1 symptom to 5 or more symptoms) was fairly equal. Thus, even using best estimate approaches, symptoms of depression are more commonly endorsed than symptoms of CD in this sample of nine-year-old girls. At one level, these symptom rates are not surprising given that the sample was selected to have higher than average rates of

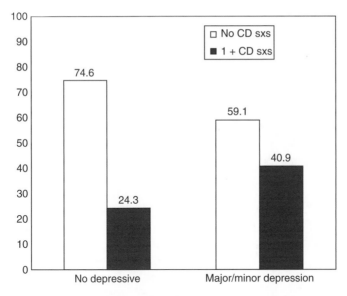

Figure 5.1 Overlap of major/minor depression and CD symptoms among 9-year-old girls.

depression symptoms. If the co-occurrence of CD and MDD emerges concurrently, however, then we would also expect to see fairly high rates of CD symptoms in this sample as well.

OVERLAP OF CD AND MDD DURING PREADOLESCENCE

We sought to determine the nature of the association between symptoms of MDD and CD and overlap of disorders during the preadolescent period with an eye toward answering the question of how early is comorbidity evident. Because of endorsement of conduct symptoms was relatively low and because we were interested in emerging comorbidity, we classified the sample into two groups: those with any symptoms of CD ($n = 64$, 27.7%) and those with no symptoms of CD ($n = 160$, 72.3%) at age 9. Symptoms of depression were common, and thus a sufficient number of girls met criteria for major or minor depression ($n = 44$, 19%). As depicted in Figure 5.1, the odds of have at least one CD symptom given a diagnosis of major or minor depression was 2.12 (95% $CI = 1.07$–4.22), $p < 0.05$. Close to 50% of the girls who met criteria for major/minor depression had at least one symptom of CD compared to 24.3% of the girls who did not meet criteria for major/minor depression. Thus, there is a greater overlap between MDD and CD symptoms than expected by chance, although the odds of the two disorders co-occurring is lower than that reported for adolescents (e.g., Costello *et al.*, 2003).

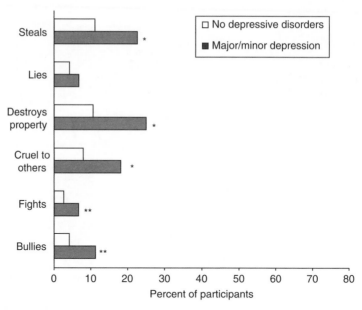

Figure 5.2 Distribution of CD symptoms for girls with or without major/minor depression.

RISK OF ENDORSEMENT OF SPECIFIC SYMPTOMS GIVEN THE PRESENCE OF MDD OR CD

Testing whether MDD increased the risk of specific CD symptoms and vice-versa was the next step. These associations were examined using logistic regression analysis. We did not include the CD symptoms for which the base rate was lower than 3% (i.e., weapon use, stealing with confrontation, cruelty to animals, truancy, and staying out late). Girls who met criteria for major/minor depression were more than twice as likely to have engaged in stealing ($OR = 2.33$, 95% $CI = 1.00-5.38$), destroyed property ($OR = 2.78$, 95% $CI = 1.22-6.35$), been cruel to others ($OR = 2.55$, 95% $CI = 1.01-6.46$), started fights ($OR = 2.88$, 95% $CI = 1.45-5.71$), and bullied others ($OR = 2.79$, 95% $CI = 1.40-5.58$) in comparison to girls who were not depressed (Figure 5.2). Thus, 5 of the 6 symptoms of CD, including both overt and covert symptoms, were more likely to occur if the girl met criteria for a depressive disorder.

The risk of specific symptoms of depression given the presence of CD symptoms was examined the same way (Figure 5.3). Having at least one CD symptom was associated with three of the nine depressive symptoms. Girls with CD symptoms were more likely to be anhedonic ($OR = 2.73$, 95% $CI = 1.17-6.37$, $p < 0.05$), have a disturbance in activity level ($OR = 2.32$, 95% $CI = 1.26-4.27$, $p < 0.01$), and have difficulty concentrating ($OR = 1.9$, 95% $CI = 1.05-3.43$, $p < 0.05$) than girls with no CD symptoms. Although the presence of CD did increase the

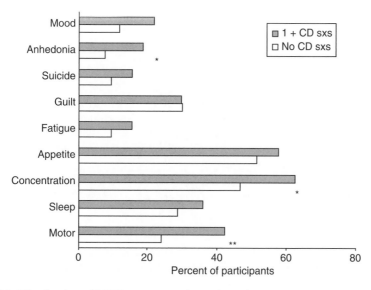

Figure 5.3 Distribution of MDD symptoms for girls with or without symptoms of CD.

risk of endorsement of three of the symptoms of depression, none were what are considered to be among the most impairing symptoms such as depressed mood, suicidal ideation, and worthless.

EFFECTS OF MDD AND CD AND THEIR CO-OCCURRENCE ON IMPAIRMENT

The next question was whether the co-occurrence of MDD and CD symptoms was associated with significantly greater levels of impairment even during this developmental period. A linear regression analysis was used with major/minor depression and 1 or more CD symptoms as the independent measures, and maternal report of the C-GAS as the dependent measure. Both major/minor depression and CD symptoms were independently and equally associated with the continuous impairment score ($\beta = -0.20$, $p < 0.01$, and $\beta = -0.25$, $p < 0.01$, respectively), accounting for 18% of the variance in impairment scores (lower score reflect greater levels of impairment). The interaction of MDD and CD symptoms, however, did not explain unique variance in level of impairment ($\beta = -0.11$). We repeated this analysis using a cut-off of 60 or lower on the C-GAS as the dependent measure, in order to test whether comorbid MDD and CD would be associated with clinically significant levels of impairment. Similarly, both MDD and CD symptoms were associated with the clinically significant impairment by mother's report: odds ratios were 12.36 (95% $CI = 1.08$–142.18) and 20.40 (95% $CI = 2.39$–174.46), respectively. The interaction of MDD and CD

Table 5.3 Effects of symptoms of MDD, CD and the interaction of MDD and CD on deficits in emotion regulation.

Dependent Measure	MDD	CD	MDD × CD	R^2
Expressive reluctance	0.30***	0.05	−0.03	0.08***
Poor awareness	0.36***	0.10	−0.00	0.15***
Inhibition of anger	0.21*	0.02	0.01	0.05*
Dysregulated anger	0.27***	0.30**	−0.16	0.11***
Inhibition of sadness	0.27***	0.08	−0.12	0.05*
Dysregulated sadness	0.06	0.13	0.04	0.03

Note: Values are standardized beta weights; MDD: 0 = no depressive disorders (81.0%); 1 = major/minor depressive disorders (19.0%); CD: 0 = no CD symptoms (72.0%); 1 = one or more CD symptoms (27.6%); *p < 0.05 **p < 0.01 ***p < 0.001.

on clinically significant impairment was not significant. At this age, therefore, we do not observe any increased risk of impaired functioning as a result of co-occurring MDD and CD.

EFFECTS OF MDD AND CD AND THEIR CO-OCCURRENCE ON DEFICIT IN EMOTION REGULATION

Regression analyses were used to test the main effects and the interaction of major/minor depression and CD symptoms on self-reported deficits in emotion regulation. As shown in Table 5.3, major/minor depression was positively associated with all measures of deficits in emotion regulation, with the exception of dysregulated sadness. CD symptoms, on the other hand, were only associated with dysregulated expression of anger. There were no interaction effects found (Table 5.3). Thus, a global set of deficits in regulation of emotion is observed in girls with depressive disorders, and these deficits are not further exacerbated by the presence of CD symptoms.

EFFECTS OF MDD AND CD ON STABILITY OF SYMPTOMS AND EMERGENCE OF DIAGNOSES ONE YEAR LATER

Finally, we examined the extent to which symptoms of CD predicted stability of MDD symptoms and emergence of disorders from ages 9–10 years, and vice-versa. One caveat to acknowledge is that there is often attenuation of symptom endorsement from time 1 to time 2 (Jensen *et al.*, 1995). In the present study, depression symptoms using the K-SADS were assessed at age 9 for the first time, whereas CD symptoms had been assessed beginning at age 5 according to caregiver report and 7 according to child report. Thus, the test-retest attenuation may have affected MDD symptoms and CD symptoms differentially.

Generalized linear models were computed with a Poisson distribution speci-fied for the dependent measure of symptom counts and robust estimators of the standard errors. Logistic regressions were computed for dependent meas-ures of diagnosis. Depression and conduct symptoms at age 9 and the interac-tion of the two were included as independent measures. Prior to computing interaction terms, the symptom variables were centered at the mean.

At age 10, MDD symptoms were predicted by age 9 MDD ($\beta = 0.219$, Wald $\chi^2 = 119.0$, $p < 0.001$) and CD ($\beta = 0.08$, Wald $\chi^2 = 18.8$, $p < 0.001$) symptoms, but not by the interaction of the two ($\beta = 0.00$, Wald $\chi^2 = 0.2$, $p = 0.668$).

Girls who met criteria for major/minor depression at age 9 were excluded prior to testing the predictive utility of MDD and CD symptoms at age 9 to diagnosis at age 10. Depressive symptoms at age 9 ($OR = 1.7$ [95% $CI = 1.2$–2.6), $p < 0.01$) but not CD symptoms ($OR = 0.9$ [95% $CI = 0.6$–1.3), $p = 0.631$), or the interaction of MDD and CD symptoms ($OR = 1.0$ [95% $CI = 0.8$–1.3), $p = 0.861$), were predictive of major/minor depression diagnoses at age 10.

In predicting stability of CD symptoms, age 9 MDD ($\beta = 0.31$, Wald $\chi^2 = 18.85$, $p < 0.001$) and CD ($\beta = 0.17$, Wald $\chi^2 = 22.45$, $p < 0.001$) symptoms, but not by the interaction of the two ($\beta = -02$, Wald $\chi^2 = 1.13$, $p = 0.287$) were significant predic-tors of CD symptoms at age 10. There were too few cases of CD at age 10 to test prediction at the diagnostic level.

CONCLUSION

Judging from the existing literature, the co-occurrence of depression and con-duct problems is a significant public health concern for females because the interaction of these two disorders appears to impact morbidity and possibly mortality for the female herself and for her offspring. Because conduct prob-lems are relatively rare in females, and few studies have been conducted with sufficient sample sizes and periods of assessment, the developmental phenom-enology of this comorbidity is poorly understood. There are data to support multiple pathways to co-occurring MDD and CD in females depending on the sample characteristics and study design. Some studies, however, have used ret-rospective recall, others have lacked clearly operationally defined measures of MDD and CD, and few have used non-clinical samples. This has left open the possibility not only for speculation as to the most common pathway to comor-bidity, but also concern that comorbidity may reflect measurement or ascertain-ment artifact (Wolf and Ollendick, 1996).

In this chapter we examined six questions relevant to the developmental comorbidity of MDD and CD in a sample of 9-year-old girls, with the aim of providing additional data on the developmental interface of MDD and CD. The fact that CD and MDD symptoms were assessed in a reliable and valid way, using a community based-sample, during the preadolescent period is useful with regard to providing clues as to the nature of the co-occurrence of the two disorders early in development. Based on these data, we found that:

- CD symptoms are less common than MDD symptoms during preadolescence among girls, as are rates of disorder
- There is a statistically significant overlap between having at least 1 CD symptom and major/minor depressive disorders in preadolescent girls
- Girls with major/minor depression are at increased risk of engaging in nearly all the overt and covert aggressive CD symptoms that had base rates above 3%
- Girls with CD symptoms are at increased risk for a minority of MDD symptoms including anhedonia, motor disturbance, and concentration problems, none of which are the most impairing symptoms
- Major/minor depression and CD symptoms are both associated with parent-reported impairment, but the co-occurrence of these problems does not explain unique variance in impairment
- Major/minor depression is associated with nearly all deficits in emotion regulation, CD symptoms are associated with dysregulated expression of anger, but no other deficits, and the co-occurrence of these problems does not explain unique variance in deficits in emotion regulation
- MDD and CD symptoms at age 9 accounted for variance in MDD symptoms at age 10, but only MDD symptoms predicted the emergence of new cases of depression, and the interaction of MDD and CD was not a predictor of MDD symptoms or disorders at age 10.

Together, these results point toward MDD preceding CD as a common pathway to comorbidity.

First, although there is a sub-sample of girls who are manifesting problems in both areas at this age, the most common condition is to have one problem or the other, and a substantial number of girls at this age are already meeting criteria for a depressive disorder; this is not the case for CD. On the other hand, the risk for having at least one CD symptom is doubled among girls with a depressive disorder in comparison to girls who have no depressive disorder. We may be capturing, therefore, a developmental period within which comorbidity is emerging, with a fully expressed conduct disorder (i.e., three symptoms) developing over the next few years. This is certainly possible, as symptoms such as truancy and staying out late become part of the girls' developmental repertoire of CD symptoms. In fact, a recent study using the PGS data revealed that the vast majority of girls who do develop DSM-IV CD, manifest their first symptom in childhood (Keenan *et al.* (*in press*), and that "adolescent-onset" might be better conceptualized as elaboration or exacerbation of CD problems during adolescence.

Second, few symptoms of depression were associated with CD at this age, and of those that were associated with CD, none are considered among the most impairing symptoms. The opposite was true for major/minor depression, which was associated with nearly all the CD symptoms tested including both overt and covert symptoms (e.g., stealing, vandalism). This is important because among boys, covert symptoms are predictive of continued dysfunction in adulthood.

Third, at this point in development, we do not observe any increased rate of impairment as a result of co-occurring MDD and CD. Nor do we see any distinct pattern of deficits in emotion regulation among girls with co-occurring MDD and CD. The fact the girls meeting criteria for major/minor depression are characterized as having deficits in most domains of emotion regulation, also lends support to the hypothesis that depression paves the way for the development of CD in girls.

Fourth, although CD symptoms at age 9 do explain variance in later depression symptoms at age 10, the magnitude of the effect was less than that observed for age 9 depression symptoms. This was not the case in predicting CD symptoms at age 10. Results from that analysis demonstrated that CD and MDD symptoms were relatively equally predictive of later CD symptoms. In both cases, the interaction of MDD and CD symptoms at age 9 did not predict age 10 MDD or CD. These data again support the hypothesis that when CD and MDD do occur together, MDD precedes the onset of CD. Moreover, the co-occurrence of MDD and CD symptoms during this period of development does not appear to confer the same risk for negative outcomes that have been observed in cases of comorbid MDD and CD at older ages.

If longitudinal data support the hypothesis that MDD commonly precedes CD, then it is possible that preventing or treating depression may result in preventing the onset of CD in a sizable population of girls. Available data on the treatment of conduct problems in girls is fairly limited, partly because developmental pathways to CD are not well documented for girls (Hipwell and Loeber, 2006). Determining how the treatment of one disorder affects the development of another is needed given the relatively high rates of heterotypic continuity in girls (Costello *et al.*, 2003). A study of school-age boys and girls referred to a day treatment program for disruptive behavior demonstrated that boys reported a decrease in depression and hopelessness following treatment, but girls did not (Grizenko and Pawliuk, 1994). Similarly, a comparison of boys and girls who were referred for Multisystemic Therapy revealed that girls rated themselves as having significantly more internalizing problems than did boys at the post-treatment, after controlling for pretreatment scores (Ogden and Hagen (2009)). Such findings suggest that boys' depression symptoms may be secondary to their disruptive behavior, and thus responsive to treatment for disruptive behavior. The same may not be true for the majority of girls.

The other issue that is partially addressed by these results is the etiology of comorbid CD and MDD in girls. Fergusson and colleagues (1996) reported that the vast majority of co-occurrence of MDD and CD could be attributed to the presence of common risk factors, such as negative life events, association with deviant peers, and a family history of antisocial behavior. Overbeek *et al.* (2006) found that expectations of failure explained co-occurring depression and conduct problems in boys and girls in mid-adolescence. Although developmental timing does not rule out the possibility that two disorders share causal factors, it would call into question whether the disorder that preceded the other confers risk either directly or via risk factors that are unique to the preceding disorder.

Sex differences in the rate of CD suggest that depressive symptoms may play a causal role in the development of CD. Although the rate of CD is lower in girls than in boys, the risk factors appear to be similar (van Hulle *et al.*, 2007). Therefore, there may need to be additional vulnerabilities in place, such as depression, in order for the transition from exposure to risk to expression of disorder to take place. It is also possible, however, given the type of data presented in this chapter, that a specific set of risk factors must be present at the time of the onset of MDD in order for CD to develop. If those factors are not present, then depression will develop without co-occurring CD.

These are complicated pathways to map, and will require an assessment of symptomatology and risk factors that begin early in life. Comorbidity is a dynamic process and symptom level as well as disorder must be part of the evolving phenomenon that is studied. Given the amount of individual variability that we observed in 9-year-old girls in depressive symptoms, and to a lesser extent conduct symptoms, uncovering the temporal unfolding of these two disorders will require multiple data points from childhood through adolescence. The data on the long-term prognosis for females with comorbid MDD and CD is persuasive, but what has not yet been determined is the dose response curve of CD symptoms. Does any level of symptomotology for any period of time impact morbidity, or is there a symptom threshold at or critical period during which the co-occurrence of symptoms significantly changes the risk for suicide, early pregnancy, or academic failure? Generating data that allows for greater specification will result in more refined profiles of risk that in turn can be used to support more targeted interventions.

REFERENCES

American Psychiatric Association (1994). *Diagnostic and Statistical Manual of Mental Disorders* (4th ed.). Washington, DC.

Birmaher, B., Ryan, N. D., Williamson, D. E., *et al.* (1996). Childhood and adolescent depression: A review of the past 10 years, Part I. *Journal of the American Academy of Child & Adolescent Psychiatry, 35,* 1427–1439.

Bjorkqvist, K., Lagerspetz, M. J., and Kaukiainen, A. (1992). Do girls manipulate and boys fight? Developmental trends in regard to direct and indirect aggression. *Aggressive Behavior, 18,* 117–127.

Cairns, R. B., Peterson, G., and Neckerman, H. J. (1988). Suicidal behavior in aggressive adolescents. *Journal of Clinical Child Psychology, 17,* 298–309.

Capaldi, D. M. (1991). Co-occurrence of conduct problems and depressive symptoms in early adolescent boys: I. Familial factors and general adjustment at Grade 6. *Development and Psychopathology, 3,* 277–300.

Cassidy, B., Zoccolillo, M., and Hughes, S. (1996). Psychopathology in adolescent mothers and its effects on mother-infant interactions: A pilot study. *Canadian Journal of Psychiatry, 41,* 379–384.

Chambers, W. J., Puig-Antich, J., Hirsch, M., *et al.* (1985). The assessment of affective disorders in children and adolescents by semi-structured interview. *Archives of General Psychiatry, 42,* 696–702.

Conseur A., Rivara F., Barnoski R., *et al.* (1997). Maternal and perinatal risk factors for later delinquency. *Pediatrics, 99,* 785–790.

Costello, E., Mustillo, S., Erkanli, A., *et al.* (2003). Prevalence and development of psychiatric disorders in childhood and adolescence. *Archives of General Psychiatry, 60,* 837– 844.

Crick, N. R., and Grotpeter, J. R. (1995). Relational aggression, gender, and social-psychological adjustment. *Child Development, 66,* 710–722.

Crick, N. R., Ostrov, J. M., and Werner, N. E. (2006). A longitudinal study of relational aggression, physical aggression, and children's social-psychological adjustment. *Journal of Abnormal Child Psychology, 34*(2), 131–142.

de Graaf, R., Bijl, R. V., ten Have, M., *et al.* (2004). Pathways to comorbidity: The transition of pure mood, anxiety and substance use disorders into comorbid conditions in a longitudinal population-based study. *Journal of Affective Disorders, 82,* 461-467.

Fergusson, D. M. Lynskey, M. T., and Horwood, L. J. (1996). Origins of comorbidity between conduct and affective disorders. *Journal of the American Academy of Child & Adolescent Psychiatry, 35,* 451–460.

Fombonne, E., Wostear, G., Cooper, V., *et al.* (2001). The Maudsley long-term follow-up of child and adolescent depression: II. Suicidality, criminality and social dysfunction in adulthood. *British Journal of Psychiatry, 179,* 218–223.

Frick, P. J., Bodin, S. D., and Barry, C. T. (2000). Psychopathic traits and conduct problems in community and clinic-referred samples of children: Further development of the Psychopathy Screening Device. *Psychological Assessment, 12,* 382–393.

Gadow, K. D., and Sprafkin, J. (1994), *Child Symptom Inventory.* Stony Brook, NY: State University of New York at Stony Brook.

Galen, B. R., and Underwood, M. K. (1997). A developmental investigation of social aggression among children. *Developmental Psychology, 33,* 589–600.

Gotlib, I., and Hammen, C. L. (1991). *Psychological Aspects of Depression: Toward a Cognitive-interpersonal Integration.* London: John Wiley & Sons, Inc.

Grizenko, N., and Pawliuk, N. (1994). Depression and hopelessness in children with disruptive behaviour disorders. *Canadian Journal of Psychiatry, 39,* 277–282.

Harrington, R. (2004). Developmental perspectives on depression in young people. In M. Power (ed.), *Mood Disorders: A Handbook of Science and Practice* (pp. 79–98). Chichester, UK: John Wiley & Sons, Inc.

Hipwell, A. E., and Loeber, R. (2006). Do we know which interventions are effective for disruptive and delinquent girls? *Clinical Child and Family Psychology Review, 9,* 221–255.

Jensen, P., Roper, M., Fisher, P., *et al.* (1995). Test-retest reliability of the Diagnostic Interview Schedule for Children (DISC 2.1): Parent, child, and combined algorithms. *Archives of General Psychiatry, 52,* 61–71.

Joffe, R. T., Offord, D. R., and Boyle, M. H. (1988). Ontario Child Health Study: Suicidal behavior in youth age 12-16 years. *American Journal of Psychiatry, 145,* 1420–1423.

Kaufman, J., Birmaher, B., Brent, D. A., *et al.* (1997). Schedule for Affective Disorders and Schizophrenia for School-Age Children-Present and Lifetime Version (K-SADS-PL): Initial reliability and validity data. *Journal of the American Academy of Child & Adolescent Psychiatry, 36,* 980–988.

Keenan K., Hipwell, A. E., Duax, J., *et al.* (2004). Phenomenology of depression in young girls. *Journal of the American Academy of Child and Adolescent Psychiatry, 43,* 1098–1106.

Keenan, K., Coyne, C., and Lahey, B. B. (2008). Should relational aggression be included in the DSM-IV nosology for disruptive behavior disorders? *Journal of the American Academy of Child and Adolescent Psychiatry, 47,* 86–93.

Keenan, K., Wroblewski, K., Hipwell, *et al.* (*in press*). Age of onset, symptom threshold, and expansion of the nosology of conduct disorder for girls.

Kovacs, M., Paulauskas, S., Gatsonis, *et al.* (1988). Depressive disorders in childhood: III. A longitudinal study of comorbidity with and risk for conduct disorders. *Journal of Affective Disorders, 15,* 205–217.

Kovacs, M., Obrosky, D. S., and Sherrill, J. (2003). Developmental changes in the phenomenology of depression in girls compared to boys from childhood onward. *Journal of Affective Disorders, 74*, 33–48.

Lahey, B. B., Loeber, R., Burke, J. D., *et al.* (2005). Predicting future antisocial personality disorder in males from a clinical assessment in childhood. *Journal of Consulting and Clinical Psychology, 73*, 389–399.

Lahey, B. B., Schwab-Stone, M., Goodman, S. H., *et al.* (2000). Age and gender differences in oppositional behavior and conduct problems: A cross-sectional household study of middle childhood and adolescence. *Journal of Abnormal Psychology, 109*, 488–503.

Lahey, B. B., Loeber, R., Burke, J. D., *et al.* (2002) Waxing and waning in concert: Dynamic comorbidity of conduct disorder with other disruptive and emotional problems over 17 years among clinic-referred boys. *Journal of Abnormal Psychology, 111*, 556–567.

Laukkanen, E., Korhonen, V., Peiponen, S., *et al.* (2001). A pessimistic attitute towards the future and low psychosocial functioning predict psychiatric diagnosis among treatment seeking adolescents. *Australian and New Zealand Journal of Psychiatry, 35*, 160–165.

Lynam, D. R. (1997). Pursuing the psychopath: Capturing the fledgling psychopath in a nomological net. *Journal of Abnormal Psychology, 106*, 425–438.

McCarty, C. A., Vander Stoep, A., and McCauley, E. (2007). Cognitive features associated with depressive symptoms in adolescence: Directionality and specificity. *Journal of Clinical Child and Adolescent Psychology, 36*, 147–158.

Mandell, D. S., Guevara, J. P., Rostain, A. L., *et al.* (2003). Economic grand rounds: Medical expenditures among children with psychiatric disorders in a Medicaid population. *Psychiatric Services, 54*, 465–467.

Maughan, B., Rowe, R., Messer, J., *et al.* (2004). Conduct disorder and oppositional defiant disorder in a national sample: Developmental epidemiology. *Journal of Child Psychology and Psychiatry, 45*, 609–621.Moffitt, T. E., Caspi, A., Rutter, M., *et al.* (2001). *Sex Differences in Antisocial Behaviour. Conduct Disorder, Delinquency and Violence in the Dunedin Longitudinal Study*. Cambridge: Cambridge University Press.

Moos, R. H., and Cronkite, R. C. (1999). Symptom-based predictors of a 10-year chronic course of treated depression. *Journal of Nervous and Mental Disease, 187*, 360–368.

Murray, C. J., and Lopez, A. D. (1997). Mortality by cause for eight regions of the world: Global Burden of Disease Study. *The Lancet, 349*, 1269–1276.

Nock, M. K., Kazdin, A. E., Hiripi, E., *et al.* (2006). Prevalence, subtypes, and correlates of DSM-IV conduct disorder in the National Comorbidity Survey Replication. *Psychological Medicine, 36*, 699–710.

Ogden, T. and Hagen, C. A. (2009). What works for whom? Gender differences in intake characteristics and treatment outcomes following Multisystemic Therapy. *Journal of Adolescence, 32*, 1425–1435.

Overbeek, G., Biesecker, G., Kerr, M., *et al.* (2006). Co-occurrence of depressive moods and delinquency in early adolescence: The role of failure expectations, manipulativeness, and social contexts. *International Journal of Behavioral Development, 30*, 433–443.

Pajer, K. A. (1998). What happens to "bad" girls? A review of the adult outcomes of antisocial adolescent girls. *American Journal of Psychiatry, 155*, 862–870.

Pajer, K. A., Kazmi, A., Gardner, W. P., *et al.* (2007). Female conduct disorder: health status in young adulthood. *Journal of Adolescent Health, 40*, 84e1–84e7.

Pardini, D., Obradovic, J., and Loeber, R. (2006). Interpersonal callousness, hyperactivity/impulsivity, inattention, and conduct problems as precursors to delinquency persistence in boys: A comparison of three grade-based cohorts. *Journal of Clinical Child and Adolescent Psychology, 35*, 46–59.

Penza-Clyve, S., and Zeman, J. (2002). Initial validation of the Emotion Expression Scale for children (EESC). *Journal of Clinical Child and Adolescent Psychology, 31*, 540–547.

Puig-Antich, J. (1982), Major depression and conduct disorder in prepuberty. *Journal of the American Academy of Child and Adolescent Psychiatry 21*, 118–128.

Robins, L. (1986). The consequences of conduct disorder in girls. In D. Olweus, J. Block, and M. Radke-Yarrow (eds), *Development of Antisocial and Prosocial Behavior: Research, Theories and Issues*. Orlando, FL: Academic Press.

Schrum, C. L., and Salekin, R. T. (2006). Psychopathy in adolescent female offenders: an item response theory analysis of the psychopathy checklist: Youth version. *Behavioral Sciences and the Law, 24*, 39–63.

Setterberg, S., Bird, H., Gould, M., et al. (1992). *Parent and interviewer versions of the Children's Global Assessment Scale*. New York: Columbia University.

Shaffer, D. (1988). The epidemiology of teen suicide: An examination of risk factors. *Journal of Clinical Psychiatry, 49*(Suppl), 36–41.

Stewart, S. M., Kennard, B. D., Lee, P. W. H., et al. (2005). Hopelessness and suicidal ideation among adolescents in two cultures. *Journal of Child Psychology and Psychiatry, 46*, 364–372.

Storvoll, E. E., and Wichstrøm, L. (2003). Gender differences in changes in and stability of conduct problems from early adolescence to early adulthood. *Journal of Adolescence, 26*, 413–429.

Teplin, L. A., Abram, K. A., and McClelland, G. M. (1997). Detecting mentally disordered women in jail: Who receives services? *American Journal of Public Health, 87*, 604–609.

van Hulle, C. A., Rodgers, J. L., D'Onofrio, B. M., et al. (2007). Sex differences in the causes of self-reported adolescent delinquency. *Journal of Abnormal Psychology, 116*, 236–248.

Weiss, B., Weisz, J. R., Politano, M., et al. (1992). Relations among self-reported depressive symptoms in clinic-referred children versus adolescents. *Journal of Abnormal Psycholog, 101*, 391–397.

Wolf, J. C., and Ollendick, T. H. (2006). The comorbidity of conduct problems and depression in childhood and adolescence. *Clinical Child and Family Psychology Review, 9*, 201–220.

Xie, H., Cairns, R. B., and Cairns, B. D. (2002). The development of social aggression and physical aggression: A narrative analysis of interpersonal conflicts. *Aggressive Behavior, 28*, 341–355.

Zeman, J., Shipman, K., and Penza-Clyve, S. (2001). Development and initial validation of The Children's Sadness Management Scale. *Journal of Nonverbal Behavior, 25*, 187–205.

Zeman, J., Shipman, K., and Suveg, C. (2002). Anger and sadness regulation: Predictions to internalizing and externalizing symptoms in children. *Journal of Clinical Child and Adolescent Psychology, 31*, 393–398.

Zoccolillo, M. (1993). Gender and the development of conduct disorder. *Development and Psychopathology, 5*, 65–78.

PART 3

Girls' Problem Behavior and Relationships

CHAPTER 6

Deviancy Training in a Sample of High-Risk Adolescent Girls in The Netherlands

Annika K. E. de Haan and Geertjan Overbeek
Utrecht University, The Netherlands

Karin S. Nijhof and Rutger C. M. E. Engels
Radboud University Nijmegen, The Netherlands

We are deeply grateful for the participation of all staff and especially girls from the facility and the high school, without whom this study would not have been possible. We would like to thank Tom Hollenstein and Ischa van Straaten for their help with the conversion of the observation data files to trajectories suitable for analyses with GridWare.

Girls persistently demonstrate lower levels of delinquent behaviour than boys (e.g., Hartung and Widiger, 1998; Bongers *et al.*, 2004; Vazsonyi and Keiley, 2007; Martino *et al.*, 2008). Girls' relatively small share in delinquent behaviour is presumably underlying their previous neglect in delinquency research. Since the 1990s, when several researchers noticed that female delinquency was on the rise, more attention for girls has emerged in this field (Hoyt and Scherer, 1998; Keenan, Loeber, and Green, 1999; Pleydon and Schner, 2001; Hipwell *et al.*, 2002; Kerpelman and Smith-Adcock, 2005).

The increasing female–male ratio of delinquency is worrisome, because various adverse outcomes are associated with adolescent delinquent behavior. Both delinquent boys and girls are more likely to demonstrate school drop-out, teenage parenthood, poor physical and mental health, substance abuse and dependence, antisocial personality disorder, and increased likelihoods of arrests and criminal activity in adulthood (e.g., Robins, Tripp, and Pryzbeck, 1991; Lewis *et al.*, 1991; Kovacs, Krol, and Voti, 1994; Zoccolillo, Tremblay, and Vitaro,

Understanding Girls' Problem Behavior: How Girls' Delinquency Develops in the Context of Maturity and Health, Co-occurring Problems, and Relationships, Edited by Margaret Kerr, Håkan Stattin, Rutger C. M. E. Engels, Geertjan Overbeek and Anna-Karin Andershed © 2011 John Wiley & Sons, Ltd.

1996; Booth and Zhang, 1997; Bardone *et al.*, 1998; Pajer, 1998). Moreover, girls showing externalizing behaviour are more likely to end up in romantic relationships with a deviant partner (Moffitt, 1993; Quinton *et al.*, 1993; Krueger *et al.*, 1998). In turn, this increases the likelihood that these girls' offspring will suffer from similar adverse home circumstances (e.g., poor parenting practices such as low supervision; low levels of parental warmth; permissive or overly harsh disciplining and living in poor and disadvantaged neighborhoods) that were factors in the development of their own problem behaviour (Richters and Martinez, 1993).

Although boys and girls are partly vulnerable to the same risk factors, recent advances in research on girls' problem behavior suggests a gender-specific phenotype. First of all, delinquent girls more often seem to have a history of maltreatment – particularly sexual abuse – than boys (e.g., Dembo *et al.*, 1998; Reebye *et al.*, 2000; McCabe *et al.*, 2002; Baker and Purcell, 2005; Handwerk *et al.*, 2006). Moreover, girls are more likely to be raised in tumultuous, chaotic, dysfunctional families, characterized by high levels of conflict and seriously disrupted parenting (Henggeler, Edwards, and Borduin, 1987; Silverthorn and Frick, 1999; Connor *et al.*, 2004). Finally, delinquent girls are much more likely than delinquent boys to suffer from co-occurring mental health problems, in particular internalizing problems such as depression, anxiety, self-harming behavior, and suicide attempts (Chamberlain and Reid, 1994; Timmons-Mitchell *et al.*, 1997; Barton *et al.*, 2001; Stewart and Trupin, 2003; Weis, Whitemarsh, and Wilson, 2005; Handwerk *et al.*, 2006). This gender-specific phenotype may imply different developmental pathways for girls. Therefore, research unravelling the processes and mechanisms underlying these pathways to delinquent behavior is highly necessary.

One possible pathway concerns association with deviant peers (e.g., Dishion, McCord, and Poulin, 1999; Patterson, Dishion, and Yoerger, 2000; Gifford-Smith *et al.*, 2005). Although this appears to be important for boys' and girls' problem behavior, girls may even be more vulnerable to peer influences due to the greater intimacy and loyalty of their friendships (Buhrmester and Furman, 1987; Hartup, 1996). Peer influences are exerted both in informal and formal settings, such as treatment groups. Several studies, of which the Cambridge Somerville Youth study is one of the most famous, reveal negative effects associated with the aggregation of deviant youth in treatment groups (e.g., Dishion *et al.*, 1999; McCord, 2002; Gifford-Smith *et al.*, 2005; Leve and Chamberlain, 2005; see for reviews Arnold and Hughes, 1999; Weiss *et al.*, 2005). In the Cambridge Somerville Youth study, a stay in a summer camp was embedded in a comprehensive intervention program. The results indicated that deviant youngsters who went to summer camp at least twice were more likely to show negative outcomes, such as higher self-reported delinquency, even after 30 years (McCord, 2002). Likewise, in a study of Chamberlain and Reid (1998), participation in a foster care program predicted fewer official and self-reported delinquency during the first year after termination of the program than participation in peer group treatment. These studies provide evidence for the assumption that affiliation with deviant peers leads to an increase in externalizing behavior.

One presumed mechanism underlying the influence of peers on deviant behavior, is a process referred to as "deviancy training" (Dishion et al., 1996; Dishion et al., 1997; Dishion, Poulin, and Burraston, 2001; Patterson et al., 2000). The core of this process consists of the presumption that peers reinforce one another's deviant or rule-breaking behavior (i.e., all behavior that goes against prevailing norms or seems inappropriate for the task or setting).

With one exception (Granic and Dishion, 2003), previous studies on deviancy training focused on boys. From a prevention and treatment point of view it is however very important to gain insight into the causes and precursors of female delinquency. Since several studies showed that deviancy training is related to later delinquency (Dishion et al., 1995; Dishion et al., 1996; Dishion et al., 1997), one way to gain more insight into female delinquency is to assess the deviancy training process in girls.

Dishion and colleagues (Dishion et al., 1996; Dishion et al., 1997; Granic and Dishion, 2003) developed an observation task to assess the process of deviancy training in interactions of adolescents. In this task reinforcement of deviant talk and behavior is assessed through registration of the amount of laughing and other encouraging behavior, like a "thumbs up" sign or a "high five." The tendency to engage in deviant talk and reinforcement of this behavior appears to be uniquely associated with violence and increases in self-reported substance use and delinquency in adolescence and later on, in young adulthood (Dishion et al., 1995; (Dishion et al. 1996; (Dishion et al. 1997).

A previous study with these observation tasks in a sample of adolescent boys indicated that delinquent dyads engaged more often in deviant talk than non-delinquent and mixed dyads (Dishion et al., 1996). In addition to these descriptive analyses, matching law analyses were conducted. In that particular study matching law analyses revealed a linear relationship between contingent positive reactions to and engagement in rule-breaking talk. This suggests that these positive reactions function as a catalyst for engagement in rule-breaking talk. Furthermore, sequential analyses revealed that non-delinquent dyads showed less positive reinforcement in response to rule-breaking talk than delinquent and mixed dyads.

With the rising popularity of dynamic systems theory, Granic and Dishion (2003) argued that the analyses as conducted in previous work did not provide full insight into the temporal pattern of interactions. Whereas previous studies relied on central tendency measures such as means and narrow temporal contingencies of behavior in sequential analyses, dynamic systems theorists argue that the overall temporal patterning of an interaction is crucial in the study of dyadic interactions (Granic and Hollenstein, 2003). As a first step to take dynamic systems principles into account, Granic and Dishion (2003) developed "a temporally sensitive measure that captures the extent to which deviant talk, over the course of a conversation, functions as an absorbing state for antisocial adolescents" (Granic and Dishion, 2003, p. 316). In dynamic systems theory an absorbing state, denoted with the term "attractor", is a specific situation or behavior subjects are repeatedly drawn to. Over time it becomes increasingly hard to withdraw from that particular state, situation or behavior. In their study Granic and Dishion (2003) created an index of attractor strength for all dyads by deriving slope values from time series of each successive episode of rule-breaking talk over the course of the inter-action. They found that adolescents with externalizing problems showed a positive and significantly higher slope value than adolescents without exter-nalizing problems. This indicates that adolescents with externalizing prob-lems showed increasingly longer episodes of rule-breaking talk over the course of the interaction. Rule-breaking talk in other words, was an attractor for these dyads.

The attempt to take dynamic systems principles into account in the study of deviancy training was taken a step further by performing state space grid anal-yses on similar observation data (Dishion *et al.*, 2004). State space grids is a recently developed methodology inspired on dynamic systems theory, allow-ing for a visual depiction of the course of an interaction (Lamey *et al.*, 2004). With regard to dyadic interactions, the state space is comprised of all possible joint states of two individuals. All coded behavior of the first person is plotted on the x-axis and the coded behavior of the second person is plotted on the y-axis. The grid encompasses cells which reflect all possible combinations of states; each cell represents a specific combination of behavior of the two sub-jects (Hollenstein, 2007). Dishion and colleagues (2004) conducted state space grid analyses on observation data as collected with the task mentioned before. Their focus was on interpersonal processes in male adolescent friendships. Their results showed that in general the interactions of antisocial boys were less organized (high dispersion over the grid; behavior occurs in a considerable number of cells) and included more rule-breaking talk than the interactions of well-adjusted control boys. However, those antisocial boys with well-organized interactions and elevated levels of rule-breaking talk, were most likely to dis-play antisocial behavior in adulthood.

THE PRESENT STUDY

Although the last two studies (Granic and Dishion, 2003; Dishion *et al.*, 2004) extended the literature on deviant talk, the response of the interaction partner to episodes of rule-breaking talk was not taken into account. As mentioned before, the core of the deviancy training process consists of the presumption that peers positively reinforce one another's deviant or rule-breaking behavior. Therefore, it is crucial to take the response of the interaction partner into account when studying deviancy training. Our study is the first to apply the dynamic systems principles to the study of deviancy training in girls, as assessed with an observation task similar to the one used by Dishion and colleagues (1996). In addition to regular descriptive analyses at the individual and dyadic level and sequential analyses, we analysed the interactions with the state space grid methodology with a focus on both deviant content of the interaction and the response of the interaction partner.

At the individual level we hypothesized that non-delinquent girls would show more rule-breaking talk in interaction with a delinquent partner compared with their behavior in interaction with a non-delinquent partner. At the dyadic level we expected that delinquent and mixed dyads (i.e., a non-delinquent girl in interaction with a delinquent girl) would show more rule-breaking talk than non-delinquent dyads. Sequential analyses were performed to test the hypothesis that delinquent dyads would respond to rule-breaking talk more often with rule-breaking talk or laughing than mixed and non-delinquent dyads. State space grid analyses were performed to examine whether delinquent and mixed dyads show greater dispersion over the grid, since these dyads would visit more cells on the grid. Furthermore, we expected that non-delinquent dyads would return less often and less quickly to the "deviancy-training region," in which deviant talk is coupled with a reinforcing response of the interaction partner, after their first visit than mixed and delinquent dyads. Finally, we expected that delinquent and mixed dyads would stay longer in this deviancy-training region.

Method

Participants and procedure

Two groups of adolescent girls participated in the current study. The "facility group" consisted of 17 adolescent girls with severe behavioral difficulties living in a residential care facility, ranging in age from 14.97 to 18.0 years (M = 16.50, SD = 0.90). The 17 participating girls from the facility lived in two residential groups consisting of ten girls each (parents of two girls refused participation and despite several attempts one girl did not complete the questionnaire). The "high-school group" consisted of 88 girls in six school classes of a Dutch vocational training school (VMBO) in the eastern part of the Netherlands. A vocational training school was chosen because most girls of the facility group attended a similar level of education. These high-school girls ranged in age from 14.23 to 17.40 years (M = 15.52, SD = 0.70). Before the start of the study parents or guardians were informed by letter about the goal and purpose of the study. A passive informed consent procedure was employed. As mentioned before, for the facility group, parents of two girls refused participation in the study. For the high-school group, parents of one adolescent refused participation.

Two introductory visits were made to both residential girls groups to explain the purpose and goal of the study. Girls were told that the researchers were primarily interested in the way adolescents discuss day-to-day topics with each other. Approximately two weeks after our last visit, girls in both residential groups completed a questionnaire on delinquency. Approximately six weeks after completion of the questionnaire, the observations were conducted at the facility. All observations were scheduled on one afternoon. The high-school students were given a short verbal introduction about the goal and purpose of the study before completion of the questionnaire on delinquency, similar to the introduction given to the girls in the facility. One week after completion of the questionnaire the first observations were conducted. Appointments were made with students by telephone or email, without interference of the school.

The first page of the questionnaire consisted of a form, on which girls could indicate whether they wanted to participate in the observation study, for which they were paid eight euro's. Seven of the "facility girls" (41.2 %) agreed to participate in the observation study. Unfortunately, one of these girls was the only one of her residential group who agreed to participate. Because there was no interaction partner for this girl, since she was the only one in her group who agreed to participate, this girl was excluded from the study. Facility girls who agreed to participate in the observation study did not differ from girls who refused participation in respect of age or delinquency score. The 62 (70.5%) high-school students who subscribed for the observation study differed from students who refused participation in the observation study in age and delinquency scores. T-tests revealed that high-school students who were willing to participate in the observation study were significantly younger (M = 15.43, SD = 0.73) than girls who refused participation in the observation study (M = 15.74, SD = 0.59, t (84) = 1.87, p < 0.10, d = 0.44). Furthermore, students who subscribed for the observation study had higher scores on the self-report questionnaire on delinquency (M = 8.63, SD = 9.86) than girls who refused participation in the observation study (M = 4.31, SD = 5.40, t (79.80) = −2.64, p < 0.01, d = −0.49).

Based on the results of the self-report questionnaire on delinquency, girls were classified as either delinquent or non-delinquent. This classification was used to form delinquent, non-delinquent and mixed dyads for participation in the observation study.

For the facility group, of the six participating girls, three were classified as delinquent (scores ranging from 42 to 70, M = 55.00, SD = 14.11). The remaining three girls were classified as non-delinquent (scores ranging from 0 to 14, M = 7.66, SD = 7.09). Although the high-school students were told that youngsters who subscribed for the observation study were selected randomly for actual participation in the observation study, selection was in fact based on the scores on the self-report questionnaire on delinquency. From each class, the two most delinquent and the two least delinquent girls were selected for participation in the observation study. The 12 high-school girls who were identified as delinquent had scores ranging from 10 to 41 (M = 21.25, SD = 12.57), whereas the 12 high-school girls who were classified as non-delinquent had scores ranging from 0 to 3 (M = 0.75, SD = 0.87).

An observation task highly comparable to the Peer Interaction Task developed by Dishion and colleagues (Poe *et al.*, 1990) was employed in the current study. A pilot study among 16 dyads at another high-school in the eastern part of the Netherlands gave rise to minor adjustments in our initial procedure.

All participants in the observation study interacted twice with a different group or class mate. They participated once with a partner from their own "delinquency group" (in a delinquent or non-delinquent dyad) and once with a partner from the other delinquency group (in a mixed dyad). Eventually, this resulted in 24 high-school dyads (six delinquent, six non-delinquent, and 12 mixed dyads) and five facility dyads (one delinquent, one non-delinquent, and three mixed dyads). In both groups, the facility group and the high-school group, the observations were conducted in a quiet room. Participants were seated next to each other at a table, on which were some tea-bags, two pens, and a plasticized card on which the first task was printed. Approximately two meters in front of them, a camera was installed on a tripod, standing on a table. After entrance to the observation room, participants were given instructions about the purpose of the task. Each individual received two forms, one listing topics adolescents regularly have quarrels about with adults (e.g., drugs and alcohol; smoking; pocket money) and one list of topics youngsters regularly have quarrels about with their friends or peers (e.g., clothes; appearance; trust). Both girls chose one topic of each list, resulting in four topics to be discussed. After the general introduction, the completion of the forms and the introduction of the first task – planning a fun activity – the experimenter left the room. After each five-minute episode she returned to the room to introduce the next topic. The order of topics was constant; after the warm up task of planning a fun activity, youngsters started discussing topics adolescents have quarrels about with adults. Finally, topics youngsters have quarrels about with friends and peers were discussed. The youngster who started discussing the topic related to adults, started with the topic related to peers as well.

Coding procedure

A coding scheme similar to the Peer Topic Code (Poe *et al.*, 1990) was used in this study. All dyadic observations were coded in real-time with software application Observer XT (Noldus). Main objects of the coding scheme were rule-breaking talk and laughing. All dyads were coded by the first author and after a thorough training and instruction two undergraduate students coded 12 dyads each (approximately 41% of all dyads in the study). These dyads were used for the purpose of calculating inter-rater reliability. Reliability analyses were conducted with an earlier version of the software application; Observer 5.0 (Noldus). Cohen's kappa was determined for each of the 12 double coded high-school dyads separately. Reliability was very good, with all kappas over 0.90. At the moment of coding all observers were unaware of the delinquency status of the dyads.

Measures

Delinquency The Self-report Delinquent Behavior questionnaire (in Dutch "Zelfrapportage Delinquent Gedrag", ZDG-vragenlijst) was administered with both groups. This questionnaire consists of 30 items on several forms of delinquent behaviour. Examples of items are "How often in the last six months did you injure a person with a weapon", "How often in the last six months did you steal a bike?" and "How often in the last six months did you sell hard drugs like heroin or cocaine?" Participants answered on a five-point scale; zero times, one time, two times, three through ten times, more than ten times. Earlier research with this questionnaire revealed sufficient reliability with alphas over 0.80.

Rule-breaking talk Rule-breaking talk was defined as all verbal and nonverbal behavior consisting "of any reference to violations of legal or conventional norms, any inappropriate behavior during the taped interaction, and any activities violating the instructions given for the task" (Dishion et al., 2004, p. 655). Importantly, all verbal responses to rule-breaking talk of the interaction partner were also coded as rule-breaking talk, unless the utterance was intended to stop the rule-breaking talk of the interaction partner. All talk or behavior that was not coded as rule-breaking was coded normative. Two variables were used in the analyses; the total duration of rule-breaking talk during an interaction in seconds and the frequency of episodes of rule-breaking talk over the course of an interaction. Because both members of each dyad were coded separately, individual and dyadic scores on the variables were computed. Dyadic scores are the sum of the scores of both members of the dyad. For the double coded dyads, mean scores of both observers were used in the analyses, for both individual and dyadic scores.

Laughing All audible and visible instances of laughing and smiling were coded as laughing, irrespective of the preceding behavior of the interaction partner. Similar to rule-breaking talk, a default state was created for this construct; not laughing.

Strategy of analyses

Analyses were performed in four steps. First, analyses at the individual level were performed. Paired t-tests were executed to assess whether non-delinquent individuals behaved differently in both types of dyads. Second, analyses at the dyadic level were performed, followed by sequential analyses. Finally, state space grid analyses were performed. Both the dyadic analyses and the state space grid analyses started with t-tests to compare the facility dyads and the high-school dyads. After these t-tests, multivariate analyses of variance were performed with dyad type as factor, to assess differences between non-delinquent dyads and the two other dyad types; mixed and delinquent dyads.

Sequential analyses   All dyads were submitted to a sequential analysis. In case a dyad was coded by two observers, one data file was randomly selected for the sequential analysis. If a behavior code occurred in the file within five seconds after the preceding behavior, this was considered a sequence. All four types of behavior were taken into account; rule-breaking talk, normative behavior, laughing, and not laughing. Because not laughing is not a positive reaction to the preceding behavior, all instances of not laughing were considered normative. Initially, a three by three crosstab was constructed with the following three behavior categories; rule-breaking behavior, normative behavior (including not laughing), and laughing. For each dyad two crosstabs were constructed, one for which the behavior of girl A was antecedent and one for which the behavior of girl B was antecedent. After manually identifying all sequences and completing the three by three cross tabs, the three categories were converted into a two by two cross tab with the categories rule-breaking talk and normative behavior. Because laughing is considered a positive, or reinforcing response to rule-breaking talk, all rule-breaking – laughing sequences were collapsed in the rule-breaking – rule-breaking category. The laughing – rule-breaking sequences were collapsed in the normative – rule-breaking category. All laughing – normative, laughing – laughing, and normative – laughing sequences were collapsed into the normative – normative category.

State space grids   As explained before, state space grids is a relatively new methodology based on dynamic systems principles. In the present study the two coded variables, rule-breaking talk and laughing and their counterparts normative behavior and not laughing, were combined into four categories; (1) normative – not laughing, (2) normative – laughing, (3) rule-breaking talk – not laughing, and (4) rule-breaking talk – laughing. Behavior of a subject always occurs in one of these four categories. The four categories result in a grid consisting of 16 cells, with each cell representing a particular combination of the behavior of girl A and girl B. The interaction, as it occurs in real time is plotted on the grid. Any time there is a change in the behavior of one of the interaction partners a new point is plotted in the cell representing that behavior and a line connecting the new and the previous point is drawn. This results in a behavioral trajectory, or a depiction of the sequence of combinations of behavioral states on the grid (Hollenstein, 2005; Hollenstein and Lewis, 2006).

GridWare (Lamey *et al.*, 2004), the computer application that is able to produce these state space grids, was used to analyse all dyadic interactions. In case a dyad was coded by two observers, one data file was randomly selected for the state space grid analyses. A number of measures for each dyad or interaction were derived from GridWare. Six of them were used in regular statistical analyses. The first is Dispersion, this is a measure that denotes the variation of the interaction. This measure has a value ranging from 0 to 1, where 0 means that there is no dispersion at all; all behavior occurs in one cell of the grid, whereas a value of 1 means that there is maximal dispersion over the grid. The second measure is Duration, which denotes the time a dyad stays in the selected deviancy-training region, in which, as mentioned before, rule-breaking talk is coupled with a positive response of the interaction partner (either laughing or engaging in rule-breaking talk). The third measure is the number of Events in the selected region. An event is a distinct episode occupying a particular cell. The fourth measure is the number of Visits to the selected region. A visit starts upon entry into the selected region and ends with the dyad's exit from the selected region. The fifth measure is the Return time to the selected region after the first visit. The smaller the Return time, the faster a dyad returns to the selected region. The last measure concerns the number of Return visits to the region after the first visit.

Traditionally, alpha levels are set at 0.05 to reduce the risk of type one errors. Over the last few decades however, several researchers have argued to refrain from this static significance testing, since the value of p is strongly influenced by the number of cases in a study (see, for example, Olejnik and Algina, 2000). In very large samples significant effects are rather easily obtained, whereas this significance does not necessarily reflect a large difference in terms of effect sizes. Since alpha levels do not provide any information about the effect size, we decided to include effect size measures for all of our analyses. The effect size of t-tests is denoted with Cohen's d. If this value is larger than 0.20 the effect size is considered small, when d is 0.50 or higher, the effect size is considered medium and a Cohen's d larger than 0.80 indicates a large effect (Cohen, 1988). The effect size of analyses of variance and contrasts is assessed with eta squared. Due to our small sample size, we decided to consider alpha levels below 0.15 significant. With the given sample size ($n = 29$) this alpha level is appropriate to detect large differences in the population, while maintaining a power of 0.80 (Cohen, 1988).

Results

Preliminary analyses

As noted in the preceding section, participants were classified as delinquent or non-delinquent. Overall, t-tests revealed that girls classified as non-delinquent had significantly lower scores on the delinquency questionnaire than girls classified as delinquent (M non-delinquent girls = 2.13, SD = 4.00, M delinquent girls = 28.00, SD = 18.65, t (15.28) = -5.25, $p < 0.001$, $d = -1.92$). Due to their stay in a facility for youngsters with severe behavior problems, we reasoned that overall, girls from the facility would have higher scores on the self-report questionnaire on delinquency than the high-school girls. This is exactly what a *t*-test revealed (M high-school girls = 11.00, SD = 13.62, M facility girls = 31.33, SD = 27.78, t (5.62) = -1.74, $p < 0.15$, $d = -1.19$).

Individual level analyses

We expected that non-delinquent girls would engage longer and more frequent in rule-breaking talk in a mixed dyad than in a non-delinquent dyad. The results partly confirmed our hypothesis; non-delinquent girls showed more frequent episodes of rule-breaking talk in interaction with a delinquent partner ($M = 8.43$, $SD = 6.99$) than in interaction with a non-delinquent partner ($M = 3.82$, $SD = 4.54$, t (13) $= -2.43$, $p < 0.05$, $d = -0.78$). No significant differences however, were found for the duration of rule-breaking talk. Moreover, the difference was in the opposite direction (M in non-delinquent dyad $= 130.62$ seconds, $SD = 308.47$, M in mixed dyad $= 89.71$ seconds, $SD = 131.31$).

Dyadic level analyses

At the dyadic level 29 dyads were the unit of analysis. First, the facility group was compared with the high-school group. Due to the overall higher level of delinquency among the facility group, we expected longer and more frequent engagement in rule-breaking talk in girls from this group. T-tests indeed revealed that dyads from the facility group engaged longer in rule-breaking talk than the high-school dyads ($M = 725.97$ seconds, $SD = 623.18$ vs. $M = 109.94$ seconds, $SD = 159.54$, t (4.11) $= -2.20$, $p < 0.10$, $d = -2.19$). Although the difference was in the expected direction, the facility and high-school dyads showed no significant difference in the frequency of rule-breaking talk episodes (M facility dyads $= 24.20$, $SD = 8.87$, M high-school dyads $= 15.73$, $SD = 15.12$).

Second, multivariate analyses of variance were performed on the same dependent variables to assess differences between the three dyad types (i.e., non-delinquent, delinquent, and mixed dyads). We expected that non-delinquent dyads would show less rule-breaking talk than delinquent and mixed dyads, both in duration and frequency. Concerning the frequency of rule-breaking talk, the dyad types differed from each other ($F(2, 28) = 3.04$, $p < 0.10$, $\eta^2 = .19$). Simple contrast testing with non-delinquent dyads as reference group, revealed that non-delinquent dyads differed significantly from delinquent ($F(1, 26) = 6.00$, $p < 0.05$, $\eta^2 = 0.19$) and mixed dyads ($F(1, 26) = 2.71$, $p < 0.15$, $\eta^2 = 0.09$). As shown in Table 6.1 delinquent and mixed dyads engaged more often in rule-breaking talk than non-delinquent dyads did. Concerning the total duration of rule-breaking talk the different dyad types did not differ from each other. However significant, the differences were not in the expected direction. Non-delinquent dyads engaged longer in rule-breaking talk than delinquent and mixed dyads did.

Sequential analyses

The preceding analyses provided a description of the total duration and frequency of rule-breaking talk during the interactions. However, those analyses do not provide insight into the relation between rule-breaking talk and

Table 6.1 Means and standard deviations for duration and frequency of rule-breaking talk (RB).

	Non-delinquent dyads			Delinquent dyads			Mixed dyads			
	N	Mean	SD	N	Mean	SD	N	Mean	SD	F
Duration RB	7	261.24	641.83	7	207.88	200.08	15	198.97	264.33	0.07
Frequency RB	7	7.64	9.09	7	25.36*	16.49	15	17.83†	13.71	3.04*

Note: Asterisks refer to significant differences with the reference group; the group of non-delinquent dyads. *F* refers to the omnibus *F*.

† $p < 0.15$; * $p < 0.10$; ** $p < 0.05$; *** $p < 0.01$.

accompanying positive or reinforcing reactions, such as laughing. We expected that in delinquent dyads, the interaction partner would more often respond positively to an episode of rule-breaking talk, by either engaging in rule-breaking talk or by laughing, than in mixed and non-delinquent dyads.

Remember that two by two cross tabs were constructed by collapsing all rule-breaking – laughing sequences (laughing in response to rule-breaking talk) into the rule-breaking – rule-breaking category. This way all positive reactions of the interaction partner to rule-breaking talk; laughing and engaging in rule-breaking talk, were taken up in the rule-breaking – rule-breaking category. Because we were primarily interested in positive reactions to rule-breaking talk, we focused on that particular sequence. Transitional probabilities of the target behavior (rule-breaking talk of the "responding" interaction partner) were compared with simple probabilities of the target behavior. The use of Allison-Liker binomial z scores (Gottman and Roy, 1990) is common in sequential analysis. Therefore, this statistic was applied to assess the statistical significance of the difference between the transitional and the simple probability of the target behavior: rule-breaking talk. If the transitional probability: the chance that rule-breaking talk was preceded by rule-breaking talk of the interaction partner, is greater than the simple probability: the chance of overall occurrence of rule-breaking talk by the responding girl, it can be stated that it is likely that the response to rule-breaking talk consists of rule-breaking talk or laughing.

Contrary to our hypotheses, all dyads showed a significant level of rule-breaking talk in response to rule-breaking talk of the interaction partner (non-delinquent dyads $z = 10.09$, delinquent dyads, $z = 10.58$, and mixed dyads, $z = 13.05$, $p < 0.05$). The same results were obtained for the comparison between facility and high-school dyads (facility dyads $z = 8.85$, high-school dyads $z = 17.68$, $p < 0.05$). These results indicate that for all dyads the probability that rule-breaking was preceded by a rule-breaking behavior was significantly larger than the probability of the overall occurrence of rule-breaking talk; all dyads were likely to positively reinforce their interaction partner's rule-breaking talk.

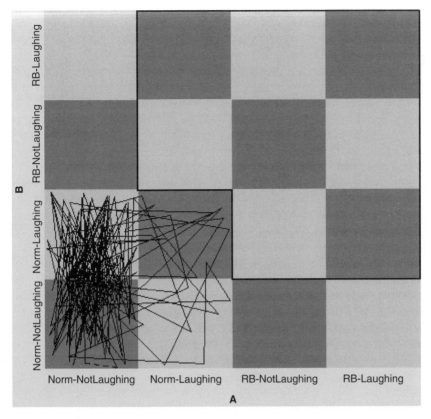

Figure 6.1 State space grid for a non-delinquent high school dyad.

State Space Grid Analyses

As explained before, the two observed constructs, rule-breaking talk and laughing and their counterparts normative behavior and not-laughing were combined in a state space grid. In Figures 6.1 and 6.2 the region that was of special interest in our analyses is marked; in this deviancy-training region rule-breaking talk of one of the interaction partners co-occurred with rule-breaking talk or laughing of the interaction partner. Figure 6.1 shows the course of an interaction for a non-delinquent dyad. All behavior during this interaction occurs exclusively in the quadrant in the bottom left of the grid, where normative – not laughing and normative – laughing are paired with normative – not laughing or normative – laughing of the interaction partner. So, both members of this non-delinquent high-school dyad engaged exclusively in normative behavior. Dispersion over the grid is limited, because behavior is restricted to this normative quadrant. Figure 6.2 shows the state space grid for a delinquent dyad. It is obvious that this dyad visited many more cells, and as a result showed greater dispersion over the grid than the non-delinquent dyad. As opposed to the non-delinquent dyad, this dyad visited the deviancy-training region several times.

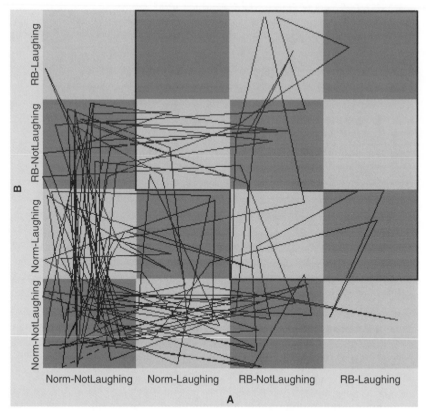

Figure 6.2 State space grid for a delinquent facility dyad.

Table 6.2 Descriptive statistics for the state space grid variables, categorized according to group.

	Facility group			High-school			
	N	Mean	SD	N	Mean	SD	*t*-value
Dispersion	5	0.52	0.25	24	0.20	0.16	3.74***
Duration	5	312.79	300.00	24	23.70	43.40	2.15*
Duration/E	5	9.25	5.88	24	1.71	2.15	2.83**
Duration/V	5	35.65	35.51	24	2.26	3.17	2.10⁺
Events	5	28.80	28.49	24	7.54	10.24	1.65
Visits	5	8.60	6.43	24	5.92	8.05	0.70
Return time	4	8.75	1.11	16	185.42	485.10	−0.71
Return visits	4	3.96	0.82	16	4.02	1.76	−0.07

Note: Duration/E = Duration per event; Duration/V = Duration per visit.
⁺ $p < 0.15$; * $p < 0.10$; ** $p < 0.05$; *** $p < 0.01$.

As described in the method section, several variables were derived from these state space grids. First, t-tests were performed to assess differences between the facility group and the high-school group. Due to the overall higher level of delinquency of the facility girls, we expected that they would spend more time in the deviancy-training region, and that they would visit this region more often. Because it was presumed that these dyads would visit the deviancy-training region more than the high-school dyads, we expected that delinquent dyads would show larger dispersion over the grid. In Table 6.2 an overview of the descriptive statistics is provided for both the facility group and the high-school group. T-tests revealed four significant differences between the groups. First, Dispersion over the grid was larger for the facility dyads than for the high-school dyads (t (27) = 3.74, $p < 0.05$, d = 1.84). Second, the facility dyads stayed longer in the deviancy-training region (t (4.04) = 2.15, $p < 0.10$, d = 2.37). Third, the Duration per Event in the deviancy-training region was longer for the facility dyads (t (4.23) = 2.83, $p < 0.05$, d = 2.51). Finally, the Duration of their Visits to the deviancy-training region lasted significantly longer than those of the high-school group (t (4.01) = 2.10, $p < 0.15$, d = 2.39). As can be seen in Table 6.2, only 20 dyads have values for Return time and Return visits. This discrepancy is caused by the fact that nine dyads (four non-delinquent, two delinquent and two mixed high-school dyads and one mixed facility dyad) did not visit the selected deviancy-training region at all. In accordance with our hypotheses, although not significant, facility dyads displayed more events and visits in the deviancy-training region, moreover, they returned faster to this region than the high-school dyads. Contrary to our hypotheses, high-school dyads made slightly more return visits to the deviancy-training region, although this was not significant.

Multivariate analyses of variance were conducted to assess differences between the three dyad types. We expected that non-delinquent dyads would visit the deviancy-training region less often and less long than mixed and delinquent dyads. Consequently, we expected that delinquent and mixed dyads would show larger dispersion over the grid than non-delinquent dyads. Moreover, we hypothesized that non-delinquent dyads would return less often and less quickly to the deviancy-training region after their first visit than mixed and delinquent dyads. In Table 6.3 an overview of the descriptive statistics for the state space grid variables is provided for each dyad type. In the first set of analyses the following variables were included: Dispersion, Duration, Events, and Visits. The omnibus F-test revealed no significant differences between the three dyad types. Simple contrast testing however, revealed one significant difference. Delinquent dyads made more Visits to the deviancy-training region than non-delinquent dyads (F (1, 26) = 2.33, $p < 0.15$, η^2 = 0.08). Remarkable to note is that overall, however not significant, non-delinquent dyads stayed considerably longer in the deviancy-training region than delinquent and mixed dyads. The second set of variables included Duration per Event and Duration per Visit. Neither the analysis of variance nor simple contrast testing revealed significant differences between the three dyad types. The third set of variables

Table 6.3   Descriptive statistics for the state space grid variables, categorized according to dyad type.

	Non-delinquent dyads			Delinquent dyads			Mixed dyads		
	N	Mean	SD	N	Mean	SD	N	Mean	SD
Dispersion	7	0.21	0.27	7	0.30	0.23	15	0.25	0.19
Duration	7	114.87	298.93	7	60.53	75.81	15	60.34	107.82
Events	7	12.43	27.89	7	13.14	11.75	15	9.73	11.85
Visits	7	2.86	4.63	7	9.14[†]	7.86	15	6.73	8.63
Duration/E	7	1.67	3.94	7	3.21	3.19	15	3.54	4.69
Duration/V	7	10.51	27.15	7	5.06	5.52	15	8.24	19.23
Return time	3	525.54	895.47	5	8.77[†]	1.09	12	115.11	367.86
Return visits	3	2.63	2.46	5	4.30	.55	12	4.24[†]	1.61

Note: Asterisks refer to significant differences with the reference group; the group of non-delinquent dyads.
Duration/E = Duration per event; Duration/V = Duration per visit.
[†] $p < 0.15$; * $p < 0.10$; ** $p < 0.05$; *** $p < 0.01$.

included Return time and Return visits. As mentioned before, the discrepancy in number of dyads is caused by the fact that nine dyads did not visit the deviancy-training region at all. Although the omnibus F-test revealed no significant differences between the three dyad types, simple contrast testing revealed two significant differences. First, non-delinquent dyads differed from delinquent dyads in Return time to the deviancy-training region ($F (1, 17) = 2.75, p < 0.15, \eta^2 = 0.14$). Non-delinquent dyads had a higher return time, which means that once non-delinquent dyads visited the deviancy-training region, it took them a longer period of time to return to the selected region than delinquent dyads. Second, non-delinquent dyads made significantly fewer Return visits to the deviancy-training region than mixed dyads ($F (1, 17) = 2.54, p < 0.15, \eta^2 = 0.13$) after their first visit to this region.

Discussion

In the current study the real time process of deviancy training was assessed among two groups; a group of high-risk adolescent girls and a group of high-school girls. Non-delinquent, delinquent, and mixed dyads were formed to participate in an observation task. Analyses with a varying level of complexity and innovativeness were performed.

Individual analyses

In line with previous studies suggesting that individuals, especially adolescents, adapt their behavior to others (see for a classic study Asch, 1952), we found that non-delinquent girls displayed more episodes of rule-breaking talk in a mixed dyad than in a non-delinquent dyad. Our hypothesis that these non-delinquent girls would engage in rule-breaking talk for a longer period of time in a mixed dyad was not confirmed. Presumably, the absence of a significant difference for the overall duration of rule-breaking talk is caused by the presence of two non-delinquent facility girls, who engaged the majority of the time in rule-breaking talk with their non-delinquent group mate. When only non-delinquent high-school girls are considered, a significant difference does emerge for duration of rule-breaking talk. Non-delinquent high-school girls adapt their behavior to their delinquent interaction partner both in respect of duration and frequency of rule-breaking talk.

Dyadic analyses

The finding that individual non-delinquent girls adapt their behavior to their delinquent interaction partner provides additional evidence for previous studies showing negative effects of peer group treatment (e.g., Chamberlain and Reid, 1998; McCord, 1992). With this knowledge in mind, it is interesting to determine whether delinquent and mixed dyads show more rule-breaking talk than non-delinquent dyads. In accordance with findings of Dishion and colleagues (1996) we found that delinquent and mixed dyads showed more frequent episodes of rule-breaking talk than non-delinquent dyads. Although the direction of the differences is in accordance with the results of Dishion and colleagues (1996), it is important to note that the rates of rule-breaking talk per minute diverge enormously. The rates adolescent boys in their study showed were at least seven times the rates girls in our study showed. There are at least two explanations for this difference. First, Dishion and colleagues (1996) conducted their study with boys. Although no gender differences were found in another study (Granic and Dishion, 2003), there is reason to assume that boys are more likely to show rule-breaking talk, since research has repeatedly shown that boys have more externalizing problems (e.g., Bongers *et al.*, 2004; Vazsonyi and Keiley, 2007; Martino *et al.*, 2008). Engagement in rule-breaking talk might be one expression of underlying externalizing problems. This same presumption holds for at-risk adolescents. Both the study that Dishion conducted in the nineties as well as his study that failed to show any gender differences were conducted exclusively with at-risk adolescents recruited from neighborhoods with high densities of reported delinquency.

Our hypothesis that delinquent and mixed dyads would engage longer in rule-breaking talk than non-delinquent dyads would was not confirmed. A closer inspection of the descriptive statistics revealed that the means were not in the expected direction. Analogue to the results at the individual level, this unexpected finding is explained through the presence of one non-delinquent facility dyad, whose members engaged almost exclusively in rule-breaking talk during the interaction. Although the means were in the expected direction after exclusion of this dyad, most effects remained non-significant. Due to our small sample size, we decided not to exclude this dyad from the analyses. Moreover, we ran the same analyses with high-school dyads only. Although the means were in the expected direction, the difference was still not significant. With caution, we argue that there is a trend in our data that delinquent and mixed dyads engage longer in rule-breaking talk than non-delinquent dyads. In contrast to the frequency of rule-breaking talk, we saw that over all dyads, the duration of rule-breaking talk over the interaction was comparable to the duration as found in at-risk boys (Dishion *et al.*, 1997).

With regard to the comparison between facility and high-school dyads, our results indicate that facility dyads engaged longer, but not more frequently in rule-breaking talk than high-school dyads. Presumably, once facility dyads start engaging in rule-breaking talk, it takes them longer to disengage from it. This reasoning is supported by the fact that their rule-breaking episodes lasted on average significantly longer than the mean rule-breaking episodes of high-school dyads. This finding might be in line with the results from a study by Granic and Dishion (2003) in which they found that for delinquent dyads rule-breaking talk was an attractor. The more episodes of rule-breaking talk occurred, the longer these episodes became. The same phenomenon might have manifested itself in our study.

Sequential analyses

The results of our sequential analyses suggest that all dyads, regardless of their level of delinquency, positively reinforce rule-breaking talk. This is not in line with sequential analyses performed by Dishion and colleagues (1996) on the same type of data. They found that non-delinquent dyads, in contrast to delinquent and mixed dyads, did not positively reinforce rule-breaking talk. Dishion and colleagues' (1996) study was conducted with boys. Research has repeatedly shown that interpersonal relationships are of greater importance for girls than for boys. Instead, boys attach more value to the larger peer group (Gavin and Furman, 1989). Girls' concerns with interpersonal relationships might have urged individual girls to follow an interaction partner in rule-breaking talk to maintain or obtain a good relationship with the interaction partner. Boys in Dishion and colleagues' study participated in the observation task with one of their best friends. Since boys attach more value to the larger peer group they might have felt less inclined to follow their friend in rule-breaking talk. Support for our results can be found in a study of Buehler and colleagues (1966). Their results too seem to indicate that delinquent or deviant behavior is positively reinforced by all adolescent girls, regardless of their level of delinquency. Another explanation for the absence of a difference in reinforcement between the different dyad types is methodological in nature. Our time slot of five seconds is quite arbitrary, it might take individuals more than five seconds to respond to the behavior of their interaction partner. Moreover, only the first behavior that occurred within five seconds of the preceding behavior was considered a consequent behavior. Presumably, as the state space grid analyses showed, sequential analyses rely too heavily on narrow temporal contingencies.

State space grid analyses

In contrast to the sequential analyses, the state space grid analyses revealed differences between dyad types. Delinquent dyads made more visits to the deviancy-training region and returned faster to the region after their first visit than non-delinquent dyads. Further, mixed dyads made more return visits to the deviancy-training region than non-delinquent dyads.

The dyadic analyses already showed that facility dyads engaged longer in rule-breaking talk than high-school dyads. In addition to this finding, state space grid analyses revealed that facility dyads also stayed longer in the deviancy-training region, in which rule-breaking talk is positively reinforced by the interaction partner. This suggests that in interactions of facility dyads more reinforcement of rule-breaking talk occurs than in high-school dyads. These findings do not fit with the results of the sequential analyses and illustrate the additive value of the state space grid analyses. Instead of relying on narrow temporal contingencies, the state space grid analyses took the overall pattern of an interaction into account (Granic and Patterson, 2006), which resulted in a better understanding of the process.

The current study is a step forward in the deviancy training literature due to several factors. First, the application of state space grid methodology is new in this type of research. The additive value of this methodology concerns the possibility for inspection of the overall temporal patterning of the course of an interaction on a state space grid (as shown in Figures 6.1 and 6.2). In addition, GridWare (Lamey *et al.*, 2004) determines several measures that reflect the temporal organization of an interaction. Dishion and colleagues (Granic and Dishion, 2003; Dishion *et al.*, 2004) suggested that since nearly all adolescents engage in rule-breaking talk, the temporal patterning might be more predictive of later antisocial behavior. Granic and Dishion (2003) found support for this reasoning; in their study the attractor index of rule-breaking talk was more predictive of later antisocial behavior than the duration adolescents engaged in rule-breaking talk during an interaction. Our results underscore the presumed importance of the temporal organization of an interaction. Whereas the sequential analyses failed to detect differences, state space grid analyses succeeded in showing differences between the different dyad types.

Another unique characteristic of the current study concerns the inclusion of composed dyads. In the original studies adolescents brought in one of their best friends for participation in the observation task. We coupled adolescents based on their level of delinquency and let them interact twice, to assess the possibility that participants behaved differently in the two types of dyads. A major advantage of this approach is that one can determine with relative certainty that individual behavior is influenced by the interaction partner. So far, most studies on deviancy training focused at the dyadic level. To assess the possibility that individuals adapt their behavior to peers, a presumption central in the theory of peer contagion, more individual analyses are necessary in future studies.

Due to the inclusion of the facility group, we were able to provide some insight into the feared effects of aggregating deviant youth in treatment groups (see Dishion *et al.*, 1999). Our results suggest that this worry is justified. As expected, we found that non-delinquent girls showed more rule-breaking talk in interaction with a delinquent partner than in interaction with a non-delinquent partner. Moreover, delinquent and mixed dyads showed more frequent episodes of rule-breaking talk than non-delinquent dyads, and facility dyads showed (1) a longer duration of rule-breaking talk and (2) more reinforcement of rule-breaking talk as reflected in a longer stay in the deviancy-training region. In short, this means that in delinquent and facility dyads, there are more instances for peers to positively reinforce one another's deviant behavior. Exactly this reinforcement plays an important role in the development and maintenance of deviant behavior. Although the sample size is too limited to make any firm statements about the results, this study offers potential implications for practice. If these results are replicated in a larger sample, it indicates that it is important to restrict utterances with a deviant content to a minimum in group treatment. Moreover, given the importance of positive reinforcement in the development and maintenance of deviant behavior, it is recommended to prevent such reinforcement by group members. We are aware that this is a very difficult challenge, since the results of a study by Buehler and colleagues (1966) suggest that the frequency of reinforcement provided by peers greatly outnumbers the reinforcement provided by staff. This makes sense since even in facilities adolescents spend the majority of their time in company of peers.

Although informal observations suggested that girls were at ease and not disturbed by the camera, the observation task remains a rather artificial situation to capture an interaction as it would unfold in "real life." Therefore, it is desirable to study the process of deviancy training in real life situations. Furthermore, research with larger sample sizes in different situations is required to gain more insight into the exact process of deviancy training.

Despite these limitations, our study showed that the deviancy-training process found in boys seems to apply for girls as well. With regard to the frequency of rule-breaking talk episodes, girls in the present study showed less frequent episodes than the boys in Dishion and colleagues' studies. However, the total duration of rule-breaking talk episodes for the girls in our study is similar to the duration of boys' engagement in rule-breaking talk. In other words, boys and girls engaged in the same amount of time in rule-breaking talk, but girls did this in fewer episodes. This could suggest that for girls engaging in rule-breaking talk is a stronger attractor than it is for boys, as it is apparently harder for girls to disengage from rule-breaking talk when it appears. This phenomenon may be caused by girls' greater orientation towards or emphasis on interpersonal relationships (Buhrmester and Furman, 1987). Their need to preserve the close relationship, might lead adolescent girls to reinforce their friend's behavior. When an interaction partner brings up a deviant topic (e.g., being drunk), girls may, for example, feel more inclined than boys to ask questions about the situation (e.g., "What did you drink?" "How did you feel?"), thereby reinforcing their interaction partner's rule-breaking talk.

A similar reinforcement mechanism seems to apply to internalizing behavior. In particular, studies found that depressive feelings of best friends are associated with adolescents' own depressive symptoms (Hogue and Steinberg, 1995; Stevens and Prinstein, 2005). Moreover, Rose (2002) found that girls actually spend more time than boys do "extensively discussing and revisiting problems, speculating about problems and focusing on negative feelings" (Rose, 2002, p. 1830) with their friends. By actively paying attention to each other's "problem talk," the rumination process that is so strongly associated with the development of internalizing problems, is dyadically reinforced. In this way, this specific reinforcement process is comparable to that of deviancy training. Adolescent girls are especially at risk for the negative effects associated with co-rumination, since their friendships are characterized by higher levels of intimacy and self-disclosure, which is a premise for engagement in co-rumination (Buhrmester and Furman, 1987). So, the relatively strong interpersonal orientation of girls might make them more vulnerable to detrimental interactions in a dyadic peer context.

Since delinquent girls suffer more often than boys from co-occurring internalizing problems (Barton *et al.*, 2001; Handwerk *et al.*, 2006; Stewart and Trupin, 2003; Timmons-Mitchell *et al.*, 1997), it is important to assess whether deviancy training and co-rumination co-occur in adolescent girls' dyadic relationships. Moreover, future studies should address the relationship between these reinforcement mechanisms and the interplay in their respective developmental pathways.

REFERENCES

Arnold, M. E., and Hughes, J. N. (1999). First do no harm: Adverse effects of grouping deviant youth for skills training. *Journal of School Psychology, 37*, 99–115.

Asch, S. E. (1952). *Social Psychology*. Englewood Cliffs, NJ: Prentice-Hall.

Baker, A. J. L., and Purcell, J. F. (2005). New York State residential treatment center admissions: Differences in histories of maltreatment, behavioral problems, and mental health problems. *Residential Treatment for Children and Youth, 22*, 39–53.

Bardone, A. M., Moffitt, T. E., Caspi, A., *et al.* (1998). Adult physical health outcomes of adolescent girls with conduct disorder, depression and anxiety. *Journal of the American Academy of Child and Adolescent Psychiatry, 37*, 594–601.

Barton, G., Rey, J. M., Simpson, P., *et al.* (2001). Patterns of critical incidents and their effect on outcome in an adolescent inpatient service. *Australian and New Zealand Journal of Psychiatry, 35*, 155–159.

Bongers, I. L., Koot, H. M., Van der Ende, J., *et al.* (2004). Developmental trajectories of externalizing behaviors in childhood and adolescence. *Child Development, 75*, 1523–1537.

Booth, R. E., and Zhang, Y. (1997). Conduct disorder and HIV risk behaviors among runaway and homeless adolescents. *Drug and Alcohol Dependence, 48*, 69–76.

Buehler, R. E., Patterson, G. R., and Furniss, J. M. (1966). The reinforcement of behavior in institutional settings. *Behaviour Research and Therapy, 4*, 157–167.

Buhrmester, D., and Furman, W. (1987). The development of companionship and intimacy. *Child Development, 58*, 1101–1113.

Chamberlain, P., and Reid, J. B. (1994). Differences in risk factors and adjustment for
male and female delinquents in treatment foster care. *Journal of Child and Family
Studies, 3*, 23–39.

Chamberlain, P., and Reid, J. B. (1998). Comparison of two community alternatives to
incarceration for chronic juvenile offenders. *Journal of Consulting and Clinical
Psychology, 66*, 624–633.

Connor, D. F., Doerfler, L. A., Toscano, P. F., *et al.* (2004). Characteristics of children and
adolescents admitted to a residential treatment center. *Journal of Child and Family
Studies, 13*, 497–510.

Cohen, J. (1988). *Statistical power analysis for the behavioral sciences*. New York: Academic
Press.

Dembo, R., Shemwell, M., Guida, J., *et al.* (1998). A longitudinal study of the impact of a
family empowerment intervention on juvenile offender psychosocial functioning:
A first assessment. *Journal of Child and Adolescent Substance Abuse, 8*, 15–54.

Dishion, T. J., Capaldi, D., Spracklen, K. M., *et al.* (1995). Peer ecology of male adolescent
drug use. *Development and Psychopathology, 7*, 803–824.

Dishion, T. J., Spracklen, K. M., Andrews, D. W., *et al.* (1996). Deviancy training in male
adolescent friendships. *Behavior Therapy, 27*, 373–390.

Dishion, T. J., Eddy, M., Haas, E., *et al.* (1997). Friendships and violent behavior during
adolescence. *Social Development, 6*, 207–223.

Dishion, T. J., McCord, J., and Poulin, F. (1999). When interventions harm: Peer groups
and problem behavior. *American Psychologist, 54*, 755–764.

Dishion, T. J., Poulin, F., and Burraston, B. (2001). Peer group dynamics associated with
iatrogenic effects in group interventions with high-risk young adolescents. *New
Directions for Child and Adolescent Development, 91*, 79–92.

Dishion, T. J., Nelson, S. E., Winter, C. E., *et al.* (2004). Adolescent friendship as a dynamic
system: Entropy and deviance in the etiology and course of male antisocial behavior.
Journal of Abnormal Child Psychology, 32, 651–663.

Gavin, L. A., and Furman, W. (1989). Age differences in adolescents' perceptions of their
peer groups. *Developmental Psychology, 25*, 827–834.

Gifford-Smith, M., Dodge, K. A., Dishion, T. J., *et al.* (2005). Peer influences in children
and adolescents: Crossing the bridge from developmental to intervention science.
Journal of Abnormal Child Psychology, 33, 255–265.

Gottman, J. M., and Roy, A. K. (1990). *Sequential analysis. A guide for behavioral researchers.*
Cambridge: Cambridge University Press.

Granic, I., and Dishion, T. J. (2003). Deviant talk in adolescent friendships: A step toward
measuring a pathogenic attractor process. *Social Development, 12*, 314–334.

Granic, I., and Hollenstein, T. (2003). Dynamic systems methods for models of developmental psychopathology. *Development and Psychopathology, 15*, 641–669.

Granic, I., and Patterson, G. R. (2006). Toward a comprehensive model of antisocial
development: A dynamic systems approach. *Psychological Review, 113*, 101–131.

Handwerk, M. L., Clopton, K., Huefner, J. C., *et al.* (2006). Gender differences in adolescents in residential treatment. *American Journal of Orthopsychiatry, 76*, 312–324.

Hartung, C. M., and Widiger, T. A. (1998). Gender differences in the diagnosis of mental
disorders: Conclusions and controversies of the *DSM-IV. Psychological Bulletin, 123*,
260–278.

Hartup, W. W. (1996). The company they keep: Friendships and their developmental
significance. *Child Development, 67*, 1–13.

Henggeler, S. W., Edwards, J., and Borduin, C. M. (1987). The family relations of female
juvenile delinquents. *Journal of Abnormal Child Psychology, 15*, 199–209.

Hipwell, A. E., Loeber, R., Stouthamer-Loeber, M., *et al.* (2002). Characteristics of girls
with early onset disruptive and antisocial behaviour. *Criminal Behaviour and Mental
Health, 12*, 99–118.

Hogue, A., and Steinberg, L. (1995). Homophily of internalized distress in adolescent peer groups. *Developmental Psychology, 31*, 897–906.

Hollenstein, T. (2005). *Using state space grids to display, describe, quantify, and analyze synchronized time series or event sequences.* Paper presented at the 5th International Conference on Methods and Techniques in Behavioral Research, Wageningen, The Netherlands.

Hollenstein, T. (2007). State space grids: Analyzing dynamics across development *International Journal of Behavioral Development, 31*, 384–396.

Hollenstein, T., and Lewis, M. D. (2006). A state space analysis of emotion and flexibility in parent-child interactions. *Emotion, 6*, 656–662.

Hoyt, S., and Scherer, D. G. (1998). Female delinquency: Misunderstood by the juvenile justice system, neglected by social science. *Law and Human Behavior, 22*, 81–107.

Keenan, K., Loeber, R., and Green, S. (1999). Conduct disorder in girls: A review of the literature. *Clinical Child and Family Psychology Review, 2*, 3–19.

Kerpelman, J. L., and Smith-Adcock, S. (2005). Female adolescents' delinquent activity. The intersection of bonds to parents and reputation enhancement. *Youth & Society, 37*, 176–200.

Kovacs, M., Krol, R. S. M., and Voti, L. (1994). Early onset psychopathology and the risk for teenage pregnancy among clinically referred girls. *Journal of the American Academy of Child and Adolescent Psychiatry, 33*, 106–113.

Krueger, R. F., Moffitt, T. E., Caspi, A., *et al.* (1998). Assortative mating for antisocial behavior: Developmental and methodological implications. *Behavior Genetics, 28*, 173–186.

Lamey, A., Hollenstein, T., Lewis, M. D., *et al.* (2004). GridWare (Version 1.1).

Leve, L. D., and Chamberlain, P. (2005). Association with delinquent peers: Intervention effects for youth in the juvenile justice system. *Journal of Abnormal Child Psychology, 33*, 339–349.

Lewis, D. O., Yeager, C. A., Cobham-Portorreal, C. S., *et al.* (1991). A follow-up of female delinquents: Maternal contributions to the perpetuation of deviance. *Journal of the American Academy of Child and Adolescent Psychiatry, 30*, 197–201.

McCabe, K. M., Lansing, A. E., Garland, A., *et al.* (2002). Gender differences in psychopathology, functional impairment, and familial risk factors among adjudicated delinquents. *Journal of the American Academy of Child and Adolescent Psychiatry, 41*, 860–867.

McCord, J. (1992). The Cambridge Somerville Study: A pioneering longitudinal experimental study of delinquency prevention. In J. McCord and R. E. Tremblay (eds), *Preventing Antisocial Behavior* (pp. 196–206). New York: The Guildford Press.

McCord, J. (2002). Counterproductive juvenile justice. *The Australian and New Zealand Journal of Criminology, 35*, 230–237.

Martino, S. C., Ellickson, P. L., Klein, D. J., *et al.* (2008). Multiple trajectories of physical aggression among adolescent boys and girls. *Aggressive Behavior, 34*, 61–75.

Moffitt, T. E. (1993). Adolescence-limited and life-course-persistent antisocial behavior: A developmental taxonomy. *Pscychological Review, 100*, 674–701.

Noldus. The Observer (Version 5). Wageningen, The Netherlands: Noldus Information Technology.

Noldus. The Observer (Version XT). Wageningen, The Netherlands: Noldus Information Technology.

Olejnik, S., and Algina, J. (2000). Measures of effect size for comparative studies: Applications, interpretations, and limitations. *Contemporary Educational Psychology, 25*, 241–286.

Pajer, K. A. (1998). What happens to bad girls? A review of the adult outcomes of antisocial adolescent girls. *American Journal of Psychiatry, 155*, 862–870.

Patterson, G. R., Dishion, T. J., and Yoerger, K. (2000). Adolescent growth in new forms of problem behavior: Macro- and micro-peer dynamics. *Prevention Science, 1*, 3–13.

Pleydon, A. P., and Schner, J. G. (2001). Female adolescent friendship and delinquent behavior. *Adolescence, 36,* 189–205.

Poe, J., Dishion, T. J., Griesler, P., *et al.* (1990). Topic Code. Unpublished coding manual. Available from Oregon Social Learning Center, 160 East 4th Avenue, Eugene, OR 97401-2426.

Quinton, D., Pickles, A., Maughan, B., *et al.* (1993). Partners, peers, and pathways: Assortative pairing and continuities in conduct disorder. *Development and Psychopathology, 5,* 763–783.

Reebye, P., Moretti, M. M., Wiebe, V. J., *et al.* (2000). Symptoms of posttraumatic stress disorder in adolescents with conduct disorder: Sex differences and onset patterns. *Canadian Journal of Psychiatry, 45,* 746–751.

Richters, J. E., and Martinez, P. E. (1993). Violent communities, family choices, and children's chances: An algorithm for improving the odds. *Development and Psychopathology, 5,* 609–627.

Robins, L. N., Tripp, J., and Pryzbeck, T. (1991). Antisocial personality. In L. N. Robins and D. A. Regier (eds), *Psychiatric Disorders in America: The Epidemiologic Catchment Area Study.* New York: The Free Press.

Rose, A. J. (2002). Co-rumination in the friendships of girls and boys. *Child Development, 73,* 1830–1843.

Silverthorn, P., and Frick, P. J. (1999). Developmental pathways to antisocial behavior: The delayed-onset pathway in girls. *Development and Psychopathology, 11,* 101–126.

Stevens, E. A., and Prinstein, M. J. (2005). Peer contagion of depressogenic attributional styles among adolescents: A longitudinal study. *Journal of Abnormal Child Psychology, 33,* 25–37.

Stewart, D. G., and Trupin, E. W. (2003). Clinical utility and policy implications of a statewide mental health screening process for juvenile offenders. *Psychiatric Services, 54,* 377–382.

Timmons-Mitchell, J., Brown, C., Schulz, S. C., *et al.* (1997). Comparing the mental health needs of female and male incarcerated juvenile delinquents. *Behavioral Sciences and The Law, 15,* 195–202.

Vazsonyi, A. T., and Keiley, M. K. (2007). Normative developmental trajectories of aggressive behaviors in African-American, American-Indian, Asian-American, Caucasian, and Hispanic children and early adolescents. *Journal of Abnormal Child Psychology, 35,* 1047–1062.

Weis, R., Whitemarsh, S. M., and Wilson, N. L. (2005). Military-style residential treatment for disruptive adolescents: Effective for some girls, all girls, when, and why? *Psychological Services, 2,* 105–122.

Weiss, B., Caron, A., Ball, S., *et al.* (2005). Iatrogenic effects of group treatment for antisocial youth. *Journal of Consulting and Clinical Psychology, 73,* 1036–1044.

Zoccolillo, M., Tremblay, R., and Vitaro, F. (1996). DSM-III-R and DSM-III criteria for conduct disorder in preadolescent girls: Specific but insensitive. *Journal of the American Academy of Child and Adolescent Psychiatry, 35,* 461–470.

CHAPTER 7

Girls' Aggressive Behavior Problems: A Focus on Relationships

Debra Pepler and Jennifer Connolly
York University, Canada

Wendy Craig
Queen's University, Canada

Depeng Jiang
University of Manitoba, Canada

This research was supported by Canadian Institutes of Health Research New Emerging Team Grant entitled, "Preventing Violence in the Lives of Girls and Women". The data for this paper were gathered with funding from the Ontario Mental Health Foundation. We are grateful to the staff of the Toronto Board of Education, to the students who participated in this research, and to the many undergraduate and graduate students who have assisted with the large research project.

As research on girls' aggression gained momentum, there has been an increased focus on relationships as a critical context for the expression and development of aggressive behavior problems. In our research and health promotion efforts, we are exploring the thesis that healthy development depends on healthy relationships. In this chapter, we focus on the relationships of aggressive girls to examine evidence on: (1) the nature of aggressive girls' relationships, (2) the link between girls' unhealthy development of aggressive behaviors and their unhealthy relationships, and (3) the implications of the growing understanding about aggressive girls' relationships for efforts to promote their healthy development. We include some of our research on girls who bully, because we view this as a particular form of

Understanding Girls' Problem Behavior: How Girls' Delinquency Develops in the Context of Maturity and Health, Co-occurring Problems, and Relationships, Edited by Margaret Kerr, Håkan Stattin, Rutger C. M. E. Engels, Geertjan Overbeek and Anna-Karin Andershed   © 2011 John Wiley & Sons, Ltd.

aggression that unfolds in the context of relationships; therefore, we specifically define bullying as a relationship problem (Pepler *et al.*, 2004a). In this review, we attempt to build an understanding of aggressive girls' developmental pathways with the emerging picture of aggressive girls' relationships from our own and others' research. Although fewer girls than boys exhibit consistently high levels of aggressive behavior problems, those girls who are highly aggressive tend to experience a range of psychosocial problems that are similar to or greater than their male counterparts (Moffitt *et al.*, 2001; Odgers *et al.*, 2008). Research, programming, and policy initiatives to understand and meet the developmental needs of aggressive girls are essential because aggressive behavior problems in childhood are strongly correlated with similar problems in adulthood for both girls and boys (Kokko and Pulkkinen, 2005; Odgers *et al.*, 2008).

With our focus on relationships, we have come to recognize the complexity involved in supporting children in their development of the capacity to form healthy relationships through socialization experiences. Compared to lessons in reading and arithmetic, with step-by-step processes that enable most children to acquire the skills, the lessons for successful social interactions are much more complex and not currently well understood. They require developing an understanding of one's own thoughts, emotions, and behaviors, as well as the thoughts, emotions, and behaviors of others. Those with whom children interact are highly variable and often unpredictable: even a single person varies from day to day in warmth, responsiveness, and emotions. The complexity of social interactions highlights the need to provide extensive, dynamic, and ongoing socialization support to children to enable them to relate positively to others, be effective in achieving social goals, and use their interpersonal power positively, rather than negatively.

As we consider aggressive girls' relationships, psychosocial problems, and healthy development, we are guided by a developmental-contextual perspective (Cairns, 1979; Magnuson, 1988; Ford and Lerner, 1992). First, developmental theory directs us to focus on the individual girl who is experiencing aggressive behavior problems. This focus highlights behaviors, motivations, and challenges that change with development and provides insight into the specific risk and protective processes in individual girls' lives. Within the present chapter, we consider what it might be in the make-up and behavioral patterns of aggressive girls themselves that may interfere with their development of healthy relationships. Secondly, the contextual perspective highlights interactions within the salient relationships or systems in which girls are developing. This focus highlights girls' relationships and leads us to consider how interactions within the family, peer group, school, and neighbourhood might be contributing to aggressive girls' behavior problems. Within this chapter, we consider what features of aggressive girls' relationships with their parents are associated with continuing aggressive problems through childhood and into adolescence. The developmental-contextual perspective informs programming by directing us to provide supports not only for individual girls' relationship capacity, but also to mobilize and transform the salient systems in their lives to promote healthy relationships.

THE NATURE OF AGGRESSIVE GIRLS' RELATIONSHIPS

In childhood, there are well marked gender differences in aggression: physical aggression comprises a higher proportion of boys' aggressive acts and indirect, non-physical aggression comprises a higher proportion of girls' aggressive acts (Bjorkqvist, Osterman, and Kaukiainen, 1992). These gender differences may be based, in part, on the different socialization experiences of girls and boys: aggression is tolerated more in boys and actively discouraged in girls, for whom prosocial behaviors are highly encouraged (Eron, Huesmann, and Zelli, 1991). For girls, in particular, a persistent pattern of relating to others with physical aggression may signal a significant gap in their socialization experiences. Aggressive girls may not have developed the social skills, social cognitions, and behavioral and emotional regulation that are required to relate competently to others, which may, in turn, put them at a substantial disadvantage as they meet developmental challenges in later childhood, adolescence, and adulthood. In the following section, we consider what aggressive girls bring to their relationships within the salient contexts for socialization – the family and the peer group.

Aggressive Girls' Contribution to Relationships

Aggressive girls, similar to aggressive boys, lack critical social skills that provide the foundation for positive interactions. In our naturalistic observations on the school playground, we found that aggressive children not only engaged in more frequent aggression than their non-aggressive peers, but they were also less predictable in social interactions. We observed that the aggressive children engaged in more "mixed" behaviors: initiating a prosocial behavior followed immediately by an antisocial behavior or visa versa before the other child even had time to respond (Pepler, Craig, and Roberts, 1988a). This style of ambivalent behaviors may make interactions with aggressive children unpredictable and unsettling for their peers. As expected, we observed that the aggressive children engaged in more frequent aggression than non-aggressive children. They also initiated more frequent touching of peers, which we coded as prosocial or neutral, but which may or may not have been welcomed by their peers. These behavior patterns, observed in both girls and boys, seem to reflect a lack of emotional and behavioral regulation and perhaps aggressive children's hostile perceptions and lack of awareness of the impact of their own behaviors on others. Aggressive children's lack of social skills and social understanding may constrain their potential for positive interactions and consequently limit the quality of their relationships with both parents and peers.

There is substantial evidence that aggressive children have troubled relationships with both their parents and peers. In an analysis of aggressive girls within the Canadian National Longitudinal Survey of Children and Youth (NLSCY), we found that aggressive girls' and boys' relationships were similarly strained – with reports of more conflicts with parents, siblings, and peers compared to non-aggressive children (Pepler and Sedighdeilami, 1998b). Aggressive girls and boys also had significantly fewer peer contacts and less positive peer relations compared to non-aggressive children within this nationally representative sample.

The strain that aggressive girls experience in their family and peer relationships may cause substantial distress because it interferes with the central social goal for girls and women – having close relationships (Maccoby, 1998; Underwood, 2003). Whereas boys generally have goals of social dominance, for which aggression might be somewhat adaptive (Hawley, 2003), girls' goals for social connectedness are most likely to be compromised by their aggression within these relationships. There is a paradox for aggressive girls: they are motivated to have close relationships and yet they are most likely to be aggressive towards those with whom they are closest, rather than towards unfamiliar people (Ehrensaft, 2005). In a recent analysis of the Canadian data from the World Health Organization's Health Behaviors of School-aged Children survey (HBSC), Craig and her colleagues found that girls' physical fights were most likely to be within the context of close relationships rather than with a stranger (10% for boys and 3% for girls) (Craig and McCuaig-Edge, 2007). When girls reported getting into a physical fight, 47% of the time it was with siblings, 33% of the time with a friend or acquaintance, 4% of the time with an adult family member, and 4% with a boyfriend or girlfriend. Within the family context, a higher proportion of girls who reported physical fighting indicated that they had fought with a sibling compared to boys (47% vs. 19%, respectively). The sibling relationship differs from peer relationships in many ways that may increase the likelihood of girls being aggressive in this context. Unlike friendships, this familial relationship is enduring and cannot be discontinued following a serious altercation. Therefore, within the intimacy of a sibling relationship or other family relationships, girls may be less inhibited to express aggression and less likely to suffer a disruption of these social connections because of their aggressive behaviors.

Bullying: A Relationship Problem

In our research on bullying over the past 20 years, we have come to understand bullying as a relationship problem that requires relationship solutions (Pepler *et al.*, 2006a). Girls and boys who persistently bully their siblings or peers experience daily lessons in the use of power and aggression to distress and control others. We are concerned that the relationship problems evident in

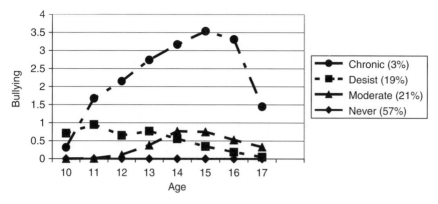

Figure 7.1 Developmental trajectories for girls' bullying.

bullying transform into sexual harassment and dating aggression in adolescence. For those aggressive youth who fail to develop the capacity for healthy relationships, we are also concerned that the interactional style of using power and aggression will transfer to marital, parenting, and workplace relationships in adulthood. Because it is a form of aggression that unfolds in the context of a relationship, bullying may be a key indicator of relationship difficulties. Children and youths' tendency to use power and aggression to control and distress others through bullying may create substantial strain on their relationships in all of the contexts where they live, learn, and play.

In our longitudinal research, we have been able to examine the developmental pathways in bullying from age 10 to 17 (Pepler *et al.*, 2008). For the present chapter, we plotted the development of girls' bullying separately from that of boys and we found four distinct pathways as depicted in Figure 7.1. A consideration of these four groups of girls highlights the relationship difficulties experienced by aggressive girls.

The majority of girls (57%) seldom if ever reported bullying their peers from late elementary through the end of high school. We expect that these girls have developed social skills, self control, and social understanding through healthy relationships at home and at school. Because their relationship contexts have presumably been healthy and have promoted the development of social competence, we expect girls not involved in bullying to have the least strained relationships with their parents and others.

A small group of girls (3%) reported chronically high levels of bullying with a peak in frequency at ages 14 and 15 and only a slight decline by age 17. It appears as if these girls are those for whom we should be most concerned. Their aggressive interpersonal behavior patterns may have developed within a troubled family context, as well as within a peer context of reinforcement for bullying within the peer group (Craig and Pepler, 1997). Without the appropriate support, these girls have not been able to learn the critical social skills, self control, as well as the social understanding and moral standards essential for contributions within a civil society.

Approximately one in five girls reported moderate bullying that persisted through the late elementary and high school years. We are concerned that these girls who bully at a lower but persistent frequency might not be detected by parents or teachers because they are not bullying with high frequency and may be more socially skilled than those girls who bully most frequently and persistently. Nevertheless, their tendency to use power and aggression within their relationships may create substantial problems for them as they try to establish relationships and as others try to cope with their bullying approach to some relationships.

THE LINK BETWEEN UNHEALTHY DEVELOPMENT AND UNHEALTHY PARENT–DAUGHTER RELATIONSHIPS

The basic tenet for our research program is that healthy development depends on healthy relationships. In our own research, we are able to examine the development of girls' aggression and the quality of their relationships longitudinally. With our data on girls' (and boys') development from late elementary (age 10) through late high school (age 17), we can examine associations between (un) healthy development and (un)healthy relationships, but fall short of providing strong causal evidence for our central theme. For this chapter, we were interested in examining whether girls who develop an interpersonal style of using power and aggression also develop patterns of aggressive conflicts with their parents using our longitudinal data. We examined girls' responses on three questions that specifically tap into aggressive conflicts including: disagreed and fought; yelled at each other; stayed angry a long time after arguing. A four group trajectory model emerged (see Figure 7.2). Five percent of girls fell onto a trajectory with consistently high aggressive conflicts with their parents; 17% fell onto a trajectory with increasing conflicts from age 10 to 17; 34% fell onto a trajectory with some aggressive conflict over these years; and 44% of girls reported low levels of conflict with their parents.

Having identified these pathways in the development of bullying and in the development of parent-daughter aggressive conflict within our longitudinal data, we were able to link the two developmental trajectories and compare transitional probabilities across the bullying groups (see Figure 7.3). In this way, we were able to look at the overlap between girls' bullying problems and their conflict with their parents.

In the chronic bullying group, 32% of the girls fell onto a trajectory of consistently high conflict with their parents, 68% fell onto a trajectory of increasing conflict, and none fell onto the lower conflict trajectories. In the group of girls whose bullying desisted, 20% followed a trajectory of consistently high conflicts with parents, but the other 80% had moderate or low conflict with their

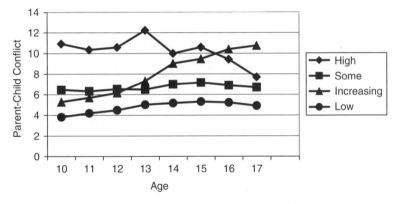

Figure 7.2 Developmental trajectories of parent–daughter aggressive conflicts.

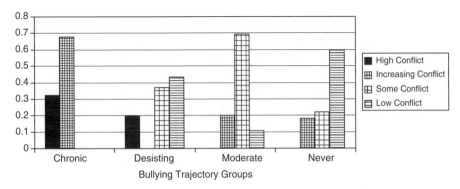

Figure 7.3 Probabilities linking girls' bullying and parent–daughter conflict trajectory groups.

parents. Although none of the girls who fell onto the moderate trajectory also fell onto the 'high conflict with parents' trajectory, 20% were on a trajectory with conflict that increased from late childhood to early adolescence and 69% were on trajectory with some conflict with their parents. The majority of girls who were on the never bullying trajectory fell onto a trajectory of low conflict with their parents from elementary through the end of high school.

Similar to other forms of aggression, a smaller proportion of girls than boys follow a pathway of high and consistent bullying through the late elementary and high school years, suggesting that this form of aggression is quite atypical for girls. Our research indicates that those girls who use power and aggression with peers at a consistently high rate are likely to experience similar problems of aggressive conflict with their parents. This association is most likely attributable to both the girls' social competence and aggressive interactional style and to the family contexts in which they are growing up. There is strong evidence that difficulties within the family, a child's primary social context, contribute to the development of aggression (Patterson, 1982; Loeber and Stouthamer-Loeber, 1986). The family risks in childhood, such as ineffective parenting and troubled family contexts, appear to operate similarly for boys and girls in contributing to antisocial behavioral problems (Moffitt *et al.*, 2001). When considering the potential processes within parent–child interactions that might foster the development of bullying, we can turn to the evidence that harsh and punitive parenting is linked to children's aggressive behavior problems (Olweus, 1978; Smith and Myron-Wilson, 1998). Parents are in a position of power relative to children; therefore, when they use harsh punishment, they model the use of power and aggression for their children, who may then transfer these lessons to bullying peers. Farrington (1993) identified an intergenerational link in bullying: Parents who had bullied in childhood were likely to have children who also bullied their peers. The family relationships of children who persistently bully are likely to be strained, with frequent conflict, lack of closeness, and poor monitoring in adolescence (Farrington, 1993; Olweus, 1993; Baldry, 2003). Our longitudinal research suggests that girls who bully at a high or moderate rate are at risk for high or increasing aggressive conflicts with their parents. Therefore, the very relationship that has the potential to help girls deal with the challenges of adolescence and promote healthy development is highly conflictual and unlikely to be protective.

Children's development is continually shaped through an interaction between their own behaviors and the relationship contexts in which they develop. Our research suggests that children with aggressive behavior problems approach relationships with a disadvantage in their capacity to form and maintain healthy relationships. The relationships in which they live on a day-to-day basis create a context in which the aggressive behavior and negativity are sustained, often reinforced, and may be exacerbated. In a recent transactional analysis of maternal negativity and child externalizing behavior, we found that children and mothers influenced each others' behaviors, with the impact of children's aggressive behaviors on mothers' negativity being stronger than the reciprocal effect (Yaghoub-Zadeh, Jenkins, and Pepler, 2010). This finding illustrates children's effects on their relationship contexts. The reciprocal effects between parents and children within these analyses occurred over three years, rather than a moment-to-moment basis as described by Patterson and his colleagues in their description of coercive processes relating to antisocial development (1992). The processes in the moment may accumulate and translate over time in similar ways: When one partner in a relationship is negative and hostile, the other is likely to respond by escalating his/her own negativity. The strong links between the developmental trajectories of girls' bullying and the developmental trajectories of conflict within their relationships with parents most likely arise from reciprocal influences of the aggressive girls and their parents, who themselves may be ill-equipped to support and monitor their troubled daughters.

A negative family context may be especially salient for girls' development of aggressive behavior problems. Girls tend to be more tied into the family and spend more time at home than boys (Maccoby, 1998). Given girls' motivation for close relationships and their time spent with family, it follows that family risks may be more strongly associated with girls' than with boys' aggression. Research points to several relevant family relationship risk processes for the development of aggression in girls including: parent-child conflict, poor problem-solving, weak attachment, and rejection by caregivers (Brook, Whiteman, and Finch, 1993; Pakaslahti *et al.*, 1998; Pepler and Sedighdeilami, 1998; Sprott and Doob, 1998). In the next section, we examine the risk for girls' healthy development associated with living in family relationships character- ized by these types of relationship risks.

The Link Between Unhealthy Development and Unhealthy Relationships for Aggressive Girls

The research cited above, together with a substantial body of evidence, provides empirical support for a developmental-contextual perspective on aggressive behavior problems (Cairns and Cairns, 1991; Magnusson, 1988). In considering the potential link between unhealthy development and unhealthy relationships specifically for aggressive girls, we can only speculate at this point about how these strained and ineffective relationships within the family might contribute to a range of health problems.

In starting to build an understanding of the association between girls' unhealthy development and unhealthy relationships, we can turn to research showing the strong link between girls' experiences of abuse and their develop- ment of aggression, particularly for sexual abuse. In a meta-analysis on girls' experiences of sexual abuse, Kendall-Tackett and her colleagues (1993) found the highest effect sizes for links to externalizing behaviors, such as sexualized behaviors and aggression. Almost half the victims of child sexual abuse exhi- bited aggressive or antisocial symptoms (Kendall-Tackett, Williams, and Finkelhor, 1993). Girls who are chronically exposed to abuse either directly, or indirectly by witnessing family violence, may not only develop aggressive interactional styles, but may also experience post traumatic stress symptoms, which would register as health problems on questionnaire reports. In addition to this specific link through trauma, girls who grow up in strained and disor- ganized families may experience problems simply as a function of their rela- tionship contexts. With ineffective parenting, these girls may lack consistency in their daily living and in the required scaffolding support from their parents, both of which are essential to the development of health-promoting behaviors. We explored these potential links within a recent paper in which we hypothe- sized that aggressive girls who report difficulties in their family relationships are at even greater risk for health problems than similarly aggressive girls with few family relationships difficulties (Pepler *et al.*, 2006b).

In exploring the thesis that healthy development depends on healthy relationships, we expected that aggressive girls growing up in strained rela- tionships would experience a range of physical and mental health problems.

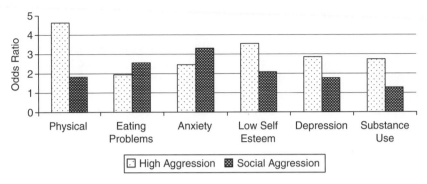

Figure 7.4 Odds ratios of having elevated health problems for aggressive girls relative to non-aggressive girls.

There is considerable evidence for the link between girls' aggression and health problems from both concurrent and longitudinal research. In the Dunedin study, Bardone and her colleagues (1998) found that girls who were aggressive at age 15 reported poorer general health at age 21 than non-aggressive girls. At the age 32 follow-up on this sample, Odgers and colleagues (2008) found that both women and men on the life course persistent antisocial pathway (starting early and continuing through adolescence) were engaging in serious violence in adulthood and had significant mental and physical health problems. There is also evidence that aggressive girls experience more gender-specific health difficulties. They are more likely than non-aggressive girls to have: experienced gynecological problems, more sexual partners, contracted a sexually transmitted disease, used birth control pills, and experienced pregnancy by late adolescence (Bardone *et al.*, 1998; Serbin *et al.*, 1991).

In our research, we examined whether aggressive early adolescent girls had indications of emerging health problems and whether these health problems were linked to difficulties in the girls' primary family relationships – with their parents (Pepler *et al.*, 2006b). We started by investigating whether aggressive girls are more likely to have physical and emotional health problems than non-aggressive girls. Through a Latent Class Analysis, we identified three distinct groups of girls: those who were generally high on aggression (both physical and social aggression) (13%), those who were only high on social aggression (26%), and those who were non-aggressive (60%). As can be seen in Figure 7.4, both high aggressive and socially aggressive girls had elevated odds ratios for physical health, emotional health, and substance use problems. Compared to non-aggressive girls, the highly aggressive girls were almost five times more likely to have physical health problems, two times more likely to have eating problems, two and a half times more likely to have anxiety problems, three and a half times more likely to have low self esteem, almost three times more likely to suffer from depressive symptoms and to use cigarettes, alcohol, and/or drugs. Compared to non-aggressive girls, the socially aggressive girls were almost two times more likely to have physical health problems, three and a half times more likely to have eating problems, over three times more likely to have anxiety problems, two times more likely to have low self esteem, and almost two times more likely to suffer from depressive symptom. All of these differences were significant. These data leave little doubt that girls who are aggressive, either generally high on aggression or high on social aggression only, suffer from a wide range of physical and mental health problems.

From a developmental-contextual perspective, we can think about potential mechanisms that might underlie the associations between girls' aggressive behavior problems and health problems. This perspective directs us to focus on characteristics of individual girls as well as on the characteristics of the relationship contexts in which they are growing up.

In considering the individual characteristics of girls who are highly aggressive, we can only speculate as to what within their makeup would interfere with healthy physical and emotional development. The link between physical aggression and lack of self regulation of thought, behaviors, and emotions (Seguin and Zelazo, 2005) may in part account for the association between aggression and health, at least for physically aggressive girls. Those girls who are at risk for being physically aggressive because they cannot or do not regulate their thoughts, behaviors, and emotions, may be at risk for similar self-regulation problems when it comes to health behaviors (e.g., hygiene, eating behaviors, risk-taking behaviors). The chronic difficulties that aggressive girls experience in regulating their thoughts, behaviors, and emotions raise concerns about their abilities to become self-sufficient and capable of planfulness in meeting their health needs through adolescence and into adulthood.

There is considerable evidence that social cognitions, understanding, and perspectives pose problems for aggressive children and adolescents. In our own research, adolescents who were persistently high on bullying from elementary through high school were 16 times more likely to report problems with moral disengagement (e.g., not caring about the well being of someone whom one has hurt) compared to adolescents who never bullied (Pepler et al., 2008). The research of Dodge and colleagues identified the tendency of aggressive children to view others around them with hostility (Dodge et al., 1990). Similarly, Downey and colleagues have shown that some youth and adults expect others to reject them and are highly sensitive to others' negative behaviors, which engenders hostility (Downey et al. 2004). The social-cognitive perspectives and understandings of aggressive children is an area in need of further research to identify whether these cognitive states mediate aggressive children's health problems through increased stress reactivity or other mechanisms, such as increased likelihood for risk taking or associating with similarly aggressive peers.

Following a consideration of individual characteristics that might help explain the link between girls' aggression and health problems, we now turn to a consideration of the relationship contexts in which aggressive girls develop. Our study of the links between aggression and health posed a question similar

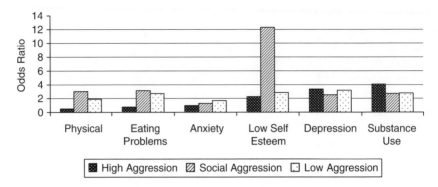

Figure 7.5 Odds ratios of having elevated health problems for girls with high levels of conflict with parents (Relative to girls with low conflict with parents).

to the focus on bullying: Do aggressive girls have more problems with their parents than non-aggressive girls? Consistent with the associations between bullying and parent-daughter conflict, we found a significant association between parent-daughter conflict and girls' aggression with the comparison of highly aggressive, socially aggressive, and non-aggressive girls. Using the three items discussed above (i.e., disagreed and fought with their parents, yelled at each other, and stayed angry a long time after arguing), we found that a third of highly aggressive girls reported high levels of aggressive conflict with their parents, compared to a quarter of the socially aggressive girls and less than a fifth of the non-aggressive girls.

Given our thesis that healthy development depends on healthy relationships, we finally investigated whether the quality of the parent-daughter relationship plays a role in the association between girls' aggression and their health problems? We computed the odds ratios of having elevated health outcomes comparing the girls within each group who reported high conflict with their parents to those who reported low or no conflict. The data for the three groups of girls are presented in Figure 7.5.

For the highly aggressive girls, reports of high conflict with their parents significantly increased their odds of having elevated levels of depression and substance use (by four times). For socially aggressive girls, the relative risk of health problems associated with high conflict with parents was found to be significant for all problems except anxiety. Socially aggressive girls who reported high conflict with their parents were more likely to have elevated physical, eating, self esteem, depression, and substance use problems compared to socially aggressive girls who reported low conflict with their parents. Similar patterns were found for the non-aggressive girls: compared to those with low conflict with parents: those who reported high conflict had significantly elevated odds of having eating, self esteem, depression, and substance use problems.

These analyses provide preliminary support for our contention that healthy development depends on healthy relationships. Although we are not able to make a causal inference within the present study, we can begin to understand the association between strained relationships and girls' health problems. It is interesting to note that the differences between the high and low parent-daughter conflict groups were found across fewer domains for the highly aggressive group of girls. These girls, who are high on both physical and social aggression, experience the most elevated health and parent-daughter aggressive conflict problems and even the physically and socially aggressive girls with less strained relationships with parents seem to have compromised health status.

IMPLICATIONS FOR PREVENTION AND INTERVENTIONS TO PROMOTE HEALTHY DEVELOPMENT

There is emerging evidence that we can begin to weave together in support of our hypothesis that healthy development depends on healthy relationships. In line with a developmental-contextual-perspective, this research indicating that healthy relationships may be critical to healthy development might provide important direction for the development of interventions for aggressive girls.

Research on effective interventions for aggressive girls is just beginning to emerge. Over the past ten years, there have been a few reviews of intervention strategies that are responsive to girls' developmental and relationship issues. In 1998, the Gender-Specific Programming for Girls Advisory Committee of the US Office of Juvenile Justice and Delinquency Prevention completed a review and set out some key principles for programs for antisocial girls. They recommended: taking girls' developmental needs and challenges into account; teaching girls relationship and decision making skills; and empowering girls to speak for themselves and see options in their lives. In a recent review, Hubbard and Matthews (2008) considered two different perspectives on programming for antisocial girls. One perspective is that there are established interventions that are known to work for antisocial youth that target known risk factors and these are adequate for girls as well as boys. The therapeutic approaches generally include behavioral, social learning, and cognitive strategies. The other perspective has been developed by those who advocate for gender-responsive programming. They recommend program elements that include: education, life skills, health and sexual behavior, assertiveness, self-esteem enhancement, and relationship building. Hubbard and Matthews conclude that programming for antisocial girls should draw from evidence-based elements from both of these perspectives.

In this paper, we have focused on understanding the nature of aggressive girls' relationships, which requires not only a consideration of the girls' capacity to engage in relationships, but also a consideration of the relationship contexts in which they are growing up. There is substantial evidence that aggressive girls lack many of the key social-emotional capacities for engaging in and maintaining positive relationships. They are more frequently aggressive than their non-aggressive peers and they are less predictable in social interactions. Aggressive girls' problems reflect a lack of emotional and behavioral regulation and perhaps a lack of awareness of the impact of their own behavior on others. From a developmental-contextual perspective, it appears as if these girls have failed to develop the skills required for age-appropriate relationships. Their lack of skills, in turn, may contribute to the difficulties that they experience in their relationships within the family and peer group contexts.

The research leaves little doubt that aggressive girls, themselves, need support to learn, practise, and integrate critical social-emotional skills and social understanding. In her review on the development of conduct problems in girls' relationships, Ehrensaft (2005) recommended that treatment for girls focus on building positive skills to steer troubled girls from a pathway of intense, unstable, and high conflict relationships. From a developmental-contextual perspective, we recognize that efforts to support aggressive girls' development of positive skills are necessary, but not sufficient. There also needs to be a focus on enhancing positive aspects of the primary and secondary relationship contexts in which these girls are growing up, through parent training and family support, outreach to schools, and efforts to promote positive peer relationships at school and in the community.

The SNAP® Girls Connection (GC) program is one example of a gender-sensitive intervention designed to promote the development of relationship capacity for young aggressive girls. Using the Early Assessment Risk List for Girls (EARL-21G; Levene *et al.*, 2001), we have learned that girls in the SNAP® GC come from chaotic families with high levels of mother-daughter conflict and experience multiple separations from their primary caregivers (Yuile, 2007). Such family stressors contribute to strained relationships, disrupted attachment, and limit the girls' development of healthy internal working models of relationships and interactional styles.

The SNAP® GC program has two primary components: a cognitive-behavioral intervention for the young aggressive girls and a complementary parent training intervention. The SNAP® GC for the girls focuses on skill development, social problem solving, emotion regulation, and anger management, with an emphasis on behavioral rehearsal and generalization activities. By promoting girls' social skills, the SNAP® GC aims to increase their capacity for positive interactions and improve the quality of their relationships with parents and peers. The concurrent SNAP® Parenting program is based on positive relationship development and focuses on helping parents develop contingent responses, effective monitoring, and anger management and relationship skills so that they are able to support the girls' acquisition of prosocial behaviors. In addition to these two primary components, the SNAP® GC also includes a program entitled, Girls Growing Up Healthy, a mother-daughter group designed to address sexual and physical health issues and enhance mother-daughter relationships. Adjunct services, such as school advocacy, tutoring, and family counseling, are also offered to meet the needs and interests of individual girls and their families (for a fuller description of the SNAP® GC program see Walsh, Pepler, and Levene 2002; Pepler, Walsh, and Levene, 2004b; Pepler *et al.*, 2010).

In an evaluation of the SNAP® GC program (Pepler *et al.*, 2010), we found that participating girls were rated as showing significant improvements compared to a waiting list group on externalizing, internalizing, and social problems. In addition, both parents and their daughters reported significant improvements in parenting as measured by consistent, rational and effective parenting skills. These treatment effects remained stable for the treatment group at the six-month follow-up assessment.

The girls who are referred to clinical programs for aggressive behavior problems, such as the SNAP® GC, are likely to be similar to the highly aggressive girls identified in our longitudinal study, with high levels of both physical and social aggression. Therefore, in developing programs that are sensitive to aggressive girls' problems, it is also important to consider their physical and mental health profiles. In our research, the highly aggressive girls, when compared to non-aggressive girls, were almost five times more likely to have physical health problems, two times more likely to have eating problems, two and a half times more likely to have anxiety problems, three and a half times more likely to have low self esteem, and almost three times more likely to suffer from depressive symptoms and to use cigarettes, alcohol, and/or drugs. Although this constellation of health problems may not be apparent upon referral, the girls' physical and mental health difficulties should be considered in assessments and in treatment planning. Our research suggests that some of these health difficulties may improve if the girls' relationships with their mothers improve, because of the strong link between these two factors. Therefore, the Girls Growing Up Healthy component of the SNAP® GC program described above may be beneficial for improving both mother-daughter relationships and girls' health prospects. Our research on that program is in progress.

Interventions focused only on the girls are necessary, but not sufficient. The present review provides substantial evidence that the relationships in which aggressive girls live on a day-to-day basis create a context in which their aggressive behaviors and negativity are likely to be sustained and exacerbated over time. Aggressive girls' relationships with their parents tend to be characterized by high levels of aggressive conflicts, disagreements and fighting, yelling, and staying angry for a long time. Aggressive girls also report fights with their siblings. In addition, it appears as that not only the girls' social-emotional well being, but also their physical and mental healthy may be jeopardized by strain in the quality of their relationships with their parents. Parents, therefore, also need support in their efforts to provide a nurturing and non-aggressive home environment for their children. Observations of mother-child interactions for boys and some girls who had participated in the SNAP® program showed that the quality of the interactions improved following treatment, especially the ability of the dyad to repair – moving from mutually negative interactions to more positive ones (Granic *et al.*, 2007).

CONCLUSION

In our research programs and our social change efforts, we are exploring the thesis that healthy development depends on healthy relationships. In leading the national Promoting Relationships and Eliminating Violence Network (www.prevnet.ca), we have come to believe that the most effective means to promote healthy relationships and prevent bullying for children and youth is to improve the practice of adults who are responsible for them. We understand that knowledge about the critical role of healthy relationships for children's healthy development is required by all adults in all settings where children live, learn, play, and work. These adults play a critical role socializing and supporting children and youth: they serve as role models, mentors, guides, and teachers.

The collective work on aggressive girls provides a window to understanding the links between healthy development and healthy relationships. In this paper, we have highlighted both the problems that aggressive girls bring to their relationships and the strained family contexts in which they grow up. Consistent with a developmental-contextual perspective, it is most likely that both the girls' own lack of self-control and social understanding, as well as the stressful family context in which they live, contribute to their physical and mental health problems. Taken together, the research reviewed in this chapter highlights the pressing need to identify aggressive girls early in their development. By identifying girls with relationship difficulties in the family, the peer group or at school, we may be able not only to promote healthy relationship contexts for them, but also to prevent the development of serious psychological and physical health problems. In addition, if we are able to foster positive relationship skills for these high-risk girls, we may be able to interrupt the inter-generational transfer of aggressive behavior problems.

The historical lack of attention to the risks and outcomes for aggressive girls may relate to the fact that girls do not accelerate to the high levels of delinquency and criminality that aggressive boys reach and, therefore, do not pose as salient a social concern. Nevertheless, if girls' development is left unsupported and if they grow up in troubled relationships, these girls may become young women with undeveloped social capacity – who are poorly equipped to become the mothers of the next generation.

REFERENCES

Baldry, A. C. (2003). Bullying and exposure to domestic violence. *Child Abuse and Neglect*, 27, 713–732.

Bardone, A. M., Moffitt, T. E., Caspi, A., *et al.* (1998). Adult physical health outcomes of adolescent girls with conduct disorder, depression, and anxiety. *Journal of the American Academy of Child and Adolescent Psychiatry*, 37, 594–601.

Bjorkqvist, K., Osterman, K., and Kaukiainen, A. (1992). The development of direct and indirect aggressive strategies in males and females. In K. Bjorkqvist and P. Niemela (eds), *Of Mice and Women: Aspects of Female Aggression* (pp. 51–64). San Diego: Academic Press.

Brook, J. S., Whiteman, M., and Finch, S. (1993). Role of mutual attachment in drug use: A longitudinal study. *Journal of the American Academy of Child and Adolescent Psychiatry, 32*, 982–989.

Cairns, R. B. (1979). *Social development: The origins and plasticity of interchanges.* San Francisco, CA: W. H. Freeman.

Cairns, R. B., and Cairns, B. D. (1991). Social cognition and social networks: A developmental perspective. In D. J. Pepler and K. H. Rubin (Eds.), *The development and treatment of childhood aggression* (pp. 249–278). Mahwah: Lawrence Erlbaum Associates, Inc.

Craig, W. M. and McCuaig Edge, H. (2007). *Bullying and Fighting in Canada.* World Health Organization Report on Health of Youth in Canada.

Craig, W. and Pepler, D. (1997). Observations of bullying and victimization in the schoolyard. *Canadian Journal of School Psychology, 2*, 41–60.

Dodge, K. A., Price, J. M., Bachorowski, J., *et al.* (1990). Hostile attributional biases in severely aggressive adolescents. *Journal of Abnormal Psychology, 99*, 385–392.

Downey, G., Irwin, L., Ramsey, M., *et al.* (2004). Rejection sensitivity and girls' aggression. In M. Moretti and C. Odgers (eds), *Girls' Aggression: Contributing Factors and Intervention Principles* (pp. 7–25). Washington, DC: American Psychological Association Press.

Ehrensaft, M. K. (2005). Interpersonal relationships and sex differences in the development of conduct problems. *Clinical Child and Family Psychology Review, 8*, 39–63.

Eron, L. D., Huesmann, L. R., and Zelli, A. (1991). The role of parental variables in the learning of aggression. In D. J. Pepler and K. H. Rubin (eds), *The Development and Treatment of Childhood Aggression* (pp. 169–88). Mahwah: Lawrence Erlbaum Associates, Inc.

Farrington, D. P. (1993). Understanding and preventing bullying. In M. Tonry (Ed.), *Crime and Justice* (Vol. 17, pp. 381–458). Chicago: University of Chicago Press.

Ford, D. H., and Lerner, R. M. (1992). *Developmental Systems Theory: An Integrative Approach.* Newbury Park: Sage Publications.

Gender-Specific Programming for Girls Advisory Committee (1998). http://www.ojjdp.ncjrs.org/pubs/principles/ch3_3.html. Accessed on June 19, 2008.

Granic, I., O'Hara, A., Pepler, D., *et al.* (2007). A dynamic systems analysis of parent-child changes associated with successful "real-world" interventions with aggressive children. *Journal of Abnormal Child Psychology, 35*, 845–857.

Hawley, P. H. (2003). Prosocial and coercive configuration of resource control in early adolescence: A case for the well-adapted Machiavellian. *Merrill-Palmer Quarterly, 49*, 279–309.

Hubbard, D. J. and Matthews, B. (2008). Reconciling the differences between the "Gender-Responsive" and the "What Works" literatures to improve services for girls. *Crime and Delinquency, 54*, 225–258.

Kendall-Tackett, K. A., Williams, L. M., and Finkelhor, D. (1993). Impact of sexual abuse on children: A review and synthesis of recent empirical studies. *Psychological Bulletin, 113*, 164–80.

Kokko, K., and Pulkkinen, L. (2005). Stability of aggressive behavior from childhood to middle age in women and men. *Aggressive Behavior, 31*, 485–97.

Levene, K. S., Augimeri, L. K., Pepler, D. J., *et al.* (2001). *Early Assessment Risk List for Girls: EARL-21G, Version 1, Consultation Edition.* Toronto: Earlscourt Child and Family Centre.

Loeber, R., and Stouthamer-Loeber, M. (1986). Family factors as correlates of and predictors of juvenile conduct problems and delinquency. In N. Morris and M. Tonry (eds), *Crime and justice: An annual review of research* (Vol. 7, pp. 29–149). Chicago: University of Chicago Press.

Maccoby, E. E. (1998). *The two sexes: Growing up apart, coming together.* Cambridge, MA: Harvard University Press.

Magnusson, D. (1988). *Individual development from an interactional perspective: A longitudinal study*. Hillsdale, NJ: Lawrence Erlbaum Associates.

Moffitt. T. E., Caspi, A., Rutter, M., *et al.* (2001). *Sex differences in antisocial behavior*. Cambridge, UK: Cambridge University Press.

Odgers, CL., Moffitt, T. E, Broadbent, J.M., *et al.* (2008). Female and male antisocial trajectories: From childhood origins to adult outcomes. *Development and Psychopathology*, *20*, 673–716.

Olweus, D. (1978). *Aggression in the schools: Bullies and Whipping Boys*. New York: John Wiley & Sons, Inc.

Olweus, D. (1993). *Bullying at School: What we know and what we can do*. Oxford: Blackwell.

Pakaslahti, L., Spoof, I., Asplund-Peltola, R. L., *et al.* (1998). Parents' social problem-solving strategies in families with aggressive and non-aggressive girls. *Aggressive Behavior, 24*, 37–51.

Patterson, G. R. (1982). *Coercive family processes: A social learning approach*. Eugene, OR: Castalia.

Patterson, G., Reid, J., and Dishion, T. (1992). *Antisocial Boys*. Eugene, OR: Castalia.

Pepler, D. J., Craig, W. M., and Roberts, W. L. (1998a). Observations of aggressive and nonaggressive children on the school playground. *Merrill-Palmer Quarterly, 44*, 55–76.

Pepler, D. J., and Sedighdeilami, F. (1998b). *Aggressive Girls in Canada*. Working paper W-98-30E, Applied Research Branch, Human Resources Development Canada.

Pepler, D. J., Craig, W., Yuile, A., *et al.* (2004a). Girls who bully: A developmental and relational perspective. In M. Putallaz and J. Kupersmidt (eds), *Aggression, Antisocial Behavior, and Violence Among Girls* (pp. 90–109). New York: Guilford Publications.

Pepler, D. Walsh, M., and Levene, K. (2004b). Interventions for aggressive girls: Tailoring and measuring the fit. In M. Moretti, C. Odgers, and M. Jackson (eds), *Girls and Violence: Contributing Factors and Intervention Principles. Perspectives in Law and Psychology* series (pp. 131–145). New York: Kluwer Academic/Plenum Press.

Pepler, D. J., Craig, W. M., Connolly, J. A. *et al.* (2006a). A developmental perspective on bullying. *Aggressive Behavior, 32*, 376–384.

Pepler, D. J., Waddell, J., Jiang, D., *et al.* (2006b). Aggressive Girls' Health and Parent-Daughter Conflict. *Women's Health and Urban Life Journal. 5*, 25–41.

Pepler, D. J., Jiang, D., Craig, W., *et al.* (2008). Developmental trajectories of bullying and associated factors. *Child Development, 79*, 325–338.

Pepler, D., Walsh, M., Yuile, A., *et al.* (2010). Bridging the gender gap: Interventions with aggressive girls and their parents. *Prevention Science*. DOI 10.1007/s11121-009-0167-4.

Seguin, J.R., and Zelazo, P.D. (2005). Executive function in early physical aggression. In R. E. Tremblay, W. W. Hartup, and J. Archer (eds), *Developmental Origins of Aggression* (pp. 307–329). New York: Guilford Press.

Serbin, L. A., Peters, P. L., McAffer, V. J., *et al.* (1991). Childhood aggression and withdrawal as predictors of adolescent pregnancy, early parenthood, and environmental risk for the next generation. *Canadian Journal of Behavioral Science, 23*, 318–331.

Smith, P. K., and Myron-Wilson, R. (1998). Parenting and school bullying. *Clinical Child Psychology and Psychiatry, 3*, 405–417.

Sprott, J., and Doob, A. (1998). *Who are the most violent ten and eleven year olds?* Working paper W-98-29E, Applied Research Branch, Human Resources Development Canada.

Underwood, M. K. (2003). *Social Aggression Among Girls*. New York, NY: Guilford Press.

Walsh, M., Pepler, D., and Levene, K. (2002). A model intervention for girls with disruptive behavior problems: The Earlscourt Girls Connection. *Canadian Journal of Counselling, 36*, 297–311.

Yaghoub-Zadeh, Z., Jenkins, J., and Pepler, D. (2010). A transactional analysis of maternal negativity and child externalizing behavior. *International Journal of Behavioral Development*, 34, 218–228.

Yuile, A. (2007). Developmental pathways of aggressive girls: A gender-sensitive approach to risk assessment, intervention, and follow-up. Doctoral dissertation, York University, Toronto, ON, Canada.

CHAPTER 8

Attachment and Aggression: From Paradox to Principles of Intervention to Reduce Risk of Violence in Teens

Marlene M. Moretti and Ingrid Obsuth
Simon Fraser University, Canada

Support for this chapter was provided by the Canadian Institutes of Health Research (CIHR), Institute of Gender and Health (IGH), New Emerging Team grant (#54020) and CIHR Operating Grant (#84567) and CIHR Senior Chair funding awarded to Dr. M. Moretti.

Virtually every developed nation is troubled by the current levels of aggression, violence and antisocial behavior among their teens and young adults. The Canadian Psychological Association (CPA), for example, identified aggression and violence as "a major contemporary concern" (CPA, 2007). In 2005 the US Center for Disease Control surveyed a nationally-representative sample of youth grades 9–12 (CDC, 2006) and found that approximately 36% reported being in a physical fight in the preceding 12 months; 19% reported carrying a weapon (gun, knife, or club) on one or more days in the preceding 30 days; and of those 5% carried a gun on one or more days in the preceding 30 days. Reports from EU countries and Australia also emphasize concerns about youth violence (National Committee on Violence, 1990; Healey, 2001; White and Mason, 2006; World Health Organization, 2006).

Even though the overall rate of juvenile violent crimes has decreased across countries over the past few years (Snyder, 2004; Statistics Canada, 2007), it remains far higher than desirable given its psychological, social and health consequences (e.g., Moretti and Odgers, 2006; Moretti, Catchpole, and Odgers, 2005; Odgers, Moretti, and Reppucci, 2005; Trulson *et al.*, 2005). Additionally, the

Understanding Girls' Problem Behavior: How Girls' Delinquency Develops in the Context of Maturity and Health, Co-occurring Problems, and Relationships, Edited by Margaret Kerr, Håkan Stattin, Rutger C. M. E. Engels, Geertjan Overbeek and Anna-Karin Andershed © 2011 John Wiley & Sons, Ltd.

decline in youth violence has not been uniform: decline in violent offences among adolescent girls has been smaller than that of adolescent boys, and in some cases, trends point to increased levels of violence in girls. For example, over the past 23 years arrest rates for female juveniles for simple and aggravated assaults in the United States have increased by approximately 10% while the rates for juvenile males decreased (Snyder and Sickmund, 2006). Similarly, in Canada between 1996 and 2002, a slight decrease occurred in the rate of violent crime committed by boys while a modest increase surfaced for girls reflecting more frequent engagement in common assaults (Statistics Canada, 2007).

These trends are disconcerting when coupled with recent surveys of young women regarding their aggressive behavior in relationships. For example, in a recent study of young adults from the United States and Mexico, Straus and Ramirez (2007) found that the prevalence for perpetration of severe physical attacks toward a partner was comparable for males (11.0%) and females (11.6%). Where only one partner in a couple reported engaging in severe aggressive acts, it was more than twice as likely to be the female (29.8%) than male (13.7%). These finding concur with Archer's (2000) meta-analytic review of 82 studies exploring gender differences in perpetration of intimate partner violence, which revealed that women were slightly more likely than men to perpetrate violence toward their partners and only slightly more likely to be injured in violent partner altercations.

Aggression is over-determined: a wide-range of risk and protective factors contribute to involvement in this behavior and risk profiles of perpetrators are heterogeneous (e.g., Tremblay et al., 2004; Brook, Duan, and Brook, 2007). However, the fact that aggression typically occurs within close interpersonal relationships may provide clues to its core etiology and function. By definition, aggression and violence are interpersonal events of immense magnitude. Moreover, while the public most fears violence at the hands of strangers, perpetrators are typically family members or intimate acquaintances. This is true for both juvenile and adult offenders. For females, the perpetration of violence is even more likely to occur within a close interpersonal relationship than it is for males. For example, juvenile justice statistics show that 90% of the victims of crime perpetrated by girls were family members compared to 64% for boys (Snyder, 1997).

Why does aggression and violence typically occur within close interpersonal relationships, particularly for girls and women? Despite extensive research on aggression and violence, both on its form and expression over the lifespan, there is limited research on the interpersonal roots and psychological mechanisms through which it develops. Rather than looking at aggression and violence through a lens of pathology, perhaps there is value in assessing the adaptive function of aggression in relationships. From this perspective, we might garner a better understanding of how normative development goes astray and results in behavioral deviance. The ubiquity of aggression in social contexts calls for an approach that examines its functional role, for as Fonagy et al. (2002) state: "The answer to the riddle of how individuals can lose restraint over their propensity to injure others must lie in what is ordinary rather than extraordinary: normal human development" (p. 91).

In this chapter, we discuss the normative expression and adaptive value of anger and aggression in relation to the attachment system. We argue that under normative or optimal conditions, anger and angry behavior typically serve adaptive functions in attachment relationships. In conditions of adversity, however, anger and angry behavior can become woven into a pattern of dysfunctional attachment behavior. Understanding aggression and violence from an attachment perspective offers new avenues for intervention, and we describe a brief manualized program that targets the attachment context of aggression and violence, and reduces risk in vulnerable teens. We also briefly touch on the possible gender differences in processes underlying therapeutic changes in aggressive and violent behaviors.

AGGRESSION AND ATTACHMENT: A PARADOX RESOLVED

Increasingly researchers have turned to attachment theory to understand the functions of social behavior, including aggression, within close relationships. Several aspects of attachment theory make it particularly valuable for understanding aggression. Although compatible with contemporary social-cognitive models of aggression, attachment theory focuses not only on the proximal cognitive processes that precede or accompany aggressive behavior, it also offers important insights into the developmental, interpersonal, and socio-emotional functions of aggressive behavior.

Bowlby's attachment theory was inspired by the work of leading ethologists, such as Konrad Lorenz and Robert Hinde and their novel approach to the understanding of animal behavior in the early 1940s. Through this collaboration Bowlby observed specific behavior patterns in non-human offspring soon after birth toward maternal caregivers, which led him to theorize that a similar biologically based system operates in humans and is essential to survival (Bowlby, [1950] (1995); Bretherton, 1992). Among monkeys and apes, for example, some of the first coordinated behaviors are grasping, clinging and sucking, which trigger maternal responses of protection and nurturance (Mason and Mendoza, 1998). These clearly patterned sequences of behavior minimize separation, which triggers arousal and distress, and maximize proximity, which soothes and brings contentment. The drive to ensure proximity and soothing is so strong, that in the absence of an animate caregiver, primates seek out surrogates and attach to an inanimate object such as a cloth-covered wire cylinder that provides no nutrition. This behavior underscores the distinct and fundamental biological basis of the attachment system apart from other drives (Harlow, 1958, 1962; Mason and Capitanio, 1988). According to Bowlby, the need for human attachment supplants other needs, including sexual and aggressive drives postulated as key needs by classic psychoanalysts and object relations theorists. Attachment, he believed, was evolutionarily selected to ensure survival and reproduction, noting that for a child "... to stay in close proximity, or in easy communication with someone likely to protect you is the best of all possible insurance policies" (Bowlby, 1988, p. 81).

The ethological origin of attachment theory raises the question of the biological basis and adaptive value of aggression and violence. The question is, given that the attachment system functions to maximize proximity and minimize separation from attachment figures, what is the function of aggression in these close relationships? Bowlby's answer to this question drew on his observations of young children's responses to separation and his experience with children and teens in clinical care. He suggested that while the naïve observer would presume that angry behavior distanced a child from his or her caregiver, it often did quite the opposite. Anger and aggressive behavior, Bowlby argued, functioned to elicit attention from a disengaged caregiver, communicating the child's or youth's need for proximity and care. In this way, it strengthened the bond between the child and the caregiver, serving a signaling function closely tied to the child's developmental status and capacity for autonomous functioning. The caregiver's prompt response to angry behavior and agitation soothed the child, providing a safe haven and a secure base for exploration outside the caregiving relationship.

Similarly, Bowlby believed that angry behavior by a parent toward a child for engaging in dangerous behavior was an expression of the attachment system, ensuring the survival of the child and preserving the attachment relationship. Anger toward a romantic partner who appears disinterested, or anger displaced onto the person perceived as a threat to the relationship, could also be understood as attachment based. In every case, these relationships provoke strong emotions, the desire to maintain the relationship and distress when it is threatened. Such observations led Bowlby (1988) to conclude that:

> at the right time, and to the right degree, anger is not only appropriate but may be indispensable. It serves to deter from dangerous behavior, to drive off a rival, or to coerce a partner. In each case, the aim of the angry behavior is the same – to protect a relationship which is of very special value to the angry person. (p. 89)

What can we learn from attachment theory about seriously aggressive and violent behavior? Bowlby observed that children whose pleas for attention were persistently ignored or rebuffed by their caregivers, frequently escalated their expressions of anger in a desperate bid to engage their caregivers. Ultimately, their increasingly aggressive and violent behavior elicited a response from their caregiver, not typically of benign care, but rather punishment and retaliation. Child and caregiver were connected but through rising displays of aggression and violence. In sum, while normative levels of anger and angry behavior can be functional in preserving and strengthening attachment relationships, extreme aggression and violence can build equally if, not stronger, but pathological bonds.

If unchecked, aggression and violence create a precarious relationship and place both child and caregiver in danger. In discussing the roots of violence, Bowlby (1973) argued that "the most violently angry and dysfunctional responses of all, it seems probable, are elicited in children and adolescents who not only experience repeated separations but are constantly subjected to the threat of being abandoned" (p. 288). He underscored the importance of threats to attachment as a determinant of aggressive behavior by drawing on Burnham's (1965) observations of extremely violent adolescents. One adolescent who murdered his mother exclaimed afterwards "I couldn't stand to have her leave me." "I decided that she would never leave me again," explained another youth who placed a bomb in his mother's luggage prior to her departure on an airplane (p. 290, cited in Bowlby, 1973). Bowlby's examples bear an uncanny resemblance to Dutton and Kerry's (1999) findings in a study of 90 incarcerated spousal killers. These murders were unplanned and occurred in the cusp of separation, often following a desperate and unsuccessful attempt of the man to convince his partner to stay in the relationship. When unsuccessful, a reactive murderous attack ensued characterized by uncontrolled rage and 'overkill' (i.e., excessive violence beyond what is required). Although less studied, it seems likely that intimate partner violence for women also occurs in the cusp of perceived or real threat of abandonment. This possibility is supported by research showing that victimization toward partners was six times higher among women classified as insecurely attached, and thus more sensitive to threats of abandonment, rather than those who are securely attached (Feerick, Haugaard, and Hien, 2002).

ATTACHMENT AND AGGRESSION: RESEARCH FINDINGS

Parenting behaviors that contribute to insecure attachment in children are very similar – if not identical – to those that contribute to aggressive and delinquent child behavior. Thus it is not surprising that studies reveal significant relationships between various types of insecure attachment and aggressive and delinquent behavior (e.g., Greenberg et al.1991; Greenberg, 1999; Guttmann-Steinmetz and Crowell, 2006; Kobak, Zajac, and Smith, 2009). Two underlying dimensions of attachment – anxiety and avoidance – are important in understanding these findings. Attachment anxiety refers to the degree of agitation experienced by individuals in relationships – whether they feel safe from or vulnerable to abandonment; attachment avoidance refers to their behavioral strategy in coping with attachment needs – whether they approach others for comfort and support or avoid them. The intersection between these two dimensions of attachment produces four prototypical attachment styles – secure attachment and three insecure styles (Bartholomew and Horowitz, 1991). Hyperactivation of the attachment system defined by the presence of high attachment anxiety, and hypersensitivity to rejection and abandonment is evident in two of these insecure styles (Shaver and Mikulincer, 2005). Anxious-fearful attachment is marked by high levels of anxiety about abandonment and rejection, coupled with the behavioral strategy of avoiding others despite a desperate desire for closeness. Anxious-preoccupied attachment is also marked by high levels of anxiety about abandonment and rejection but coupled with the behavioral strategy of persistent and often coercive pursuit of others. The third insecure pattern – avoidant-dismissing – is characterized by deactivation of the attachment system (Shaver and Mikulincer, 2005), therefore low levels of anxiety and a behavioral strategy of avoidance. Individuals with a predominantly avoidant-dismissing attachment style are not interested in relationships, they do not worry about potential rejection, nor do they seek out relationships.

Research with adolescents has revealed a relationship between anxious-preoccupied attachment and engagement in delinquent activities, including physical fights and assaults. For example, Allen *et al.* (2002) found that anxious-preoccupied attachment at age 16 predicted increasing delinquent behavior between the ages of 16 and 18 years. From an attachment perspective, it is not surprising that higher levels of anxiety and fear of abandonment coupled with a persistent pursuit of others increases risk for aggressive behavior. Because anxious-preoccupied attachment is associated with a history of unreliable and inconsistent responsiveness from caregivers, these youth learn that an effective means to elicit attention is to display heightened expressions of need that may include extreme anger, aggression and violence. Such behavior is most likely to occur in anticipation of abandonment or rejection because this naturally triggers feelings of anxiety and fuels proximity seeking. Unfortunately, the intense pursuit of others is likely to backfire and produce the very outcome that is most feared, namely abandonment and rejection.

Research also shows that avoidant patterns of attachment relate to aggressive and delinquent behavior. For example, early studies revealed that anxious-avoidant attachment was related to noncompliant behavior in very young children both concurrently and prospectively from infancy to grades one to three (Renken, Egeland, and Marvinney 1989; Speltz, DeKlyen, and Greenberg, 1999; Greenberg *et al.*, 2001). Further, Rosenstein and Horowitz (1996) found that avoidant-dismissing attachment was characteristic of male adolescents diagnosed with conduct disorder, substance abuse, and/or antisocial or narcissistic personality disorders.

From an attachment perspective, higher levels of avoidance may increase risk for aggressive behavior because of interpersonal disengagement. Youth who develop avoidant attachment keep their distance from others as they have learned that close relationships are either punitive or worthless. Having few opportunities to experience empathy from others, they thus lack the ability to understand the impact of their behaviors on those around them. Youth with avoidant attachment styles also lack close and trusting relationships to buffer them in stressful situations. Even if they desire closeness with others, as in the case of avoidant-fearful attachment, they are unskilled in establishing and maintaining close interpersonal relationships and anxious about abandonment and rejection. If they are disinterested in relationships, they have little motivation to restrain hostile impulses.

In a recent analysis of data from our longitudinal research on aggression and violence in at-risk teens (Obsuth and Moretti, 2009), we examined the relation between the two dimensions of attachment – attachment anxiety and attachment avoidance – and aggressive behavior concurrently and at a follow-up two years later in 167 incarcerated or clinically referred adolescent girls and boys, aged 12–18 years (M = 15.34; SD = 1.48; 80 females; 87 males) at high risk for aggressive behavior. Youth completed the *Form-Function Aggression Measure* (FFAM; Little, Jones, and Henrich, 2003); a self-report instrument of two forms of aggressive behavior (overt and relational). Youth also completed the *Family Attachment Interview* (FAI; see Bartholomew and Horowitz, 1991), a 1- to 2-hour long semi-structured interview modified based on the Adult Attachment Interview (AAI; see Main and Goldwyn, 1998) to tap into childhood and current experiences with caregivers. The interviews were coded by reliable coders, adhering to Bartholomew's coding system (Bartholomew and Horowitz, 1991), well validated for high-risk youth (Scharfe, 2002). Girls' scores on attachment anxiety were significantly higher than were boys' scores. In contrast, boys' scores on attachment avoidance were significantly higher than were girls' scores.

Hierarchical regression analyses revealed an interaction between gender and anxiety for both overt and relational aggression: high anxiety in girls but not in boys was related to higher levels of both overt and relational aggression concurrently, and relational aggression at the two-year follow-up. In contrast, high avoidance in boys but not in girls was related to higher levels of both overt and relational aggression concurrently, and relational aggression at the two-year follow-up.

These findings suggest that there may be important gender differences in the relation of attachment and aggressive behavior: for females, aggression may be more commonly associated with over-activation of the attachment system while for males it is possibly associated with deactivation. Research on attachment related behaviors suggests that related gender differences are present as early as in infancy. Taylor *et al.* (2000) and David and Lyons-Ruth (2005) found that female infants responded to maternal frightening behavior with approach while male infants were more likely to avoid, resist or display conflict behavior. Further, research on socialization of girls suggests that from an early age, girls are encouraged to attend to the needs and well-being of others, to use relationships to self-regulate, and to judge their self worth in terms of others opinion of them (Cross and Madson, 1997; Moretti and Higgins, 1999).

Due to socialization, and perhaps by virtue of the neurobiological propensity and evolutionary advantage for females to orient toward caregiving (Beech and Mitchell, 2005), interpersonal relationships appear to be especially salient for girls' development and adaptation. Under normative conditions that provide adequate and timely responsiveness to attachment needs, girls develop a sense of trust and healthy interdependence in close relationships. By responding to a daughter's attachment needs, which entails recognition and reflection of her psychological experience, her caregiver promotes her capacity to understand her own internal experiences and to have empathy for those around her. Fonagy and Target (1997) refer to this capacity as "reflective function": the ability to be aware of, to reflect on, and to modulate one's behavior in relation to the psychological experiences of others and as distinct, but related to one's own psychological experiences. The security and capacity for autonomous functioning that arise through this process lay the foundation for girls to venture into the world, unhampered by overactivation of the attachment system, anxiety, and vigilance in monitoring the availability of attachment figures.

Under adverse conditions where attachment needs are met only intermittently, and only when expressed through extreme behavior, girls are burdened by anxiety about abandonment, vigilant of their attachment figures' whereabouts and sensitive to signs of rejection. Anxiety pervades their experience and they lack a secure base to explore their own internal world and the psychological world of others. Perplexing as it may seem, even though anxious-preoccupied attachment entails an intense focus on others, it is inherently focused on the self and one's own safety and thus likely inhibits mentalization and empathy. Our results are consistent with findings from a study by Orcutt, Garcia, and Pickett (2005), in which they examined female perpetrators of partner violence in a large college sample and found that females high in attachment anxiety and low in attachment avoidance reported higher rates of perpetrating violence toward their partners. Similarly, in a recent study Kobak, Zajac, and Smith (2009) examined the trajectories of adolescents' impulsive and hostile behaviors and found higher rates of hostile feelings in anxious-preoccupied girls than boys.

Attachment avoidance may relate to aggressiveness in complex ways depending on whether individuals experience anxiety in conjunction with avoidance or not. By definition, the hallmark of attachment avoidance is the reluctance to engage in or express emotional experiences. There is good evidence to suggest that avoidance in the absence of anxiety about, or interest in, relationships marks the unwillingness or inability of individuals to consider the perspectives of others in regulating their own behavior. This may give rise to instrumental acts of aggression that are not triggered by personal feelings toward the victim, but rather the pursuit of other goals, such as acquiring material or other goods.

Additional findings from our research support this view: boys with a dismissing attachment, characterized by high avoidance and low anxiety, scored higher on the Psychopathy Checklist: Youth Version (PCL:YV; see Forth, Kosson, and Hare, 2003). In particular, boys who scored high on dismissingness were more likely to have a history of early behavior problems and engaging in serious and versatile criminal behavior (Catchpole and Moretti, 2008).

Like dismissing individuals, fearful individuals are also avoidant but they desire close relationships and feel anxious about rejection and abandonment. Mayseless (1991) argues that when pressed into intimacy, fearfully attached individuals may be spurred into aggression because of the anxiety this provokes and their lack of experience regulating these emotions.

In sum, there is substantial evidence from studies of children, adolescents and adults that insecure attachment is a risk factor for aggressive and violent behavior. As noted earlier, angry behavior may be functional in healthy attachment relationships; however, the degree and manner in which anger is expressed is shaped by the caregiving relationship. When children experience caregivers as inconsistently responsive, rejecting or punitive, they may escalate their expression of anger into aggressive and violent acts. Emerging evidence suggests that there are gender differences in the expression of aggression related to attachment anxiety versus avoidance. Such findings combined with extensive research on parenting practices in relation to aggressive behavior in children, have led to the development of intervention programs that target parenting and the parent–child relationship. Next, we discuss the components of these programs and their relation to clinical outcomes.

ATTACHMENT-BASED INTERVENTIONS

The past two decades have seen the emergence of numerous intervention programs based on attachment theory. The bulk of these programs are for mothers of infants to pre-school aged children, although interest has grown in programs for older children and adults. In 2003, Bakermans-Kranenburg, van IJzendoorn, and Juffer completed a comprehensive meta-analysis of 70 studies of interventions aimed at enhancing positive parenting behaviors such as responsiveness and sensitivity, and observing changes in parenting behavior and child attachment. Only intervention programs for parents of children under the age of five were included. Results showed a medium effect size for parental sensitivity and a small effect size for child attachment security. Programs that were more effective in enhancing parental sensitivity were also more effective in increasing child attachment security, and programs with a specific focus and limited number of sessions (between 5 to 16) were found to be more effective than nonspecific longer-term programs. Studies that are more recent have evaluated the effectiveness of attachment-based interventions in specific populations. For example, a recent study (Van Zeijl et al., 2006) examined the effectiveness of the Video-Feedback Intervention to Promote Positive Parenting and Sensitive Discipline (VIPP-SD) for mothers of behaviorally disturbed young children (ages 1–3 years). They found that the program helped parents to consider their child's perspective and pay attention to their child's attachment signals, particularly in situations that required discipline. Not only did the program enhance maternal sensitivity, but it also resulted in a decrease in overactive behaviors (e.g., cannot sit still, quickly shifts activity) among children from highly stressed families, and particularly for mothers of infants with reactive temperaments. Comparable findings emerged using VIPP-SD with mothers of infants between 7 and 10 months old: compared to control mothers, mothers who completed VIPP-SD became more sensitive, particularly if their infants were reactive in temperament (Klein Velderman *et al.*, 2006). These findings are especially promising given the common assumption that change is unlikely among children with severe behavior problems and difficult temperament. In fact, these results suggest quite the opposite: a reactive temperament in a child may be a sign of greater rather than lesser susceptibility to parenting practices and other social influences (Belsky, 1997).

Video-taped feedback was also used by Dozier and colleagues (Dozier *et al.*, 2006) in their Attachment and Bio-behavioral Catch-Up program (ABC Program) with caregivers of foster children ages 3 months to 3 years. This program provides parents with 10 in-home training sessions designed to enhance parenting sensitivity through helping caregivers to follow their child's lead, support their children in expressing and understanding their emotions, and appreciate the importance of touching and hugging their child. Results showed that children of foster parents who completed this program had lower cortisol levels, an important biological marker of stress, than did children of foster parents in the control condition, underscoring the impact of intervention on the bio-behavioral aspect of regulation.

Another intervention, the Circle of Security program (COS; see Marvin, *et al.*, 2002) adopts a more tailored approach based on the attachment pattern of each young child, his or her mother's working models of close family relationships, and attachment related behaviors toward the child. Parents are encouraged to reflect on and understand their child's needs for attachment and autonomy and to pay attention to the role of anxiety in provoking behavior. Video-taped feedback is used to help parents identify and reflect on sequences of caregiver-child interactions surrounding problem behavior and develop alternate parenting strategies. Toddler and preschool children whose parents completed the COS program showed significant increases in attachment organization and security (Hoffman *et al.*, 2006).

Family and peer attachment continue to play a significant role in adolescent development and adjustment to adulthood (Allen *et al.* 2002; Moretti and Peled, 2004). Yet in contrast to the number of programs developed for caregivers of infants and young children, and the growing evidence for their effectiveness, few are available for adolescents. This is surprising because attachment focused interventions have also been developed for adults, couples and families and there is growing evidence of their effectiveness as well (e.g., Bateman and Fonagy, 2003; Johnson and Whiffen, 2003; Johnson, 2004). The absence of attachment based programs for adolescents is particularly perplexing given the shifts in the nature and quality of attachment relationships during this developmental period and associated increases in vulnerability (Moretti and Holland, 2003; Moretti and Peled, 2004).

Whatever the explanation, apart from the approach we have developed and describe later in this chapter, only two manualized attachment-based programs for adolescents and their families can be found in the literature thus far: Attachment-Based Family Therapy (ABFT; see Diamond *et al.*, 2002) and Multiple-Family Group Intervention (MFGI; see Keiley, 2002).

Originally modeled on Multidimensional Family Therapy (MDFT; see Liddle, 2002), ABFT was developed based on research linking various aspects of poor parenting with insecure parent-child attachment in relation to psychopathology and risky behaviors such as teen depression, substance use, delinquent peer relationships, and risky sexual behavior. ABFT helps parents 'reframe' problem behavior in terms of relational issues, strengthen the working alliance between parent and teen, revisit and repair ruptures in the attachment relationship, and helps parents provide a secure base for autonomy development in their children. Although the evaluation of this program is limited, the results are promising. A small randomized waitlist control study showed that, compared to adolescents on waitlist, fewer adolescents met criteria for major depression following their family's completion of ABFT. In addition, family conflict dropped in families that received ABFT (Diamond, 2002; Diamond, Siqueland, and Diamond, 2003).

MFGI is also a brief manualized program, but specifically designed for caregivers of incarcerated adolescents and delivered prior to their teen's release. Keiley (2002) argues that enhancing parent-teen bonds and reducing coercive interaction patterns may promote greater attachment security and in turn reduce risk for antisocial and delinquent behavior. Borrowing from techniques used in Emotionally Focused Therapy (EFT; see Greenberg and Johnson, 1990; Johnson, 1996), through role-plays, discussion, and behavioral coaching during conflict scenarios, caregivers and teens develop affect regulation and perspective taking skills necessary to avoid the escalation of negative affect and acting out behavior. Promising findings emerged from a recent pre- and post-treatment evaluation (Keiley, 2007) of MFGI in a sample of 67 caregivers of 73 incarcerated teens. Six months post-treatment, recidivism was only 44% for the treatment group compared to the national norm of 65-85%. Results also showed significant declines in the teens' externalizing behavior and enhancement of teen-mother attachment.

As promising as these programs appear, further development of attachment-based approaches for adolescents and their families is well overdue. As previously noted, attachment theory provides insight into anger-related behavior, its adaptive value and the conditions that push anger into aggression and violence. For this reason, it is well suited as a foundation for intervention programs targeting aggressive, violent and antisocial problems in teens. What treatment components and processes are critical in developing such programs for teens? Fortunately, research on change processes underlying outcomes of attachment-based programs for young children shed light on this question.

CONNECT: AN ATTACHMENT-BASED APPROACH TO SUPPORTING PARENTS OF TROUBLED TEENS

Connect (Moretti, Braber, and Obsuth, 2009)[1] was developed in response to the growing evidence of the significance of attachment-based interventions in the treatment of externalizing problems in adolescents. Connect is a 10-week-long manualized principle-based program for parents and alternate caregivers of teens who engage in aggressive, antisocial, and delinquent behaviors. It integrates research on adolescent-parent attachment, adolescent development and effective parenting practices. Connect focuses on the enhancement of the building blocks of secure attachment shown to affect child outcomes: parental sensitivity; partnership and mutuality; parental reflective function; and adaptive dyadic affect regulation.

Each session begins with the presentation of an attachment principle that helps parents understand attachment issues related to challenging interactions with their adolescent. Through experiential activities, including role-plays and reflective exercises, parents develop skills to accurately perceive attachment needs in their adolescent's behavior; to reflect upon these needs as they relate to their child's state of mind; and to respond promptly and effectively with empathy and clear limit setting. Parents are also coached to 'step back' in emotionally charged situations and reflect on how their response to their adolescent will influence the quality of the relationship; the adolescent's receptivity to feedback, support and limit setting; and growth of adolescent autonomy. Thus, parents are encouraged to be mindful of their child's experience and to respond to their child's behavior sensitively, rather than reactively.

In line with attachment theory, parents also learn that conflict is part of attachment and it is particularly acute during times of transition in their children's development, such as the transition through adolescence, which universally introduces major changes in the parent–child relationship. Throughout the sessions, parents are encouraged to reflect upon their own experiences as teens and in their current lives. They learn to recognize and modulate their own emotional response to their youth's problem behavior and mindfully utilize parenting strategies to support their relationship with their adolescent while clearly setting limits and expectations. Increasing parental sensitivity and mindfulness assists parents in reframing conflict and increases their ability to communicate and set appropriate limits. These strategies enhance the parent–adolescent relationship by providing necessary skills for navigating conflict without defaulting to coercion and escalating dyadic aggression.

In our first evaluation of the effectiveness of Connect (Moretti and Obsuth, 2009), we completed a waitlist control study with 20 caregivers (17 females and 3 males) and their teens (7 females and 13 males, mean ages 15.06 and 14.15 years old, respectively) with follow up at 12–18 months post-treatment. Each caregiver completed measures of parenting and youth externalizing and internalizing problems, and questionnaires assessing their sense of parenting competence at four time points: at the beginning of their waitlist placement (approximately 4–6 months prior to treatment), at the beginning of treatment, at the end of treatment, and at 12–18 months after treatment.

Although a small decline in parent reports of teen problem behavior occurred over the waitlist period, this decrease was not significant. In contrast, prepost treatment comparisons revealed significant declines in caregivers' reports of youths' externalizing and internalizing problems as measured by the *Child Behavior Checklist (CBCL*; Achenbach and Edelbrock, 1981), including reductions in youths' rule-breaking behavior, aggressive behavior, oppositional defiant problems, and conduct problems as well as anxiety/depression, and social problems. Caregivers also reported significant increases in their sense of parenting efficacy and satisfaction as measured by the *Parenting Sense of Competence Scale* (PSOC; see Johnston and Mash, 1989). All post-treatment gains were maintained 12 to 18 months later at follow-up. Further, caregivers reported additional significant decreases in youths' total problems as compared to their reports immediately following treatment. Specifically, caregivers indicated that their teens' symptoms of conduct problems, rule breaking behaviors, anxiety and depression, as well as social problems dropped even further since the completion of treatment.

We further evaluated the clinical significance of our findings by examining whether teens with the highest levels of problem behavior also benefited equally from treatment. Results confirmed this to be the case: teens with internalizing and externalizing problems above the 70th percentile on the CBCL were rated by their caregivers as significantly improved at post-treatment on both scales.

The effectiveness of interventions is sometimes difficult to achieve outside the centre in which they were developed. For this reason, and to meet the growing demand for evidence based, cost-effective and accessible programs for caregivers and parents of at-risk youth, a standardized training program was developed to train mental health professionals to lead Connect groups across the province of British Columbia. Clinical supervision to ensure program adherence and certification of leaders was also established. Mandatory evaluation of the program, with standardized measures, is integrated into program delivery, and constitutes one component of the treatment manual.

Over the course of two years, 50 leaders have been trained in 17 communities to deliver Connect. Results based on pre-post-treatment reports from 309 caregivers (279 females and 30 males) of 309 adolescents (135 females and 174 males, mean ages 13.73 and 15.53 years old, respectively) confirmed the effectiveness of Connect through revealing medium to large effect sizes in changes in youth symptoms and consistently large effect sizes in changes in parenting experiences. Specifically, caregivers reported significant reductions in teens' externalizing and internalizing problems. More specifically, they reported significant reductions in youth's symptoms of conduct disorder, oppositional-defiant disorder, ADHD, and dysthymia. Caregivers also reported significant increases in their youths' prosocial functioning, including social participation, quality of relationships, school participation, and global functioning as measured by the *Brief Child and Family Phone Interview* (BCFPI; see Cunningham, Pettingill, and Boyle, 2000). By administering the *Conflict Tactics Scale-modified* (Straus, 1979; revised by Moretti, 2003 and Moore and Pepler, 2006) we assessed caregivers' reports of how aggressive their teen was toward them, both verbally and physically, and how aggressive they were toward their teen. Caregivers reported that after treatment their teens were significantly less verbally and physically aggressive toward them, and they were significantly less verbally and physically aggressive toward their teen.

Our generalization study also included measures of affect regulation (*Affect Regulation Checklist*, ARC; Moretti, 2003) and attachment anxiety and avoidance (*Comprehensive Adolescent-Parent Inventory*, CAPAI; Moretti, McKay, and Holland, 2000). Caregivers reported that following treatment teens were significantly better able to regulate their emotional arousal and to reflect on their emotional experiences. They also suppressed their emotions to a significantly lesser degree and were rated as less avoidant in their relationships with their caregivers ($p < -0.004$).

An important question regarding the impact of our program was the degree to which it eased caregiver strain, thus promoting continuity of care. To assess caregiver strain we used the *Caregiver Strain Questionnaire* (CGSQ; see Brennan, Heflinger, and Bickman, 1997). Findings showed that after treatment caregivers reported significantly less objective strain (e.g., missing work or neglecting other duties, interruption of personal time, family member(s) having to do without things, financial strain), significantly less internalized subjective strain (e.g., feelings of sadness, guilt and fatigue, worrying about the family's future and child's future), and significantly less externalized subjective strain (e.g., anger, resentment, embarrassment). Finally, following treatment caregivers reported significantly more satisfaction in parenting their teen and felt significantly more competent in doing so (PSOC).

Even though research we previously reviewed highlighted gender differences in the relation of attachment anxiety and avoidance to aggression, no differences were found in the treatment outcomes that we measured. However, it is possible that similar treatment effects may occur as a result of different change processes in the relationships of parents with their daughters versus their sons as discussed below.

Client acceptance and satisfaction with programs is essential to their success. Our community sample of 309 caregivers uniformly reported high levels of satisfaction with the program. All participants reported that the program was helpful or very helpful. Ninety-seven percent felt that Connect helped them to understand their child a great deal better and 86% noted a positive change in their relationship with their child as a result of applying what they learned in the program. Similar findings were reported in the waitlist control study. Attendance in both trials was excellent, with low dropout rates of 14% and high attendance at sessions, whereby 84% of participants (excluding those who dropped out) attended 8 or more of the 10 Connect sessions.

These are promising findings, particularly given the serious and longstanding nature of aggressive and violent behavior in these teens and the stress and difficulties experienced by themselves and their caregivers. Aggression and violence of this nature often provokes strong reactions in caregivers and clinicians to contain, control, and eradicate such behavior, if not out of anger and indignation than based on the desire of caregivers to protect and provide guidance to the teens. Yet such efforts often escalate the very problems they seek to diminish. Paradoxically, an attachment-based approach that focuses caregivers away from control and toward connection with their teens reduces aggression in teens and their caregivers. In addition, this approach has the potential to open new opportunities for building security within relationships and for facilitating the development of self-regulatory skills.

ATTACHMENT, CHANGE PROCESSES, AND GENDER

It is not yet clear what processes account for change as a result of attachment-based interventions. Research on intervention and attachment thus far suggests that caregiver sensitivity, or the ability of caregivers to cognitively represent the relation of their child's behavior to attachment needs and to respond appropriately, is central in moving children toward greater attachment security. However, other studies suggest that there may be more at play than just caregiver sensitivity (e.g, Van IJzenoorn, 1995). Over a decade ago, Van IJzendoorn (1995) posited a 'transmission gap', arguing that we were yet to understand the mechanisms that underlie transgenerational patterns of attachment. Fonagy and others (Fonagy et al., 2002; Slade et al., 2005) believe that the capacity of the caregiver to mentalize and reflect on the child's emotional state, that is the capacity for 'reflective function', is crucial to attachment security. When caregivers can understand their child's behavior in relation to their child's feelings and needs, this gives meaning to the child's emotional experiences and provides opportunities for the caregiver to modulate these states in partnership with the child, thereby providing optimal conditions for supporting attachment security and the development of healthy affect regulation. However, in order for this process to unfold successfully, caregivers must themselves be able to access, assess and modulate their own emotions states in relation to their own attachment experiences and feelings.

This research suggests that the processes that account for change in the context of intervention are complex and multi-leveled. Not only must parenting behavior change, but changes in caregivers' 'state of mind' may also be critical to treatment success. In a recent study (Moretti et al., 2009), we investigated the importance of parenting representations as a key target of intervention and an essential mechanism in the change process. Caregivers were administered the Parenting Representations Interview – Adolescence (PRI-A; see Scharf and Mayseless, 1997/2000) prior to and following their completion of Connect. The PRI-A is a semi-structured interview that assesses parental representations of the child, the parent, and the child-parent relationship. Interviews were coded along a number of dimensions related to attachment security and a host of attachment-related parenting behaviors. Preliminary findings show that following completion of the program parents viewed their relationships with their adolescents as more secure across a number of dimensions. They reported fewer conflicts and increased levels of mutuality, reciprocity, and open communication in their relationships.

As previously noted, we did not find that treatment outcomes on measures of youth emotional and behavioral functioning differed for the daughters versus sons of parents completing Connect. However, it is important to recognize that these outcomes may result from different change processes in the relationships of parents to their daughters versus their sons. Our preliminary analyses of gender differences in change processes suggest that this may indeed be the case. Results showed that decreases in girls' aggressive behaviors were related to parents' experiences of increased partnership and mutuality with their daughters; increased acceptance of parental authority by their daughters; and increased positive feelings by themselves and their daughters about their relationship. These results suggest that Connect enhances healthy connectedness between parents and daughters by supporting parents in moving closer to their daughters in a manner that expresses both parental guidance and partnership, and by enhancing positive feelings of both parents and daughters. In contrast, decreases in boys' aggressive behaviors following Connect were related to parental reports of decreased monitoring and increased autonomy support. These results suggest that the program supports parents in reducing attempts to control their sons and encouraging greater autonomy in decision making. Together the results are provocative in raising the possibility that similar outcomes may occur as a result of different processes related to child gender and parenting. Not only are these preliminary findings important in understanding the effects of this particular program, but they suggest that gender differences in change processes may be deeply embedded in other programs despite similar outcomes for girls and boys. We are currently in the process of completing one year follow-up interviews with participants to determine the extent to which treatment effects are maintained and to understand how gender plays a role in the processes that account for positive outcomes.

CONCLUSION

The fact that aggression and violence can occur in the pursuit of attachment is a paradox. In the face of aggressive behavior, we typically attempt to exercise greater control and introduce more serious consequences for misbehavior. These actions are not misguided, but in many instances they lead us away from understanding the underlying causes and processes that contribute to and sustain aggressive behavior. Perhaps we are reluctant to consider the psychological world of the aggressive teen because we feel that doing so would sanction his or her behavior. Yet, understanding our teen and our relationship with them need not preclude limit setting or reasonable consequences. More importantly, failing to consider these issues may hamper our ability to work productively and in partnership with our teens.

Attachment theory offers a perspective that helps us to understand the development and function of aggression and violence within a relational framework. It is inherently a developmental perspective and therefore provides an understanding of how behavior patterns unfold over development, within the context of caregiving relationships, and in relation to a wide range of other risk and protective factors. Furthermore, because it does not preclude other theoretical models, it provides a framework for integrating seemingly diverse perspectives. For example, an attachment perspective is not necessarily in opposition with coercion theory, which argues that aggressive behavior is shaped by parental responses to child behavior and the relational consequences of such action (Van Zeijl *et al.*, 2006).

Attachment theory provides a strong foundation that can support the development of interventions across a broad range of adolescent problems because it addresses underlying relational issues – issues that are of relevance across the lifespan and particularly during adolescence. Although attachment problems are certainly not always the *cause* of behavioral and psychological problems in children and teens, invariably psychological problems and disorders result in stress and disturbances to the parent–child relationships. Helping parents and caregivers understand the attachment issues that are relevant to the problems with which their child is struggling, and providing guidance and support to sustaining security within the parent–child relationship to the extent that this possible, is a crucial element of effective intervention.

NOTE

1   For further details about Connect, including information about training, please refer to the following webpage: www.sfu.ca/connectparentgroup.

REFERENCES

Achenbach, T. M., and Edelbrock, C. S. (1981). Behavioral problems and competencies by parents of normal and disturbed children aged four through sixteen. *Monographs of the Society for Research in Child Development, 46*, 1–78.

Allen, J. P., Marsh, P., McFarland, C., *et al.* (2002).Attachment and autonomy as predictors of the development of social skills and delinquency during midadolescence. *Journal of Consulting and Clinical Psychology, 70(1)*, 56–66.

Archer, J. (2000). Sex differences in aggression between heterosexual partners: A meta-analytic review. *Psychological Bulletin, 126(5)*, 651–680.

Bakermans-Kranenburg, M. J., van IJzendoorn, M. H., and Juffer, F. (2003). Less is more: Meta-analysis of sensitivity and attachment interventions in early childhood. *Psychological Bulletin, 129(2)*, 195–215.

Bartholomew, K., and Horowitz, L. M. (1991). Attachment styles among young adults: A test of a four-category model. *Journal of Personality and Social Psychology, 61*, 226–244.

Bateman, A., and Fonagy, P. (2003). The development of an attachment-based treatment program for borderline personality disorder. *Bulletin of the Menninger Clinic, 67,* 187– 211.

Beech, A. R., and Mitchell, I. J. (2005) A neurobiological perspective on attachment problems in sexual offenders and the role of selective serotonin re-uptake inhibitors in the treatment of such problems. *Clinical Psychology Review, 25(2),* 153–182.

Belsky, J. (1997). Theory testing, effect-size evaluation, and differential susceptibility to rearing influence: The case of mothering and attachment. *Child Development, 68(4),* 598–600.

Bowlby, J. [1950] (1995). *Maternal Care and Mental Health,* 2nd ed. 1995, *The Master Work* series, Northvale, NJ: Jason Aronson.

Bowlby J (1973). *Separation: Anxiety and Anger, Attachment and Loss* (Vol. 2). London: Hogarth Press.

Bowlby, J. (1988). *A Secure Base: Parent-Child Attachment and Healthy Human Development.* New York: Basic Books.

Brennan, A.M., Heflinger, C. A., and Bickman, L. (1997). The caregiver strain questionnaire: Measuring the impact on the family of living with a child with with serious emotional disturbance. *Journal of Emotional and Behavior Disorders, 4,* 212–222.

Bretherton, I. (1992). The origins of attachment theory: John Bowlby and Mary Ainsworth. *Developmental Psychology 28(5),* 759–775.

Brook, J. S., Duan, T., and Brook, D. W. (2007). Fathers who abuse drugs and their adolescent children: Longitudinal predictors of adolescent aggression. *The American Journal on Addictions, 16(5),* 410–417.

Burnham, D. L. (1965). Separation anxiety. *Archives of General Psychiatry, 13,* 346–358.

Canadian Psychological Association (CPA) Annual Report. Retrieved from the Canadian Psychological Association website: www.cpa.ca.

Catchpole, R. E. H. and Moretti, M. M. (2008). Attachment to caregivers and psychopathic characteristics among adolescents at risk for aggression. Unpublished manuscript. Dissertation in progress. Simon Fraser University.

Cross, S. E., and Madson, L. (1997). Models of the self: Self-construals and gender. *Psychological Bulletin, 122(1),* 5–37.

Cunningham, C. E., Pettingill, P., and Boyle, M. (2000). *The Brief Child and Family Phone Interview.* Hamilton, ON: Canadian Centre for the Study of Children at Risk, Hamilton Health Sciences Corporation, McMaster University.

David, D. H., and Lyons-Ruth, K. (2005). Differential attachment responses of male and female infants to frightening maternal behavior: Tend or befriend versus fight or flight? *Infant Mental Health Journal, 26(1),* 1–18.

Diamond, G. S., Reiss, B., Diamond, G. M., *et al.* (2002). Attachment-based family therapy for depressed adolescents: A treatment development study. *Journal of the American Academy of Child and Adolescent Psychiatry, 41,* 1190–1196.

Diamond, G., Siqueland, L., and Diamond, G. M. (2003). Attachment-based family therapy for depressed adolescents: Programmatic treatment development. *Clinical Child and Family Psychology Review, 6(2),* 107–127.

Dozier, M., Peloso, E., Lindheim, O., *et al.* (2006). Developing evidence-based interventions for foster children: An example of a randomized clinical trial with infants and toddlers. *Journal of Social Issues, 62(4),* 767–785.

Dutton, D. G., and Kerry, G. (1999). Modus operandi and personality disorder in incarcerated spousal: Killers. *International Journal of Law and Psychiatry, 22(3–4),* 287–299.

Feerick, M. M., Haugaard, J. J., and Hien, D. A. (2002). Child maltreatment and adulthood violence: The contribution of attachment and drug abuse. *Child Maltreatment, 7(3),* 226–240.

Fonagy, P., Gergely, G., Jurist, E., *et al.* (2002). *Affect Regulation, Mentalization, and the Development of the Self.* New York: Other Books.

Fonagy, P., and Target, M. (1997). Attachment and reflective function: Their role in self-organization. *Development and Psychopathology, 9(4),* 679–700.

Fonagy, P., and Target, M. (1996). Playing with reality: I. Theory of mind and the normal development of psychic reality. *International Journal of Psycho-Analysis, 77*(2), 217– 233.

Forth, A., Kosson, D. and Hare, R. (2003). *The Psychopathy Checklist: Youth Version (PCL:YV)*. Toronto: Multi-Health Systems.

Greenberg, M. T. (1999). Attachment and psychopathology in childhood. In J. Cassidy and P. R. Shaver (eds), *Handbook of Attachment. Theory, Research, and Clinical Applications* (pp. 469–496). New York: Guildford Press.

Greenberg, L. S., and Johnson, S. M. (1990). Emotional change processes in couples therapy. In: *Emotions and the Family: For Better or For Worse* (pp. 137–153). Elaine A. Blechman. Hillsdale, NJ, England: Lawrence Erlbaum Associates, Inc.

Greenberg, M. T., Speltz, M. L., DeKlyen, M., *et al.* (1991). Attachment security in preschoolers with and without externalizing problems: A replication. *Development and Psychopathology, 3*, 413–430.

Greenberg, M. T., Speltz, M. L., DeKlyen, M., *et al.* (2001). Correlates of clinic referral for early conduct problems: Variable- and person-oriented approaches. *Development and Psychopathology, 13*(2), 255–276.

Guttmann-Steinmetz, S., and Crowell, J. A. (2006). Attachment and externalizing disorders: A developmental psychopathology perspective. *Journal of the American Academy of Child and Adolescent Psychiatry, 45*(4), 440–451.

Harlow, H. F. (1958). The nature of love. *American Psychology 13*, 673–685.

Harlow, H. F. (1962). *Development of Affection in Primates. Roots of Behavior* (pp. 157–166). E. L. Bliss (ed.). New York: Harper.

Healey, J. (ed.). *Bullying and Youth Violence. Issues in Society*, Vol. 154, Thirroul, Australia: The Spinney Press.

Hoffman, K. T., Marvin, R. S., Cooper, G., *et al.* (2006). Changing toddlers' and preschoolers' attachment classifications: The Circle of Security intervention. *Journal of Consulting and Clinical Psychology. 74*(6), 1017–1026.

Johnson, S. M. (1996). *The Practice of Emotionally Focused Marital Therapy: Creating Connection*. Philadelphia, PA: Brunner/Mazel.

Johnson, S. M., and Whiffen, V. E. (eds) (2003). *Attachment Processes in Couple and Family Therapy*. New York: Guildford Press.

Johnson, S. M. (2004). *The Practice of Emotionally Focused Marital Therapy: Creating Connections* (2nd ed.). New York: Brunner/Mazel.

Johnston, C. and Mash, E. J. (1989). A measure of parenting satisfaction and efficacy. *Journal of Clinical Child Psychology, 18*, 167–175.

Keiley, M. K. (2002). The development and implementation of an affect regulation and attachment intervention for incarcerated adolescents and their parents. *The Family Journal: Counseling and Therapy for Couples and Families, 10*(2), 177–189.

Keiley, M. K. (2007). Multiple-family group intervention for incarcerated adolescents and their families: A pilot project. *Journal of Marital and Family Therapy, 33*(1), 106–124.

Klein Velderman, M., Bakermans-Kranenburg, M. J., Juffer, F., *et al.* (2006). Effects of attachment-based interventions on maternal sensitivity and infant attachment: Differential susceptibility of highly reactive infants. *Journal of Family Psychology, 20*(2), 266–274.

Kobak, R., Zajac, K., and Smith, C. (2009). Adolescent attachment and trajectories of hostile-impulsive behavior: Implications for the development of personality disorders. *Development and Psychopathology, 21*(3), 839–851.

Liddle, H. A. (2002). *Multidimensional Family Therapy for Adolescent Cannabis Users*. (DHHS Publications No. SMA 02-3660). Rockville, MD: Substance Abuse & Mental Health Services Administration, Center for Substance Abuse Treatment.

Little, T. D., Jones, S. M., and Henrich, C. C. (2003). Disentangling the 'whys' form the 'whats' of aggressive behavior. *International Journal of Behavioral Development, 27*(2), 122–133.

Main, M., and Goldwyn, R. (1998). Adult attachment scoring and classification system. (Unpublished manuscript). Berkeley: University of California.

Marvin, R., Cooper, G., Hoffman, K., et al. (2002). The Circle of Security project: Attachment-based intervention with caregiver-pre-school child dyads. Attachment & Human Development, 4(1), 107–124.

Mason, W. A., and Capitanio, J. P. (1988). Formation and expression of filial attachment in rhesus monkeys raised with living and with inanimate mother substitutes. Developmental Psychobiology, 21, 401–430.

Mason, W. A., and Mendoza, S. P. (1998). Generic aspects of primate attachments: Parents, offspring and mates. Psychoneuroendocrinology, 23(8), 765–778.

Mayseless, O. (1991). Adult attachment patterns and courtship violence. Family Relations: Journal of Applied Family & Child Studies, 40(1), 21–28.

Moore, T. E., and Pepler, D. J. (2006) Wounding words: Maternal verbal aggression and children's adjustment. Journal of Family Violence, 21(1), 89–93.

Moretti, M. M. (2003). The Affect Regulation Checklist. Unpublished measure and data. Simon Fraser University, British Columbia, Canada.

Moretti, M. M. and Holland, R. (2003). The journey of adolescence: Transitions in self within the context of attachment relationships (pp. 234-257). In: S. Johnson and V. Whiffen (eds) Attachment Processes in Couple and Family Therapy. New York: Guildford Press.

Moretti, M. M., Catchpole, R., and Odgers, C. (2005). The dark side of girlhood: Recent trends, risk factors and trajectories to aggression and violence. Canadian Child and Adolescent Psychiatry Review, 14, 32–38.

Moretti, M. M., Braber, K., and Obsuth, I. (2009). Connect: An Attachment Focused Treatment Group for Parents and Caregivers – A Principle Based Manual. © Simon Fraser University.

Moretti, M. M., and Higgins, E. T. (1999). Own versus other standpoints in self-regulation: Developmental antecedents and functional consequences. Review of General Psychology, 3(3), 188–223.

Moretti, M. M., McKay, S., and Holland, R. (2000). The Comprehensive Adolescent-Parent Attachment Inventory (CAPAI). Unpublished measure and data. Simon Fraser University, Burnaby, British Columbia, Canada.

Moretti, M. M., and Obsuth, I. (2009). Effectiveness of an attachment-focused manualized intervention for parents of teens at risk for aggressive behavior: The Connect Program. Journal of Adolescents. Special Issue: Intervention and Prevention with Adolescents, 32, 1347–1357.

Moretti, M. M., and Odgers, C. (2006). Sex differences in the functions and precursors of adolescent aggression. Aggressive BehaviorBehavior, 32(4), 373–375.

Moretti, M. M., and Peled, M. (2004). Adolescent-parent attachment: Bonds that support healthy development. Pediatrics & Child Health, 9(8), 551–555.

Moretti, M. M., Obsuth, I., Mayseless, O., et al. (2009). Reducing aggression through parent-teen relationships: effectiveness and change processes of a brief attachment focused program. Paper presented in a Symposium at the Biennial Meeting of the Society for Research in Child Development, Denver, CO.

National Committee on Violence (1990). Violence: Directions for Australia. Canberra: Australian Institute of Criminology.

Obsuth, I., and Moretti, M. M. (2009). The role of attachment and affect regulation in aggressive behaviour: Concurrent and prospective effects among at-risk adolescents. Unpublished manuscript; dissertation in progress. Simon Fraser University.

Odgers, C., Moretti, M. M. and Reppucci, N. D. (2005). Examining the science and practice of violence risk assessment with female adolescents. Law & Human Behavior, 29, 7–27.

Renken, B., Egeland, B., and Marvinney, D. (1989). Early childhood antecedents of aggression and passive-withdrawal in early elementary school. *Journal of Personality, 57(2)*, Special issue: Long-term stability and change in personality, 257–281.

Rosenstein, D. S., and Horowitz, H. A. (1996). Adolescent attachment and psychopathology. *Journal of Consulting and Clinical Psychology, 64*(2), 244–253.

Scharf, M. and Mayseless, O., (1997/2000) Parenting Representations Interview – Adolescence (PRI-A). Unpublished manuscript. University of Haifa.

Scharfe, E. (2002). Reliability and validity of an interview assessment of attachment representations in a clinical sample of adolescents. *Journal of Adolescent Research, 17(5)*, 532–551.

Schludermann, E. H., and Schludermann, S. M. (1988). *Children's Report on Parent Behavior (CRPBI-108, CRPBI-30) for Older Children and Adolescents.* (Technical Report). Winnipeg, Manitoba, Canada: University of Manitoba, Department of Psychology.

Slade, A., Grienenberger, J., Bernbach, E., *et al.* (2005). Maternal reflective functioning, attachment, and the transmission gap: A preliminary study. *Attachment & Human Development, 7(3)*, 283–298.

Snyder, H. (1997). *Serious, Violent, and Chronic Juvenile Offenders: An Assessment of the Extent of and Trends in Officially-recognized Serious Criminal Behavior in a Delinquent Population.* Pittsburgh, PA: National Center for Juvenile Justice.

Snyder, H. (2004) Juvenile justice bulletin – juvenile arrests 2002 national report. Washington, DC: US Department of Justice (Office of Justice Programs, Office of Juvenile Justice and Delinquency Prevention).

Snyder, H. and Sickmund, M. (2006) *Juvenile Offenders and Victims: 2006 National Report.* Washington, DC: US Department of Justice (Office of Justice Programs, Office of Juvenile Justice and Delinquency Prevention).

Speltz, M. L., DeKlyen, M., and Greenberg, M. T. (1999). Attachment in boys with early onset conduct problems. *Development and Psychopathology, 11*(2), 269–285.

Straus, M. A. (1979). Measuring intrafamily conflict and violence: The Conflict Tactics Scales. *Journal of Marriage and the Family, 41*, 75–81.

Straus, M. A., and Ramirez, I. L. (2007). Gender symmetry in prevalence, severity, and chronicity of physical aggression against dating partners by university students in Mexico and USA. *Aggressive Behavior, 33*(4), 281–290.

Taylor, S. E., Klein, L. C., Lewis, B. P., *et al.* (2000). Biobehavioral responses to stress in females: Tend-and-befriend, not fight-or-flight. *Psychological Review, 107*, 411–429.

Tremblay, R. E., Nagin, D. S., Séguin, *et al.* (2004). Physical aggression during early childhood: Trajectories and predictors. *Pediatrics, 114*(1), 43–50.

Trulson, C. R., Marquart, J. W., Mullings, J. L., *et al.* (2005). In between adolescence and adulthood. *Youth Violence and Juvenile Justice, 3*, 355–387.

US Department of Justice, Office of Justice Programs (1998). *Trends in Juvenile Violence in European Countries.*

Van IJzendoorn, M. H. (1995). Of the way we were: On temperament, attachment, and the transmission gap: A rejoinder to Fox. *Psychological Bulletin, 117*(3), 411–415.

Van Zeijl, J., Mesman, J., Van IJzendoorn, *et al.* (2006). Attachment-based intervention for enhancing sensitive discipline in mothers of 1- to 3-year-old children at risk for Externalizing behavior problems: A randomized controlled trial. *Journal of Consulting and Clinical Psychology, 74*(6), 994–1005.

White, R., and Mason, R. (2006). Youth gangs and youth violence: Charting the key dimensions. *Australian & New Zealand Journal of Criminology, 39*(1), 54–70.

World Health Organization (2006). *Youth Violence and Alcohol*, Fact Sheet.

CHAPTER 9

The Transfer of Developmental and Health Risk from Women with Histories of Aggressive Behavior to Their Children: Recent Results from the Concordia Longitudinal Project

Lisa A. Serbin, Dale M. Stack, Michele Hubert, and Alex E. Schwartzman
Concordia University, Canada

Jane Ledingham
University of Ottawa, Canada

Research on aggression in women and girls has accelerated rapidly over the past decade. For those of us who have worked in this field since the 1980s, when all research on aggression in the United States was delegated to the Department of Justice for funding (under the Regan administration), and girls were deliberately excluded from longitudinal research on the outcomes of aggressive behavior (because so few women were arrested in adolescence for violent crimes), things have truly changed in our field. We now have many studies in the literature on the distinctive nature and function of girlhood aggression, and have broadened the construct beyond direct physical violence

Understanding Girls' Problem Behavior: How Girls' Delinquency Develops in the Context of Maturity and Health, Co-occurring Problems, and Relationships, Edited by Margaret Kerr, Håkan Stattin, Rutger C. M. E. Engels, Geertjan Overbeek and Anna-Karin Andershed © 2011 John Wiley & Sons, Ltd.

to include studies of social exclusion, teasing, ingroup–outgroup behavior, bullying, victimization, cyber attacks, gang participation, and many other aspects of aggressive behavior that are frequently utilized by girls, as well as boys, in their social relationships. Has girlhood aggression become more frequent, or serious (in terms of consequences) over the past decades, or are we simply looking through a broader lens that now includes aggressive behaviors more typical of the females of our species? This remains unclear.

The literature indicates that rates of aggression and violent behavior in males continue to equal or surpass rates in females, regardless of the type of behavior coded, the experimental paradigm utilized, the specific environmental context, the specific population studied, or the age of the participants (Card *et al.*, 2008). Starting in early childhood, boys generally behave more aggressively than girls, particularly with respect to physical aggression, though girls may engage in more relational aggression towards peer including such behaviors as teasing, gossiping, and social ostracism. (Cairns *et al.*, 1989). However, the use of all forms of aggression by females is higher than previously reported or generally believed. Also, the form and function of female aggression may be different from males: at least after toddlerhood. Recent research, as illustrated in the present volume, has moved beyond documenting the development, form and function of aggression in the two sexes. We are now examining the *consequences* and *sequelae* of aggression in women and men, both in terms of consequences for the individual actor and for members of that individual's social circle and community, including victims, peers and family. Further, the recognition that the *sequelae* and *consequences* of early aggression may take many forms across the course of development, some *homotypic* (i.e., similar behavior) and some *heterotypic* (i.e. not obviously similar in form) has gained recognition (Moffitt *et al.*, 2001; Huesmann, Dubow, and Boxer, 2009). Finally, the idea that childhood aggression is a characteristic that may increase risk in many domains, via both direct and indirect pathways, has gained widespread interest. It is also clear from recent intergenerational studies that the continuity of aggressive behavior in childhood may be observed between generations: in terms of both similar behavior occurring in offspring at a similar age and heightened risk for a wide variety of developmental and health *sequelae*.

Conceptually it makes sense to utilize a *systems* approach in understanding a complex issue such as aggression: clearly there are simultaneous and sequential biological (genetic and non-genetic), physiological, environmental, cognitive, and social aspects of this complex behavior. *Sequelae* and outcomes are also extremely complex. However, with this conceptualization as an underlying basis for the research, we still find it practical and useful to focus on specific pathways and processes associated with aggressive behavior across development. Childhood aggressive behavior is usually part of a broad pattern of highly dysfunctional behavior, which may include atypical social relations, academic problems, attentional difficulties, problems in executive functioning, atypical stress reactivity, mental and physical health and possibly even abnormal immune system functioning. However, by focusing specific research projects on a limited number of related parts of the system, useful components of a systems model may be delineated. Accordingly, the focus of this chapter will not be on genetic or other biologically based transfer of risk. Instead we will discuss the direct and indirect pathways from childhood behavioral characteristics to conditions of child rearing, home environment characteristics, and parenting behavior. Behavioral, cognitive, and physical health outcomes in the next-generation will also be considered. In the first section, we describe the Concordia Longitudinal Risk Project. In the next section, we describe the trajectories of highly aggressive girls in the Concordia sample: from middle childhood through adolescence and early adulthood. In the subsequent sections, we examine a number of outcomes predicted after the girls had become parents: (1) parenting and environment and (2) developmental and health outcomes in the offspring. We then briefly summarize, interpret, and discuss the meaning of these results and propose suggestions for intervention and policy.

A LONGITUDINAL STUDY OF AGGRESSION IN CANADA

Participants in the studies reviewed for this chapter come from a large, community-based research sample of families whose average income level and occupational status, for the most part, are significantly below the average levels for Canada and Quebec. The Concordia Longitudinal Risk Project is an ongoing inter-generational study begun by Jane Ledingham and Alex Schwartzman (Ledingham and Schwartzman, 1981; Schwartzman, Ledingham, and Serbin, 1985) in 1976–78 with the screening of 4109 francophone school children attending grades 1, 4, and 7. The screening process involved the classification of children along the dimensions of aggression and withdrawal by means of a French translation of the Pupil Evaluation Inventory (PEI; see Pekarik *et al.*, 1976), a peer nomination instrument. Sample items for the Aggression factor included "children who are mean and cruel towards other children" and "children who fight all the time and get into trouble." Items in the Withdrawal factor include "children who are too shy to make friends easily" and "children who usually don't want to play with others." Children were asked to nominate up to four boys and four girls in their class who best matched each item on the PEI. The number of nominations received by each child was summed for both aggression and withdrawal factors. These total scores were then subjected to a square root transformation to decrease skewness. Finally, transformed scores were converted to z-scores for each sex, within each classroom to control for class size and gender differences in base rates of aggression and withdrawal. This procedure enabled appropriate comparisons of each child against the relevant norms for gender and age. There were 861 boys and 909 girls selected for ongoing participation. Approximately half of the selected participants had elevated risk profiles due to extreme patterns of aggressive or withdrawn behavior or a combination of both, while the other half was a comparison group: normative in terms of social behavior.

Findings from the Concordia study have consistently shown relatively high stability of aggression and withdrawal for both girls and boys (Moskowitz, Schwartzman, and Ledingham, 1985; Serbin *et al.*, 1991; Serbin, Peters, and Schwartzman, 1996). Aggression appears to be a general risk factor for diverse negative outcomes within the sample of participants from the Concordia Project and high levels of social withdrawal in childhood can modulate the developmental trajectory of aggression. In contrast with aggression, social withdrawal has been rarely studied as a predictor of outcomes within financially disadvantaged populations. It may predict the adoption of traditional life styles in women: specifically marriage, childbearing, and homemaking as a career (Caspi, Bem, and Elder, 1989). Although more might be known about the stability and consequences of aggression relative to social withdrawal, research suggests that both patterns of behavior can have negative *sequelae* throughout the life course depending on social, educational, and economic contexts such as family poverty (e.g., Huesmann *et al.*, 1984).

The combined pattern of aggression and withdrawal has generally shown extremely problematic outcomes during adolescence and early adulthood in most areas of functioning of participants of the Concordia sample. Aggression and social withdrawal, when they occur together, reduce the likelihood of academic success (Caspi, Elder, and Bem, 1988b; Bardone *et al.*, 1996). Through lowered educational attainment, they also indirectly increase the chances of financial disadvantage across the life course (Kokko *et al.*, 1998). Both lower educational attainment and poverty are known to limit parents' access to social resources. Parental academic competence has also been shown to be linked with offspring's subsequent academic competence (Cairns *et al.*, 1998). In the studies that are described in this chapter, childhood aggression and the pattern of elevated aggression and withdrawal in combination were examined as predictors of a variety of later risks.

THE CONCORDIA LONGITUDINAL RISK PROJECT: OVERVIEW OF DESIGN AND FINDINGS THROUGH EARLY ADULTHOOD

Unlike most longitudinal studies of childhood aggression or other childhood behavior problems, this is a community-based (rather than a clinical) sample. A community sample avoids the selection biases inherent in clinic-referred samples and is more representative of the Quebec population as a whole. Furthermore, unlike most other longitudinal studies of children from disadvantaged communities, specific atypical dimensions of social behavior (i.e., aggression and withdrawal) were initially identified, and could be followed as predictors within a population at elevated risk for a wide variety of psycho-social and health problems.

Another unique feature of the original design was the inclusion of approximately equal numbers of girls and boys. Consequently, the Concordia study is one of the few longitudinal studies, worldwide, that has followed a large sample of aggressive and withdrawn girls into adulthood. Due to the nature of the design, with some girls having patterns of atypical behavior and others with normative patterns of behavior (342 and 567 respectively), we are able to observe those factors that are predictive of both positive and negative adaptation, an important focus of recent research on risk and resiliency.

As the original participants reached their late 20s to early 30s, many became parents. Although the study of offspring and the inter-generational transfer of risk was not originally planned, the opportunity now existed. Given the unique nature of the sample and the longitudinal data set, and the likelihood that parenting may be a particularly important outcome measure, inter-generational studies of the offspring of the Concordia sample were begun virtually as soon as they started having children in the late 1980s (Serbin *et al.*, 1991). Results to date strongly suggest that psycho-social risk may be transferred between generations via the behavior, functioning, environment, and social and economic circumstances of the participants as they become parents (Serbin *et al.* 1996, 1998, 2002; Serbin and Karp, 2004; De Genna *et al.*, 2007).

Children growing up under disadvantaged conditions are likely to become the parents of another disadvantaged generation, who, like their parents, are born with a high-risk of serious psycho-social and health problems. However, longitudinal studies reveal that psycho-social risk is, as the term denotes, probabilistic. Many children from high-risk backgrounds grow up to have reasonably prosperous and productive lives, despite their poor prospects at birth (Rutter, 1990; Masten 2001). The studies described below are recent attempts to identify risk and protective factors across generations. How girls' aggression is manifested across development in terms of lifestyle, family functioning and health sequelae is underscored. The pathways through which aggression develops and the transfer of risk across generations are also included.

TRAJECTORIES FOLLOWED BY HIGHLY AGGRESSIVE GIRLS IN MIDDLE CHILDHOOD, ADOLESCENCE AND EARLY ADULTHOOD

Characteristics of Aggressive Girls

Beginning at the original point of identification of the Concordia sample in elementary school, the risk trajectories of aggression in girls has proved to be distinctive, though there are many similarities between the highly aggressive girls' and highly aggressive boys' trajectories. Recall that the highly aggressive girls in the sample were defined according to gender-based norms; that is, highly aggressive girls were more aggressive than other girls in their classes but not as aggressive as their male counterparts. It was aggressive boys who were described by peers in terms of a profile underlining public disruptive behavior perceived as intrusive, uncontrolled, and immature. Aggressive girls were described in terms of a gender-neutral profile (i.e., these characteristics were endorsed equally for boys and girls), including behaviors generally perceived as hostile and domineering (Schwartzman *et al.*, 1995).

Patterns of Aggression on the Playground

The behavior patterns of highly aggressive girls were examined in an observational study of a sample of 174 fifth and sixth grade children on the playground (a younger group identified from among the same schools and using the same methods as the original Concordia Project; see Serbin *et al.*, 1987; Lyons, Serbin, and Marchessault, 1988; Serbin *et al.*, 1993a). We found that peer-nominated aggressive girls and boys were more physically aggressive during play than non-aggressive children of either sex. In general, relatively few episodes of explicit or extreme aggression or violence were observed during this study of social interaction during recess periods. Most aggressive events were incorporated into episodes of rough-and-tumble play (e.g., tackling, pushing, hitting, or kicking during games or lining-up, etc). The peer-identified aggressive girls spent much of their time playing with boys engaged in rough-and-tumble play behavior (an atypical behavior pattern for girls at this age) and most of their observed aggressive acts were directed at boys (rather than other girls).

Aggressive play is a much more normative pattern among boys in general than among girls (Serbin, Powlishta, and Gulko, 1993b), and the peer identified aggressive girls appeared to be integrating (or attempting to integrate) into primarily male play groups. Possibly, they were excluded from girls' groups on the playground due to their uncharacteristic behavior. Gender segregation is a well documented social pattern among children of this age on the playground (see Maccoby, 1998), and again, the aggressive girls seemed to be violating a social norm with regard to their preferred play partners. Interestingly, although aggressive boys were generally liked by their same-sex classmates, aggressive girls were disliked by other girls. Most disliked among both sexes, however, were the aggressive-withdrawn children. These children of both sexes attracted more peer-initiated aggressive attacks on the playground than other children (Serbin *et al.*, 1987; Lyons *et al.*, 1988; Serbin *et al.*, 1993b). In other words, these children were most likely to be victimized during play periods. This pattern of associating with boys, especially those with aggressive play styles, and being avoided by girls may be a core element in the subsequent development of aggressive girls. Girls who are drawn to peer groups that engage in aggression and other types of risk-taking behavior in elementary school may expand their repertoire of deviant behavior as they mature, following the norms and values of their peer subgroup.

Academic Ability and Performance and Achievement

Another major consideration in projecting trajectories for aggressive girls is that highly aggressive children of both sexes were more likely to have lower IQs and lower standardized academic achievement test scores than children from the comparison or withdrawn group (Ledingham and Schwartzman, 1981; Schwartzman, Ledingham, and Serbin, 1985). In other words, aggression was associated with academic and cognitive difficulties in both sexes, beginning as early as first grade. The combination of aggression and withdrawal was particularly problematic; this group of children had the lowest average IQ and school achievement scores in the sample.

In a first follow-up study of academic outcomes three years after identification, there were few gender differences in terms of the school progress of highly aggressive children: both aggressive girls and boys were more likely to have repeated a grade, or to have been placed in a special class for children with behavioral or learning problems. Approximately 41% of the highly aggressive children had repeated a grade within three years or had been placed in a special class, while 48% of the highly aggressive and withdrawn group repeated a grade (compared with 17% of the normative comparison children and 25% of the withdrawn group; see Schwartzman, Ledingham, and Serbin, 1985).

Academic difficulties seen in elementary school continued into high school, with aggression scores predicting elevated rates of high school drop-out for both sexes, and the aggressive-withdrawn group failing at the highest rates. Aggression predicted high school dropout, even when academic ability scores were controlled statistically (Serbin *et al.*, 1998). In other words, early aggression predicted later school drop-out, even when children's cognitive and academic abilities were not impaired. Aggressive behavior seems to affect school success via patterns of peer relations, social and emotional problems, and risk-taking behavior, as discussed above. Once these children have dropped out of high school, risk of early parenthood is greatly elevated (Serbin *et al.*, 1998).

Risk-Taking Behavior

During adolescence, girls' aggression was associated with elevated rates of self-reported alcohol, and illegal drug usage (Schwartzman *et al.*, 1995). This suggests that these girls continue to seek out behaviorally compatible peer groups, probably composed of boys and girls with similar aggressive, or what could be considered pre-delinquent, behavioral styles, if not actively engaging in delinquent behavior. The aggressive girls, in general, report far less overt criminal or violent behavior than the aggressive boys during adolescence, as reflected in their much lower arrest records (Schwartzman and Mohan, 1999). However, they do have a higher arrest rate in their late teens than other girls, and their self reported risk-taking behavior, such as smoking and drug use, indicates a likelihood of continuing negative life trajectories.

Mental Health

Mental health outcomes for highly aggressive girls were examined in late adolescence and early adulthood. Interestingly, and consistent with the relatively low rates of criminal behavior in late adolescence and early adulthood by the women who were highly aggressive or both aggressive and withdrawn, were not associated with conduct disorder per se, but were predictive of elevated rates of internalizing problems such as depression and anxiety disorders (Schwartzman *et al.*, 2009).

Sexual Behavior, Gynecological Risk, and Early Parenthood

Another aspect of the high-risk behavior and peer relations typical of the highly aggressive girls in the Concordia sample relates to their sexual behavior during adolescence. Examining the adolescent health care records of 853 women, childhood aggression predicted elevated frequencies of gynecological problems and acute infections between 11 and 17 years of age, and of STDs and childbearing between the ages of 14 and 20 (Serbin *et al.*, 1991). In other words, girls' childhood aggression seems to have predicted early, unprotected sexual activity during the teen years. This pattern continued into late adolescence and early adulthood, when teen parenthood, multi-parity (defined as having more than one child by age 23), close spacing of successive births (less than two years apart), and obstetric and delivery complications were elevated risks for girls with childhood histories of aggression, and especially those with combined histories of aggression and withdrawal (Serbin *et al.*, 1998).

These fertility patterns are associated with problematic subsequent histories for both parents and children, as opportunities for continuing education and higher occupational status are curtailed, along with a probability of lower income across the life course (Furstenberg, Brooks-Gunn, and Morgan, 1987; Furstenberg, Brooks-Gunn, and Chase-Lansdale, 1989). For offspring, the risks extend to physical health and lack of social and economic support during the important prenatal period and continuing throughout childhood. As discussed below in the section describing outcomes for offspring, these concerns for the health of offspring of highly aggressive women, especially those born to teen mothers, were confirmed in an examination of pediatric medical records.

Maternal Health

Maternal health behaviors and symptoms in adults may vary as a function of childhood risk status, indicating that childhood social behavior may help predict future health outcomes and transmission of risk to the next generation. Girls who are seen as very aggressive by their peers may develop different health habits and patterns of physical ailments, which may in turn affect the physical environments for their future children. Mothers in the Concordia sample who were aggressive in childhood were more likely to have smoked during their pregnancies (De Genna *et al.*, 2006; De Genna *et al.*, 2007). Current maternal smoking in mothers of toddlers and preschoolers, which may have an impact both on these mothers' and children's current and future health, was predicted by maternal childhood aggression. Moreover, maternal childhood aggression predicted maternal respiratory complaints including at least one experience of asthma, bronchitis, pneumonia, and sinusitis (in the mothers themselves) three months prior to the time of our evaluation. Based on regression equations, the effects of childhood aggression on maternal health were above and beyond the effects of current maternal smoking. Finally, mothers high on both childhood aggression and withdrawal were more likely to currently suffer from hematological irregularities with lifestyle implications, such as anemia, hypoglycemia and diabetes (De Genna, *et al.*, 2006).

To summarize, aggressive girls were generally perceived as hostile and domineering. They had a preference for male playmates that were likely to reciprocate the rough play style, and this physical, rough-and-tumble style of play was disliked by other girls. In the academic domain, aggression was related to academic and cognitive difficulties as well as school dropout. Girl's aggression also predicted internalizing disorders in early adulthood, along with histories of adolescent risk taking behavior, including smoking, alcohol use, substance abuse, and unprotected sexual activity, as well as early parenthood. Consequently, risk taking behavior (e.g., timing of sexual activity, early pregnancy) was shown to predict health problems in the young mothers. These health problems affected their offspring's developmental outcomes and health, and contributed to the home environment (see below). In essence, the offspring's early developmental and health trajectories were affected by mothers' risk behavior, lifestyle and health problems, including events and characteristics present prior to the birth of the child.

SOME IMPLICATIONS OF GIRLHOOD AGGRESSION FOR CONTINUING ADULT DEVELOPMENT AND THE INTER-GENERATIONAL TRANSFER OF RISK

The lifestyle stress suggested by women's histories is considerable. It may involve incremental social, economic, and educational disadvantage across adolescence, and the likelihood of early parenthood with inadequate social, emotional, and financial support. Cumulative and acute stress may, in part, account for the elevated rates of mental health problems in these women. Within other longitudinal samples, the lifetime probabilities of low occupational status, frequent job changes, welfare status, single parenthood, and marital instability are all likely to be elevated in women with histories of childhood aggression (Pulkkinen and Pitkanen, 1993).

As relationships and social support are important parts of this picture, it is also not surprising that girls with childhood histories of aggression are likely to form adult relationships with male partners having similar behavioral styles to their own (Peters, 1999). Similar findings have also been replicated in a longitudinal examining assertative mating for antisocial behavior (Krueger et al., 1998)

Undoubtedly these cumulative social, educational, emotional, occupational, and economic problems in early adulthood contribute to ongoing mental and physical health difficulties, along with many other problems of social and psychological adjustment. The long-term problems of aggressive girls cannot, however, be entirely attributed to their elevated risk for school drop-out, early parenthood, and other stressful socio-economic conditions. As we will discuss below, childhood aggression seems to reflect a stable behavioral style that continues to influence social relationships into adulthood, including marital interaction patterns and parent-child relationships.

PREDICTING PARENTING AND HOME ENVIRONMENT: RISK TO A NEW GENERATION

It is clear from the preceding section that highly aggressive girls in the Concordia sample demonstrate risk-taking behavior and problematic peer relations through adolescence and into young adulthood. One route through which children are placed at risk is through the pre-, peri-, and post-natal care and environments that are provided to the developing child. The factors that surround the birth of the child can include numerous potentially important variables, ranging from nutritional status prior to conception and during pregnancy, substance ingestion during pregnancy, prematurity, birth weight, medical status at birth, birth trauma, delivery complications, length of hospitalization, multi-parity, chronic illness, injuries, and the family and home environment after birth. These factors are all associated with important outcomes in terms of children's health and development. A risk event can occur (before pregnancy, at conception, during pre-natal development, during the peri-natal period, or following birth) and be related to developmental outcome in offspring (Kopp and Kaler, 1989).

As described above, in terms of health-risk behavior, maternal childhood aggression was associated with the number of cigarettes smoked while pregnant, as well as current levels of smoking. In turn, these factors were both positively associated with maternal BMI. Moreover, larger children were more likely to have had mothers who were heavier smokers during pregnancy (De Genna et al., 2006; De Genna et al., 2007).

Adverse conditions during early development are clearly important considerations which can affect children's long-term health and developmental outcomes. Pre-, peri-, and post-birth factors may be elevated or complicated by poverty and teenage pregnancy. In the current phase of the Concordia Project, we are interested in identifying specific characteristics of the family situation, the parents, and/or the child that promote adjustment in the face of psycho-social disadvantage. Previous studies have emphasized the role of parental education as a protective factor (Furstenberg *et. al.*, 1987; Auerbach *et al.*, 1992; Serbin *et al.*, 1998). In this phase, we examined additional variables, such as parental characteristics, family relationships, and the availability of social support. Previous research (e.g., Cowen *et al.*, 1990; McLoyd, 1990), indicates that these variables may represent important buffers against negative outcomes. In the next section of the chapter, we will report on recent findings expanding our previous work to predict examine girls' childhood social behavior patterns, family risk variables, parenting, and home environment during parenthood.

CHILDHOOD AGGRESSION AS A PREDICTOR OF FAMILY DISADVANTAGE

Relations between early maladaptive behavior and later family circumstances have rarely been examined in the literature, especially from childhood into parenthood. However, maladaptive behavior patterns in childhood may influence the later life and functioning of individuals and their families through a variety of mechanisms and pathways. Primarily, they may impede a child's school functioning, performance and educational attainment, which can potentially set off a devastating chain of events across the life-course. These behavioral styles may also contribute to premature parenthood (Bardone *et al.*, 1998), to marital or family discord (Kinnunen and Pulkkinen, 2003), and consequent parental separation, family economic distress and poverty (Bardone *et al.*, 1996; Kokko and Pulkkinen, 2000). Negative outcomes in terms of educational attainment, timing of parenthood, family structure, and income may have particular importance for child rearing, with respect to the environment in which an individual becomes a parent and raises the next generation. In other words, social and behavioral patterns in childhood may have both direct and indirect implications for the conditions under which subsequent generations are raised.

Some of the specific pathways that may threaten child rearing environments are considered in the following conceptual model (see Figure 9.1).

In a study to test this model, we examined pathways from problematic behavior patterns in childhood to disadvantaged family circumstances in adulthood, conditions that may promote the intergenerational transfer of risk for disadvantage (Serbin *et al., in press*). The relations between childhood risk factors and family outcomes are likely to be complex. Therefore, direct and indirect paths from childhood behavior patterns through academic achievement, high school dropout, early parenting, and parental absence to current family poverty were considered within the predictive model (see Figure 9.1).

To test this model, observations were included from four phases across the participant's life course. Phase 1 (1976–1977) refers to middle childhood,

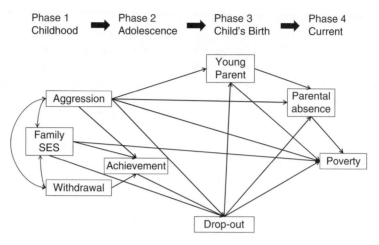

Figure 9.1   Theoretical model predicting poverty and other threats to parenting (Model from Serbin *et al.* (in press)).

specifically the age at which participants were rated by peers in terms of aggression and social withdrawal. At this time, information on the children's academic achievement and family SES were also collected. Phase 2 (1980s) refers to the participants' adolescent years and the time at which high school completion normally takes place. Phase 3 (late 1980s–1990s) refers to the time at which participants became parents. Phase 4 refers to the most recent phase of the project; information on family composition as well as poverty status during child rearing years was collected.

The subsample for this study was composed of ongoing participants in the Concordia Project who had become parents by 2003, when an update of participants' demographic records was carried out. The size of the sample was 550 parents (328 mothers and 222 fathers). Both mothers and father had a mean age of 32 and on average had completed 12.1 years of schooling. Ages at first birth ranged from 15.2 to 36.5 years (M = 24.9) for mothers and 18.5 to 37.9 years (M = 26.6) for fathers. Young parenthood was defined statistically as being in the youngest quartile of participants when becoming a parent for the first time. Of the 328 women in this sample, 202 (62%) lived with all their biological children and their children's biological father. Of the 222 men, 147 (66%) lived with all their biological children and their children's mother father. In other words, these participants had both biological parents present within the household. The remaining participants were considered to have one biological parent absent. Of the 550 families, 192 (35%) families were classified as poor, including 40% of the participating mothers' families, and 28% of the participating fathers' families.

For these analyses, models for mothers and fathers were tested separately, given that academic failure, early parenthood, parental absence, and poverty might have different predictors and inter-relations for men and women and their families.

Results from women's path model indicated that both childhood aggression and withdrawal directly predicted lower school achievement in middle childhood. In turn, girls who experienced difficulties in school were at increased risk for dropping out of high school. Girls who failed to complete high school were at greater risk for entering motherhood at a young age and parenting in poverty. A direct pathway from aggression to young motherhood persisted as well. Not only were aggressive girls at greater risk for becoming mothers early, but having children at a young age increased the likelihood that their children would be raised with one biological parent absent. Childhood aggression also directly put girls at risk for parenting in a context of parental absence. In turn, parenting a child in a non-traditional family structure with a parent absent increased the likelihood of living in poverty. When controlling for the effects of family SES, high school dropout, early parenthood, and parental absence, only a marginal effect was found for childhood aggression in the prediction of family poverty during parenthood ($\beta = 0.09$, $p < 0.10$). In other words, aggression was partly mediated by of family SES, high school dropout, early parenthood, and parental absence.

Similar to women, men's childhood aggression and withdrawal were found to predict lower school achievement in middle childhood. In turn, boys who performed less well in school were subsequently at increased risk for dropping out of high school. There was a direct path from boy's aggression to poverty during parenthood. Unlike aggressive girls, aggressive boys had a significantly increased risk of not completing their secondary educations even when controlling for school achievement. A second gender difference was that dropping out of high school predicted subsequent poverty during parenthood for women, but not for men. This could be due partly to discrepancies in the life circumstances and types of jobs available to male and female high school dropouts. The third difference between the models was the path from parental absence to poverty during parenthood. Unlike the women, men who had children being raised in a non-intact family structure did not have an increased risk for living in poverty. It should be noted that many of the children being raised under conditions of parental absence were living with their mothers (17%). Fathers were either living alone or with new partners at the time of this study. Hence these fathers were not themselves at increased risk of living in poverty, but their children may have been.

In sum, direct paths from childhood aggression to adverse parenting conditions included paths to young parenthood, parental absence and poverty for mothers and paths to high school drop-out, young parenthood, parental absence, and poverty for fathers. Indirect paths accounted for some of the relation between aggression and withdrawal and the four outcome variables. Almost three times as much of the variability in family poverty was accounted for in the model for women as in the model for men. This suggests that high school drop-out, early parenthood and parental absence may be particularly important and salient in the life-courses of women, and consequently, they may be useful in predicting risk to offspring. Aggression in childhood also appears to be an important predictor of negative life paths among women. This has particular relevance for the processes whereby psycho-social risk is transferred across generations through negative rearing conditions.

These findings support the idea that there are potential buffers that can function protectively within at-risk populations: characteristics and experiences that may protect individuals from negative outcomes, even under disadvantaged family circumstances. Most notably, in this study, basic academic skills appeared to play an important role in determining educational outcomes, controlling for both family disadvantage and children's behavioral characteristics. In turn, educational attainment predicted experiences and conditions that also played a role in successful parenting, such as age at parenthood, parental absence, and family poverty.

CHILDHOOD AGGRESSION AS A PREDICTOR OF HEALTH AND DEVELOPMENT IN THE SUBSEQUENT GENERATION

We now turn to the health and functioning of the offspring of the Concordia sample. As anticipated, these children showed a variety of elevated risks from birth onward. However, it should be noted that in the offspring generation, like their parents, risk is by definition probabilistic. Although the Concordia Project offspring may be at greater risk of developing a given problem than the general population, many of these children, even those with multiple risk indicators, will not develop serious health, developmental, or behavioral problems.

Beyond health factors, the mother–child relationship is an important contributor to the environment within which the child grows and to the child's socialization and development. Accordingly, one of the primary focuses of the Concordia Project has been the mother-child relationship in our search for important parenting and family variables that may place the offspring of the Concordia Project participants at risk. The relationship between mother and child has been understood as one of the most important in the life of a child. It is within the context of early relationships that children develop skills and strategies that will serve them for the rest of their lives (Bowlby, 1980). When this relationship is adaptive, children are likely to emerge well-adjusted and free from major pathology. When this relationship is disrupted through maternal psycho-social difficulty, maternal pathology, or family dysfunction, children are placed at risk for psycho-social disturbances (Beardslee, Keller, and Klerman, 1985; Hammen et al., 1987; Caspi and Elder, 1988a; Dumas, LaFreniere, and Serketich, 1995). During the first three years of life, important attachment processes and emotional organization take place (Emde, 1989; Sameroff and Seifer, 1992; Fogel, 1993). A parent's ability to be emotionally available, responsive, and attentive during these early years, will ultimately impact the developmental outcome of their child (Egeland and Erickson, 1987; Biringen and Robinson, 1991). In considering whether mothers' childhood aggression might interfere with their abilities to effectively parent their young children, we examined unresponsive parenting toward infants, toddlers, and school-aged offspring.

In one study, 84 women from the original sample together will their eldest children (5–12 years of age) participated in four videotaped laboratory tasks (Serbin et al., 1998). The four laboratory tasks used in this study were selected so that a range of typical mother-child interaction scenarios might be observed. They included: a free play task, a teaching task, a negotiation task, and finally, a conflict discussion task. The order of the tasks was designed to gradually move mother–child dyads from a relatively stress-free, optional interaction situation through to a potentially anxiety-provoking, highly interactive, confrontational scenario in which a topic that provoked conflict between members of the dyad was selected for discussion. The sequence of the activities, save for the presence of the first task, was drawn from the work of Granger, Weisz, and Kanneckis (1994). Using this paradigm, we examined whether maternal psycho-social difficulties in childhood would be predictive of reduced support, aggressivity, and unresponsiveness as indices of maladaptive behaviors in interactions with their offspring. In general, both childhood aggression and maternal education proved to be independent predictors of maternal behavior. Mother's childhood history of aggression was predictive of unresponsive maternal behavior, while lower education predicted mother's current aggressive behavior towards offspring, lack of supportive behavior, and unresponsiveness.

Our most recent longitudinal study of offspring, which is ongoing (e.g., Serbin, Stack, and Schwartzman, 2000), includes over 200 infant and preschool aged children, born to parents in their mid 20s to mid 30s. These families represent a broad range of backgrounds in terms of education, age at parenthood, and marital and occupational status. In this way, we are able to examine the effects of childhood variables such as aggression without confounding social and economic disadvantages (e.g., early parenthood), making it impossible to determine the specific effects of the early risk factors. In other words, because of the wider range of backgrounds represented in this subsample, we can now examine the effects of parental histories in more mature or functional families to those with having experienced earlier disadvantage or adversity.

In this sample of young children at preschool age (N = 175), there was a wide range of outcomes in terms of children's health, development, social-behavioral skills, and cognitive functioning. Approximately 53% of the offspring were found to have current developmental and/or behavioral problems. Many of these children (36%) were "multi-problem," exhibiting significant delays, family problems, and behavioral difficulties (overlap of about 40% between cognitive/language and behavioral problems). Approximately twice as many boys as girls had developmental and/or behavioral problems. In the older children from the sample (aged 4–6), the overall prevalence of difficulties (including cognitive, language and/or behavior problems) reached 73% for boys, compared with 44% for girls. However, very few of these problems had been detected or assessed by health service professionals prior to the study. Only 27% of the children having difficulties had received any developmental, psycho-educational, or speech/language services to date. The remaining

47% of the group appeared to be developing normally at the time of assessment, although an additional 11% of the total group was experiencing serious family problems, such as parental alcoholism or mental illness.

Parent reports of common physical health problems included: recurrent respiratory illness including asthma, bronchitis, upper respiratory infections, nasal allergies (30%), frequent middle ear infections (31%), severe illnesses including cancer, epilepsy, heart problems, kidney problems, thyroid problems, and lupus (10%). Boys also had histories of more physical health problems, including infant colic and middle ear infections.

Child development, social-behavioral skills, cognitive functioning, and physical health were predicted by a number of family characteristics which are briefly described below:

- Parental childhood characteristics and abilities: particularly mothers' childhood aggression, which negatively predicted outcomes for offspring (especially if combined with social withdrawal and/or low academic ability)
- Parental education: high-school completion and years of post-secondary schooling
- Family economic status (including poverty level, welfare status)
- Maternal smoking
- Parenting behavior (including mothers' responsiveness, use of supportive teaching strategies, and emotional availability)
- Cognitive stimulation provided within the home environment
- Level of family and parenting stress
- Adequacy of social and emotional support for parents

Protective factors

- Financial security (income at least 10% above Statistics Canada's definition of poverty; low income cutoff)
- Parents' level of education (high-school completion and number of years, post-secondary)
- Mothers' ability to stimulate their children's problem solving ("scaffolding")
- Home environment with many opportunities for cognitive stimulation (e.g. provision of books and educational toys)
- Parents' satisfaction with available social and emotional support

As seen in these results, the intergenerational transfer of risk is a complex process. Childhood aggression in girls does place their offspring at risk for developmental and health problems, both through "indirect" or cumulative pathways such as lowered educational, occupational achievement, income over time, and also through more direct pathways, including parenting styles, modeling of problematic interpersonal behavior, lack of effective cognitive stimulation, stress, and ongoing risk-taking behavior (e.g., smoking) within the home and parenting context. From the above results, it appears that male offspring may be more vulnerable than female offspring to the health, cognitive, and behavioral effects of family risk profiles. Proposed hypotheses to explain these sex differences include males' slower rates of biological maturation, their greater vulnerability to environmental hazards and their patterns of prenatal hormone production affecting brain development (Rutter, Capsi, and Moffitt, 2003). Differential exposure of boys and girls to environmental hazards, parenting practices, and other socialization factors are also possible contributors to the gender difference. However, the girls also showed a variety of problems, although at a lower overall rate than the boys, and parental history was predictive of problems in offspring of both sexes. Further, as with the general literature on aggression and other childhood problems such as developmental delay, the gender ratio of prevalence does not mean that girls' difficulties can be ignored. Aggressive girls in particular, with their different, milder, or less obvious problems than boys, are still likely to grow up to have negative life trajectories involving themselves and their families, as demonstrated by the results of the Concordia Project to date.

Prediction of Injuries and Health Outcomes for Offspring

Next we looked at objective measures of health in the offspring generation. We had access to children's complete records of medical visits obtained from provincial databases (Regie de l'Assurance-Maladie du Quebec).

In a first study, we focused on the 94 children who were born while their mothers were in adolescence (Serbin et al., 1996). We examined the effect of mother's early maladaptive behavior patterns on offspring's physical health outcomes using records of emergent and non-emergent medical visits as well as hospitalization received in the first four years of life. Diagnosis information was also available for the ER visits and was grouped into one of three categories: injury-related diagnoses, acute illness and infections and asthma.

Results indicated that mothers' childhood histories of aggression and aggression combined with withdrawal was predictive of annual rates of ER visits. The average rate of ER visits per year for the offspring of aggressive and aggressive-withdrawn women was 1.95 and 2.23 respectively; the offspring of women without histories of deviant social behavior had an average rate of 1.17 visits per year. Mothers' childhood histories of aggression and aggression-withdrawal were also predictive of the ER treatment of injuries, acute infections, and asthma. Children's rates of hospitalizations and emergency surgeries followed a similar pattern.

In our most recent ongoing study, preliminary findings confirm that there is a relation between mothers' early maladaptive behavior and subsequent childhood injury in a larger sample of 1322 offspring of the Concordia Project, not just those of teenage mothers. The direct and indirect effect of parents' early problem behaviour on the use of medical services for children's injury was analysed using path modeling to predict medical records of injury-related medical services of these children between the ages of one and five. Several family-level characteristics thought to mediate the effect of early maladaptive behaviors were included in the analysis including mothers' physical health, mothers' age at childbirth, child gender and neighborhood quality.

Results of the path model indicated that mother's aggression was predictive of medically attended injuries in offspring, controlling for all other variables in the model. Indirect paths from aggression to child injuries were also found via physical health and mother's age at childbirth. Child gender was predictive of injuries with boys being at an increase the risk of having medical services for injuries.

The results of these two studies suggest that early maladaptive behavior, particularly aggression, is not only detrimental to the individual but it also places the individual's offspring at risk for a variety of health problems and increases their use of medical services. Mother's history of aggression-withdrawal was only problematic for children of teenage moms.

SUMMARY OF INTERGENERATIONAL RISK

A variety of current indices of family functioning were related to children's development. Most of these findings replicate the broad literature indicating that parenting stress, parenting skills, quality of the home environment, parental smoking, and parents' mental health predict children's health, development, and behavior. What is new here, first, is the examination of how parents' childhood behavioral histories predict resources and family functioning in adulthood. Second, the results demonstrate a cumulative risk pattern, indicating additive and multiplicative relations between these historical factors and specific aspects of current family functioning as predictors within a high-risk population of children.

It is important to note that protective factors, which predict positive child outcomes, were also found, namely financial security, parents' levels of education, mothers' abilities to stimulate their children's problem solving, home environment with many opportunities for cognitive stimulation (e.g., provision of books and educational toys), and availability of social and emotional support. Education appeared to enhance family functioning and parenting abilities directly, as well as increasing the likelihood of higher income levels which impacted the well-being of family members in many important ways, including pre- and peri-natal health and the subsequent quality of the child's home environment.

Parents' childhood histories of aggression and withdrawal predicted many of the most powerful family influences on children's development. Specifically, childhood aggression predicted parenting stress, parental smoking, mothers' mental health, the quality of the home environment, and mothers' abilities to provide cognitive stimulation to their preschoolers' (scaffolding). Childhood withdrawal predicted child outcomes because of its relation to mothers' educational attainment, subsequent family income, and unexpected relations to peri-natal health, subsequent childhood illness, and parenting stress.

Within this lower SES, inner-city sample of parents and their children, parents' childhood aggression predicted future family poverty, both directly and indirectly, via lower levels of educational attainment. In other words, continuity of problematic behavioral styles from childhood into adulthood may be implicated in lowered adult occupational attainments and, in some cases, eventual welfare dependency.

In terms of current functioning, it is clear that the correlated triad of distress measures, including mother's mental and physical health problems, child behavior problems, and parenting stress, present a formidable challenge to families in this population. Improving social and economic levels of support as well as providing educational opportunities for parents may prevent or alleviate the consequences attributed to these distress factors.

CONCLUSION

The problematic life courses of aggressive girls is the focus of an increasing number of longitudinal studies currently being carried out across a diverse range of countries and regions, including ongoing projects in Canada, the United States, Britain, Scandinavia, Germany, and New Zealand. It is now acknowledged that this behavior pattern is likely to be indicative of serious social and academic difficulties for the child as well having important negative consequences (such as victimization and bullying) for peers and others living in the child's social environment. The long-term impact of girlhood aggression is just beginning to be understood in terms of life trajectories for aggressive girls themselves, as well as impact on current and future family members, society at large, and, most recently, impact on the next generation: children born to women with histories of aggressive behavior. The impact of aggression across the life course from childhood to adulthood in a given individual is clearly modulated by contextual factors, including environmental conditions, experiences, and events. Cultural, social, family, educational, and economic conditions are likely to either exacerbate or buffer outcomes of aggressive girls.

In this chapter, we have focused on a longitudinal sample growing up in inner-city Montreal, which has been followed from elementary school age into young adulthood. The women in the sample have followed a wide variety of life trajectories according to the profiles of risk and protective events and conditions they have experienced. Early aggression appears to have had negative consequences via at least two distinct routes. First, the aggressive behavioral patterns visible to peers in the children's elementary school classes seem to reflect a distinct interpersonal style, which is fairly stable across age. This style is reflected in successive social relationships, including those with peers, partners and spouses, and, eventually, offspring. The negative impact of this pattern in girls may be most obvious in continuing violent, neglectful, or coercive inter-personal relations in successive stages of the life course (e.g., bullying and coercive peer relations; dating and spousal violence; child neglect and abuse; elder abuse). It is also seen in terms of associated health risks (e.g., smoking, substance abuse, early and unprotected sexual activity) and violations of legal and social conventions (e.g., traffic infractions and other non-violent crime; school drop-out; early parenthood; unemployment; welfare dependence). Such activities are also related to modeling and support from the peer group with which aggressive girls associate. These subsequent difficulties doubtlessly maintain the negative trajectory of highly aggressive girls. Indirect effects of early aggression, via poor educational achievement, poverty, social and physical environment, and ill-health, are also visible in this sample. Again, these indirect pathways were found for both the parent and off-spring generations.

On the more positive side, however, buffering factors (notably academic ability and educational achievement) were also identified within the Concordia sample. Income (closely related to educational attainment) is also a powerful predictor and contextual modulator of the long term outcomes of girlhood aggression. Many of the women (and their offspring) are now doing relatively well, despite their poor prospects in childhood or early adolescence. The challenge for researchers in this field is to pinpoint the processes whereby risk and buffering factors operate, as well as the amount of risk for specific negative outcomes that may be quantitatively attributed to specific predictors, and to identify these in the contexts of research, social, educational, and health policy.

Although the literature on male's aggression far surpasses that of girl's, much information has been gained in recent years. Researchers should continue to follow aggressive girls across their life courses, looking at outcomes such as mental and physical health, social and occupational functioning, and family relations as important domains in middle adulthood and beyond. In addition, researchers need to gain a better understanding of the direct and indirect processes whereby these children and their families remain at risk as well as the contextual factors that modulate the risk process. More research is needed to elucidate the role of biological (e.g. genetic; neuro-developmental; neuro-endocrine) and health factors involved in aggressive behavioral styles in girls, both in terms of the origins and maintenance of aggressive behavior, and its consequences for women over the life course. Finally, parallel studies of aggressive boys should be carried out within these research contexts: Family, health, and occupational outcomes have also been understudied for aggressive boys: most of the research on aggression and conduct disorder in boys has focused on risk for delinquency, crime, substance abuse, etc.

Aggression in girls is a predictor of long-term social, academic, and health problems, that can be identified as early as grade one. Accordingly, a main implication for of these findings for social and health policy is the need to identify high-risk children early, and to provide appropriate and comprehensive intervention to families. By the time children reach elementary school with patterns of aggression, social withdrawal, and poor cognitive and language skills, it may already be too late to prevent academic and social problems. However, intensive and continuing programs to identify children with these problems and intervene appropriately are necessary as early as elementary school. In high school, academic, social and health support for high-risk girls may be useful to help them complete their secondary education and prevent early parenthood. Finally, education, social, and economic support to high-risk families with young children is needed, especially those of women with a history of aggressive social behavior.

There has been a great deal of progress in recent years in our knowledge and understanding of the complex ways in which aggressive behavior places children at risk for ongoing problems across the life course. Aggression in girls is now acknowledged as a stable indicator of risk for continuing social, emotional, occupational, and health difficulties, both for the girls and for their families. The relation between girlhood aggression and intergenerational risk is also being clarified. Girls and boys do not live on separate planets, even if we sometimes refer to the "Two Worlds" of childhood (Maccoby, 1998) to describe their separate playgroups and stereotyped roles. Differences between males and females in behavior, although often attributed to neuro-biology (Eliot, 2009), are far fewer than similarities. Regardless of the origins of gender differences, women's and men's developmental trajectories obviously intersect, particularly in adolescence and parenthood. If we are to understand the origins and sequelae of aggression in general, we need to include both females and males in our conceptual and empirical frameworks.

REFERENCES

Auerbach, J., Lerner, Y., Barasch, M., *et al.* (1992). Maternal and environmental characteristics as predictors of child behaviour problems and cognitive competence. *American Journal of Orthopsychiatry, 62*(3), 409–420.

Bardone, A. M., Moffitt, T. E., Caspi, A., *et al.* (1996). Adult mental health and social outcomes of adolescent girls with depression and conduct disorder. *Development and Psychopathology, 8,* 811–829.

Bardone, A. M., Moffitt, T. E., Caspi, A., *et al.* (1998). Adult physical health outcomes of adolescent girls with conduct disorder, depression, and anxiety. *Journal of the American Academy of Child and Adolescent Psychiatry, 37,* 594–601.

Beardslee, W. R., Keller, M. B., and Klerman, G. D. (1985) Children of parents with affective disorder. *International Journal of Family Psychiatry, 6*(3), 283–299.

Biringen, Z. and Robinson, J. (1991). Emotional availability in mother-child interactions: A reconceptualization for research. *American Journal of Orthopsychiatry, 61*(2), 258–271.

Bowlby, J. (1980). *Attachment and Loss.* Vol. 3: *Loss, Sadness and Depression.* New York: Basic Books.

Cairns, R. B., Cairns, B. D., Neckerman, H. J., *et al.* (1989). Growth and aggression: I. Childhood to early adolescence. *Developmental Psychology, 25*(2), 320–330.

Cairns, R. B., Cairns, B. D., Xie, H., *et al.* (1998). Paths across generations: Academic competence and aggressive behaviours in young mothers and their children. *Developmental Psychology, 34*(6), 1162–1174.

Card, N. A., Stucky, B. D., Sawalani, G. M., *et al.* (2008) Direct and indirect aggression during childhood and adolescence: A meta-analytic review of gender differences, intercorrelations, and relations to maladjustment. *Child Development, 79*(5), 1185–1229.

Caspi, A. and Elder, G. H. (1988a). Emergent family patterns: The inter-generational construction of problem behaviour and relationships. In R. Hinde and J. Stevenson-Hinde (eds), *Relationships within Families: Mutual Influences* (pp. 218–240). Oxford: OUP.

Caspi, A., Elder, G. H., and Bem, D. J. (1988b). Moving against the world: Life course patterns of explosive children. *Developmental Psychology, 23*, 308–311.

Caspi, A., Bem, D. J., and Elder, G. H. (1989). Continuities and consequences of interactional styles across the life course. *Journal of Personality, 157*, 375–406.

Cowen, E. L., Wyman, P. A., Work, W. C., *et al.* (1990). The Rochester Child Resilience Project: Overview and summary of first year findings. *Development and Psychopathology, 2*(2), 193–212.

De Genna, N., Stack, D. M., Serbin, L. A., *et al.* (2006). From risky behavior to health risk: Continuity across two generations. *Developmental and Behavioral Pediatrics. 27*(4), 297–309.

De Genna, N., Stack, D. M., Ledingham, J., *et al.* (2007). Maternal and child health problems: The inter-generational consequences of early maternal aggression and withdrawal. *Social Sciences and Medicine, 64*, 2417–2426.

Dumas, J. E., LaFreniere, P. J., and Serketich, W. J. (1995). Balance of power: A transactional analysis of control in mother-child dyads involving socially competent, aggressive, and anxious children. *Journal of Abnormal Psychology, 104*(1), 104–113.

Egeland, B. and Erickson, M. F. (1987). Psychologically unavailable caregiving. In M. R. Brassard, R. Germain, and S. M. Hart (eds), *Psychological maltreatment of children and youth* (pp. 110–120). New York: Pergammon Press.

Eliot, L. (2009) *Pink Brain, Blue Brain: How Small Differences Grow into Troublesome Gaps – and What We Can Do About It.* New York: Houghton Mifflin Harcourt.

Emde, R. N. (1989). The infant's relationship experience: Developmental and affective aspects. In A. J. Sameroff and R. N. Emde (eds), *Relationship Disturbances in Early Childhood* (pp. 33–51). New York: Harper Collins.

Fogel, A. (1993). *Developing Through Relationships: The Origins of Communication, Self, and Culture.* New York: Harvester Wheatsheaf.

Furstenberg, F. F. Jr., Brooks-Gunn, J., *et al.* (1987). *Adolescent Mothers in Later Life.* New York, NY: Cambridge University Press.

Furstenberg, F. F., Brooks-Gunn, J., and Chase-Lansdale, L. (1989). Teenaged pregnancy and childbearing. *American Psychologist, 44*, 313–320.

Granger, D. A., Weisz, J. R., and Kanneckis, D. (1994). Neuroendocrine reactivity, internalizing problems and control-related cognition in clinic referred children and adolescents. *Journal of Abnormal Psychology, 103*(2), 259–266.

Hammen, C. L., Gordon, D., Burge, D., *et al.* (1987). Maternal affective disorders, illness, and stress: Risk for children's psychopathology. *American Journal of Psychiatry, 144*, 736–741.

Huesmann, L. R., Dubow, E. F., and Boxer, P. (2009). Continuity of aggression from childhood to early adulthood as a predictor of life outcomes: Implications for the adolescent-limited and life-course-persistent models. *Aggressive Behavior, 35*(2), 136–149.

Huesmann, L. R., Eron, L. D., Lefkowitz, M. M., *et al.* (1984). The stability of aggression over time and generations. *Developmental Psychology, 20*, 1120–1134.

Kinnunen, U., and Pulkkinen, L. (2003). Childhood Socio-Emotional Characteristics as antecedents of Marital Stability and Quality. *European Psychologist, 8*(4), 223–237.

Kokko, H., Sutherland, W. J., Lindstroem, J., Reynolds, J. D., *et al.* (1998). Individual mating success, lek stability, and the neglected limitations of statistical power. *Animal Behaviour, 56*(3), 755–762.

Kokko, K. and Pulkkinen, L. (2000). Aggression in childhood and long-term unemployment in adulthood: A cycle of maladaptation and some protective factors. *Developmental Psychology, 36*(4), 463–472.

Kopp, C. B. and Kaler, S. R. (1989). Risk in infancy: Origins and implications. *American Psychologist, 44*, 224–230.

Krueger, R. F., Moffitt, T. E., Caspi, A., *et al.* (1998). Assortative mating for antisocial behavior: Developmental and methodological implications. *Behavior Genetics, 28*, 3, 173–186.

Ledingham, J. E. and Schwartzman, A. E. (1981). L'identification de nouvelles populations a risque élevé: Le risque du chercheur. In G. Lauzon (ed.), *Actes du Colloque sur la Recherche Sociale.* Québec: Ministere des Affaires Sociales.

Lyons, J., Serbin, L. A., and Marchessault, K. (1988). The social behaviour of peer-identified aggressive, withdrawn, and aggressive/withdrawn children. *Journal of Abnormal Child Psychology, 16* (5), 539–552.

Maccoby, E. E. (1998). *The two sexes: Growing Up Apart, Coming Together.* Cambridge, MA: Harvard University Press.

Masten, A. S. (2001). Ordinary magic: Resilience processes in development. *American Psychologist, 56*(3), 227–238.

McLoyd, V. C. (1990). The impact of economic hardship on Black families and children: Psychological distress, parenting, and socio-emotional development. *Child Development, 61* (2), 311–346.

Moffitt, T. E., Caspi, A., Rutter, M., *et al.* (2001). *Sex differences in antisocial behaviour: Conduct disorder, delinquency, and violence in the Dunedin Longitudinal Study.* Cambridge: Cambridge University Press.

Moskowitz, D. S., Schwartzman, A. E., and Ledingham, J. E. (1985). Stability and change in aggression and withdrawal in middle childhood and early adolescence. *Journal of Abnormal Psychology, 94*(1), 30–41.

Pekarik, E. G., Prinz, R. J., Liebert, D. E, *et al.* (1976). The Pupil Evaluation Inventory: A sociometric technique for assessing children's social behavior. *Journal of Abnormal Child Psychology, 4*, 83–97.

Peters, P. L. (1999). *Assortative Mating Among Men and Women with Histories of Aggressive, Withdrawn, and Aggressive-Withdrawn Behaviour.* Unpublished doctoral thesis, Concordia University, Montreal, Quebec.

Pulkkinen, L. and Pitkanen T. (1993). Continuities in aggressive behaviour from childhood to adulthood. *Aggressive Behaviour, 19*, 249–263.

Rutter, M. (1990). Psychosocial resilience and protective mechanisms. In J. E. Rolf, A. S. Masten, D. Cicchetti, *et al.* (eds), *Risk and Protective Factors in Development of Psychopathology* (pp. 181–214). New York: Cambridge University Press.

Schwartzman, A. E., Ledingham, J., and Serbin, L. A. (1985). Identification of children at risk for adult schizophrenia: A longitudinal study. *International Review of Applied Psychology, 34*(3), 363–380.

Schwartzman, A. E., Verlaan, P., Peters, P., *et al.* (1995). Sex roles as coercion. In J. McCord (ed.), *Coercion and Punishment in Long-Term Perspectives* (pp. 362–375). New York: Cambridge University Press.

Schwartzman, A. E. and Mohan, R. (1999) *Gender Differences in the Adult Criminal Behavior Patterns of Aggressive and Withdrawn Children.* Presented at the Ninth Scientific Meeting of the International Society for Research in Child and Adolescent Psychopathology, Barcelona, Spain.

Schwartzman, A. E., Serbin, L. A., Stack, D. M., *et al.* (2009). Likeability, aggression and social withdrawal in childhood, psychiatric status in maturity: A prospective study. *European Journal of Developmental Science, 3*, 1, 51–63.

Serbin, L. A., Lyons, J., Marchessault, K., *et al.* (1987). Observational validation of a peer nomination technique for identifiying aggressive, withdrawn and aggressive-withdrawn children. *Journal of Consulting and Clinical Psychology, 55* (1), 109–110.

Serbin, L. A., Moskowitz, D. S., Schwartzman, A. E., *et al.* (1991a). Aggressive, withdrawn, and aggressive/withdrawn children in adolescence: Into the next generation. In D. Pepler and K. A. Rubin (eds), *The Development and Treatment of Childhood Aggression* (pp. 55–70). New York: Guildford Press.

Serbin, L. A., Peters, P. L., McAffer, V. J., *et al.* (1991b). Childhood aggression and withdrawal as predictors of adolescent pregnancy, early parenthood, and environmental risk for the next generation. *Canadian Journal of Behavioural Science, 23*(3), 318–331.

Serbin, L. A., Marchessault, K., McAffer, V., *et al.* (1993a). Patterns of social behaviour on the playground in 9- to 11-year-old girls and boys: Relation to teacher perceptions and to peer ratings of aggression, withdrawal and likability. In C. Hart (ed.), *Children on Playgrounds: Research Perspectives and Applications*, (pp. 162–183). Albany: S.U.N.Y. Press.

Serbin, L. A., Powlishta, K., and Gulko, J. (1993b) Sex roles, status, and the need for social change. *Monographs of the Society for Research in Child Development, 58*(2), 93–95.

Serbin, L. A., Peters, P. L., and Schwartzman, A. E. (1996). Longitudinal study of early childhood injuries and acute illnesses in the offspring of adolescent mothers who were aggressive, withdrawn, or agressive-withdrawn in childhood. *Journal of Abnormal Psychology, 105*(4), 500–507.

Serbin, L. A., Cooperman, J. M., Peters, P. L., *et al.* (1998). Inter-generational transfer of phsychosocial risk in women with childhood histories of aggression, withdrawal or aggression and withdrawal. *Developmental Psychology, 34*, 1246–1262.

Serbin, L. A., Stack, D. M., and Schwartzman, A. E. (2000). Identification and prediction of risk and resiliency in high-risk preschoolers: An intergenerational study. Final Report (#6070-10-5/9515); Child, Youth and Family Health Unit, Child and Youth Division, Health Canada.

Serbin, L. A., Stack, D. M., Schwartzman, A., *et al.* (2002). A longitudinal study of aggressive and withdrawn children into adulthood: Patterns of parenting and risk to offspring. *The Effects of Parental Dysfunction on Children* (pp. 43–69). New York: Kluwer Academic/Plenum Publishers.

Serbin, L. A., and Karp, J. (2004). The intergenerational transfer of psychosocial risk: Mediators of vulnerability and resilience. *Annual Review of Psychology, 55*, 333–363.

Serbin, L. A., Temcheff, C. E., Cooperman, J. M., *et al.* (in press). Predicting family poverty and other disadvantaged conditions for child rearing from childhood aggression and social withdrawal: A 30-year longitudinal study. *International Journal of Behavioral Development.*

Sameroff, A. J. and Seifer, R. (1992). Early contributors to developmental risk. In J. Rolf, A. S. Masten, D. Cichetti, *et al.* (eds), *Risk and Protective Factors in the Development of Psychopathology* (pp. 52–66). New York: Cambridge University Press.

Index